GOLD
BAR BOB

In memory of Ken Boehm

GOLD
BAR BOB

The Downfall of the
Most Corrupt US Senator

Isabel Vincent and Thomas Jason Anderson

**DIVERSION
BOOKS**

Diversion Books
A division of Diversion Publishing Corp.
www.diversionbooks.com

The authors represent that all material in this book has been gathered from public
source documents, including court records, property and voter registrations, police
records obtained under freedom of information legislation as well as news reports,
books, and interviews. In many cases, sources would only consent to speak to us
on the condition of anonymity. They are indicated by the generic term "source"
throughout the text and in the endnotes.

Diversion Books and colophon are registered trademarks
of Diversion Publishing Corp.

For more information, email info@diversionbooks.com.

Hardcover ISBN: 9798895150115
e-ISBN: 9798895150122
First Diversion Books Edition: October 2025

Design by Neuwirth & Associates, Inc.
Cover design by David Ter-Avanesyan/Ter33Design LLC

Printed in the United States of America
1 3 5 7 9 10 8 6 4 2

Diversion books are available at special discounts for bulk purchases in the US
by corporations, institutions, and other organizations. For more information,
please contact admin@diversionbooks.com.

"What's past is prologue . . ."

—William Shakespeare,
The Tempest

CONTENTS

Never Enough

On July 16, 2024, around 11:00 a.m., a meteor flew over the Statue of Liberty. Traveling at a staggering 34,000 miles per hour, this rare morning fireball passed directly over the Manhattan Southern District courtroom where US Senator Robert "Bob" Menendez was awaiting the jury's verdict in his grueling nine-week, sixteen-count corruption prosecution. Despite the tension in the courtroom, Menendez appeared stoic, awaiting the climactic moment of his trial.

Earlier that morning, before federal marshals opened the doors to US District Court Judge Sidney H. Stein's twenty-third-floor courtroom, Menendez stood by a window in the hallway looking out onto the majestic Brooklyn Bridge, the East River, and a distant Statue of Liberty. Perhaps he was trying to summon a sense of calm as he sang the opening lyrics to "You Raise Me Up" in a low baritone. The singing of the inspirational spiritual with its message of overcoming adversity and drawing on support from loved ones was a daily occurrence in his lengthy trial, and even as he entered the courtroom, he held the tune just under his breath as he made his way to the defense table. He was a pretty good singer—"a gentle crooner," noted one critic[1]—and broke into song several times a day, according to his second wife. Years earlier, he sang in Newark federal court where he survived a thirteen-count indictment through a hung jury made up of his own constituents. In that friendlier setting, the jurors knew the US senator as their senior representative in Washington, DC, a familiar figure who had long represented their interests. But here, in the Southern District of New York, he was a stranger—a defendant in a trial that felt far removed from the place he called home.

As the foreman of the jury prepared to read the verdict, the meteor—following a steep 44-degree descent—continued beyond the heavens above Manhattan and pierced the intensely hot summer sky over Newark, leaving witnesses awestruck by its brilliance. Its journey continued as it disintegrated above the small town of Mountainside, New Jersey, marking the end of its fiery path.

Like the meteor's dramatic fall, Menendez's own trajectory was destined to meet a fiery conclusion in a guilty verdict that landed early that afternoon. The unanimity of the jury's decision was astonishing in its breadth and depth, with the charge sheet reading more like that of a Mob boss than a longtime public servant. Counts of bribery, extortion, conspiring to act as a foreign agent, obstruction of justice, and several counts of conspiracy followed the clearly dazed and shocked Menendez to a post-verdict podium. Outside the Daniel Patrick Moynihan US Courthouse, Menendez stood before a buzzing gaggle of New York City media.

"I have never violated my public oath," he said. "I am deeply, deeply disappointed by the jury's verdict."

The jury had found him guilty after sitting through a prosecution that hit hard with photographs and evidence placed directly in their hands, gathered from the modest Englewood Cliffs home he shared with his second wife and alleged accomplice. The twelve-member panel saw photos of the loot federal agents seized from the home during a raid—one of five—in the summer of 2022: a Mercedes convertible, nearly $500,000 in cash stuffed into Menendez's hiking boots and jacket pockets, and a collection of gold bars. A prosecutor handed to the jurors two bags of gold bars valued at more than $150,000 found in two closets of the couple's bedroom. The FBI team had cut through two dead bolt locks to get to the loot in the closets, the jury heard in testimony that day. One by one, the jurors turned the gold bars over in their hands, feeling their weight.

Aristotelis Kougemitros, the lead federal agent on the first raid on the senator's home, testified that the sheer volume of bills hidden in the closets proved too much to count by hand. FBI agents found a total of $486, 461 in addition to gold bars. One was wrapped in a paper towel and stuffed into a Ziploc bag, casually lying on the floor under a pile of clothes and other items.

"The amount of cash that we began to discover was so voluminous that I directed the team that we would no longer be photographing any of the cash; we would be seizing the cash, because I believed it was evidence potentially of a crime," Kougemitros said.

His team understood the gravity of their mission on that early June morning in 2022: Senator Bob Menendez was one of the most powerful elected officials in Congress. As the chairman of the Senate's Foreign Relations Committee, Menendez held sway over the sale of the most powerful arsenal of military weapons in the history of the world by the stroke of his pen. Menendez was known by everyone in the Justice Department to be an aggressive legislator willing to use the power of his office to pursue any grievance he had with high-level officials, and he could make the life of a rank-and-file member of the FBI a living hell.

"We came with unmarked vehicles," Kougemitros testified. "We didn't have a large group, which we normally have for a search. We wore subdued markings that identify us. We were sensitive that we were searching the home and executing a search warrant of a United States senator."

No one was home when federal agents quietly entered the code on the keypad of the garage where the black Mercedes convertible was parked. Tradecraft allowed them to decipher the digital code, but they had to hire a locksmith to open the locked doors throughout the property, including to the master bedroom.

The first of the raids of the senator's home occurred during a particularly sensitive time in America. Months earlier, Russia had invaded Ukraine in what Russian president Vladimir Putin called a "special operation." The world was heading toward a potential World War III, and Menendez played a pivotal role in how America would respond to what could turn into a nuclear confrontation. Putin's propagandists bragged almost by the hour that they possessed the highly touted Zircon hypersonic missile system as well as the RS-28 Sarmat, better known as the Satan II nuclear warhead. Designed to bypass the most advanced missile defense systems on Earth, Putin had test-fired a Sarmat from a silo launcher at the Plesetsk State Test Cosmodrome in the Arkhangelsk region of northern Russia just a few weeks before the raid on the Menendez home.

The world was also spiraling into chaos after emerging from the COVID pandemic, challenging the global order through strained supply chains and frayed political alliances. Inflation had taken hold of the American economy, and there were daily updates of unfolding events concerning numerous court cases and investigations related to former President Trump's first term in office. The mood in America was turning bitter as it seemed there was a new story of corruption in high offices almost weekly.

If there were rumblings of a new investigation into the senior senator from New Jersey at that time, few paid attention. The Garden State was long known for its corrupt politicians, going back to the days of Prohibition and popularized by Hollywood in *On the Waterfront* and *The Sopranos*. Menendez was just your typical Jersey pol—a stereotype that made him almost invisible in the national zeitgeist, perhaps even allowing members of the media to nearly ignore the significance of yet another federal investigation.

Menendez was also a savvy media operator. His daughter, Alicia Menendez, was a high-profile anchor on a major national news network, and Menendez knew how to play to the mainstream national media when they were focused on him. Shortly after that first raid on his home, Menendez made sure to amend his financial disclosures, noting the sale of $400,000 worth of gold bars—a maneuver that would ensure that he had a ready answer for nosy reporters and eager prosecutors if they started asking about why he had gold bullion locked in his bedroom closet.

As the tide turned against him following the series of indictments in the fall of 2023, Menendez used every ounce of his influence to remain in the Senate even though there were calls for him to resign. Senate leader and fellow Democrat Chuck Schumer distanced himself from Menendez publicly but refused to pressure him to leave the legislative body altogether. Schumer understood the strategic importance of Menendez in the Senate. In fact, Schumer allowed Menendez to continue to hold his seat in the powerful Foreign Relations Committee as well as the Banking and Judiciary Committees. Menendez was also allowed to continue to receive classified briefings even as he was accused of conspiring to act as a foreign agent for both Egypt and Qatar—a situation that many outside of the Senate found hard to believe.

The truth was that Schumer and his Senate Democrats had a political gun to their heads and didn't have much choice as long as Menendez refused to step down on his own. The Senate was split fifty-fifty between Republicans and Democrats, forcing a record number of tiebreaking votes from the US vice president on issues ranging from the Ukraine war funding to budget crises that threatened to shut down the government. In total, Kamala Harris cast twenty-six tiebreaking votes between January 2021 and January 2023—the most of any vice president in a single Congress.

With the economy on edge, and military funding necessary for supporting Ukraine against the onslaught of Russian aggression, Schumer and the Democrats couldn't afford to do anything that would cause Menendez to break ranks. Menendez had mastered the art of political leverage and was applying it to his own Democratic Caucus, forcing them to grudgingly support him in his crusade to overcome the greatest threat to his career and legacy. Menendez didn't care that he was bringing the entire party down with him during one of the nation's most trying times. He needed to appear to a potential jury as if he were innocent, which meant keeping his Senate seat and behaving as if the case against him was nothing more than political theater. He portrayed himself as a victim even though the Justice Department prosecuting him was led by an attorney general appointed by a president from his own party.

Menendez was so convinced of his own propaganda and power that he was able to force the Democrats into protecting him. By refusing to leave office, he contributed to the flagging fortunes of his own party, and may even have unintentionally helped usher in the catastrophe of the 2024 election. Shortly after his trial and historic conviction in the summer of 2024, the Democrats would suffer a series of crippling blows, losing the White House and their majorities in the House of Representatives and the Senate.

≈

In his navy suit and wire-rimmed glasses, the white-haired Menendez cracks the hint of a smile in his official portrait in front of the Greek-inspired white columns of the US Capitol. Shortly after his seventieth birthday in 2024, he had the bearing of a sober statesman and powerful foreign policy maker.

Bob Menendez had come a long way from Union City, New Jersey—the hardscrabble enclave of Latin American immigrants across the Hudson River from Manhattan where he had cut his teeth as a young politician and where he reigned throughout his career like an American caudillo.

In fact, the ambitious lawmaker had taken great pains throughout his career to create the narrative that would appeal to his Latino constituents. Although born in Manhattan, he was a working-class Cuban American who was raised in a Union City tenement and rose from the barrio to the pinnacle of power in Washington, DC. His origins resonated with immigrants in Union City, many of whom had fled the tyranny of Cuban strongman Fidel Castro, but Menendez's family was not part of that particular exodus, although he often implied that his parents and older siblings fled the Communist island because they feared confiscation of their assets.

Although there are many inaccuracies about who Bob Menendez is—some that he fabricated himself—he is undoubtedly a self-made man. His daughter, Alicia Menendez, described him as "a scrappy kid from a small town who learned to be tough as a means of survival."[2] He focused so intently on being an adult early on that he had nothing like a normal childhood, according to his daughter.

"To be the first in your family to do and be many things—a natural-born US citizen, a college graduate, an attorney, an elected official—is all a great privilege," she wrote in a letter to Judge Stein. "It is also lonelier than most people can imagine."

Menendez's lonely road is full of foggy facts, however. At Union Hill High School, he couldn't afford the books for his advanced level courses, so he supposedly convinced the school to provide them for free, demonstrating a remarkable ability to negotiate and persuade—a story that years later would prove to be false. He was a stellar student who presided over the debate team as well as the history, chess, and tennis clubs. He was student body president. At nineteen, he became the youngest candidate to run for the Union City Board of Education.

"Many from the Hispanic community look at me and think that it is possible to grow up poor, go to public schools, be the first in your entire family to go to college, and rise to be one of a hundred United States senators, in a country of 310 million people," he has often said.

Donald Scarinci, who has been friends with Menendez for more than half a century, said that Menendez's example, his "higher calling" to become a public servant, inspired him to steer away from finishing a PhD in English literature and become a lawyer.

"It is possible to change the world, and Bob Menendez did!" Scarinci said. "He broke a glass ceiling by showing people who grew up in urban areas in small apartments like us that they can be whatever they want to be and that their example, like Bob's example, can change the world one person at a time and one community at a time."[3]

But how did he go from such modest beginnings to become one of the most powerful men in the US government? How did he create a mini-American dynasty that saw his son become a congressman and his daughter a leading TV journalist married to the grandson of a Cuban president?

How Menendez attained power, how he wielded that power—nationally and globally—and how he became one of the most corrupt lawmakers in US history have preoccupied many who have closely observed his career for decades. Even before his first federal criminal indictment in 2015, many members of law enforcement and the media wondered about the senator's luxury trips abroad, his dalliance with a woman who handled investments for convicted pedophile Jeffrey Epstein, and even his own deep-seated conviction that he was a victim of an elaborate Cuban spy ring that targeted him over his hard-line policy positions with respect to the Communist island.

Menendez's power came from old-school political patronage and strategic alliances with local politicians and the leaders of the Cuban underground. He was their best friend, until it was politically expedient to turn against them—a characteristic that has marked the lawmaker's half-century career. In a desperate bid to save his own skin during his last corruption trial, he seemed to have few qualms about throwing his own wife under the bus.

That's not surprising, since he did it once before at the beginning of his career in politics in the 1970s and early 1980s. Ultimately, that single act of treachery against his most important political mentor planted the seeds of Menendez's own epic downfall nearly half a century later.

Menendez, the product of machine politics in the Garden State, saw his career begin to soar in the 1980s and 1990s. He was eventually elected to Congress, forging important ties to Hillary Clinton with whom he was so close that the former secretary of state's chief of staff referred to Menendez only half-jokingly as "Your boy" in an email. With Clinton's backing, he wielded power on the world stage, first as chair of the Senate Subcommittee on the Western Hemisphere, where he routinely blocked the appointments of ambassadors he didn't like. At one point, he had jettisoned so many ambassadorial picks in the Caribbean that most countries had to make do without a Senate-approved US representative.

He had been a fierce supporter of Israel, cosponsoring legislation in 2017 that would have made it a federal crime for Americans to encourage or participate in boycotts against the country. And he was one of only four Democratic senators to oppose the 2015 nuclear deal with Israel's enemy Iran. "President Obama continues to erroneously say that this agreement permanently stops Iran from having a nuclear bomb," he said. "Let's be clear: What the agreement does is to recommit Iran not to pursue a nuclear bomb, a promise they have already violated in the past."

But, even as he made headlines for his international policy initiatives and principled stands, he was beloved by many of his constituents because he worked hard helping them get jobs, visas, and, in some cases, saving their lives. Danny O'Brien, a former chief of staff, said his boss worked constantly, conducting constituent meetings in New Jersey on Mondays before heading to Washington to be available for the first vote of the week often at the expense of spending any real time with his children when they were young.

"On Thursdays, he would wrap up activity in Washington, then race back to New Jersey for an event," he said. "Fridays, Saturdays, and Sundays were almost all work for Bob Menendez. He logged countless miles to attend events and connect with constituents across New

Jersey. The only personal time slot he tried to carve out for himself was Sunday evenings for dinner with his children."[4]

By the time Menendez faced Judge Stein in 2024, he had twice chaired the Senate Foreign Relations Committee, historically one of the most powerful policymaking institutions of the US government that had presided over the establishment of the United Nations in 1945, ratified treaties with foreign governments, and authorized billions in aid and arms purchases around the world.

Menendez amassed power and wealth throughout his career, but then he got sloppy and precipitated his own downfall.

In 2015, Menendez was indicted for fraud along with Salomon Melgen, a shady Florida ophthalmologist, who was among his biggest political benefactors.

Menendez vigorously denied the charges, at one point alleging that they stemmed from a Cuban espionage conspiracy against him. When a New Jersey federal jury could not reach a unanimous verdict, the judge declared a mistrial in the fall of 2017.

"He is a cat with nine lives," said political strategist Hank Sheinkopf, who has known the senator for decades. "They got him time and time again, and he always managed to get away."[5]

Outside the courthouse in Newark on an overcast November afternoon, Menendez, flanked by his high-powered Washington lawyer and his daughter, Alicia, declared victory and reminded constituents that he was unbreakable and would rise to even greater heights.

"Today is resurrection day," he said.

Perhaps he thought himself invincible after that first trial, a political Jesus Christ, who was so beloved, so invulnerable that no one would dare call him to account. That air of entitlement was surely among the senator's tragic flaws.

Did he ever stop to wonder that his behavior was reckless, or was he simply emboldened by his own greatness and the adoring woman who became his second wife?

In happier times, a few years before the federal raids on his home and the lengthy corruption trial that ruined his life, Menendez traveled to India on an official government visit. Among the members of his official entourage was Nadine Arslanian, the love of his life, who was also proving to be a savvy and well-connected business partner.

In front of the Taj Mahal, the ivory mausoleum commissioned by a seventeenth-century Mughal emperor to honor his dead wife, Menendez burst into the song "Never Enough" from *The Greatest Showman*, a 2017 Hollywood film about nineteenth-century entrepreneur P. T. Barnum, who, like Menendez himself, rose from modest roots to conquer the world.

With one knee propped up on a bench behind Arslanian, his right hand holding hers, Menendez crooned the song whose ironic lyrics, which referenced "towers of gold" and stealing stars from the night sky, presaged the couple's triumph and tragedy. Amid the *click-click* of news cameras and the surprised shouts of their traveling companions, Menendez brought out a small box from his pocket and placed a ring on Arslanian's finger. They posted the video to the Robert&Nadine YouTube channel—the couple's only posting.

Federal prosecutor Paul Monteleoni might have taken his cue from the love song, making it the soundtrack for the precipitous downfall of Bob Menendez—a politician "who puts power up for sale" and reaps the benefits.

"It wasn't enough for him to be one of the most powerful people in Washington," Monteleoni told the packed federal courtroom at his trial. "It wasn't enough for him to be entrusted by the public with the power to approve billions of dollars of US military aid to foreign countries. No, Robert Menendez wanted all that power. But he also wanted to use it to pile up riches for himself and his wife."

So, Monteleoni continued, Menendez sold the most valuable thing he owned—the power of his senate office.[6]

CHAPTER ONE

Growing American Roots

"**M**y son is no good," Mario Menendez allegedly said shortly before he died on June 1, 1978. "He's a piece of shit."[7]

It was a startling confession and a terrible thing for a father to say about one of his sons. Or at least that's what stood out for Union City's Deputy Police Chief Frank Scarafile years later, when he recalled what the local handyman had said about his youngest son, Bob, at the unofficial Democratic Party clubhouse, which was housed at the Italian Cultural Center, a popular wedding venue.

Scarafile, who was a loyal soldier to the city's mayor William Musto and would be convicted alongside him and six others on corruption charges years later, never understood what led to the outburst, but he found it so disturbing that he never forgot it. He knew that Menendez—a rising star in Union City Democratic political circles at the time—did not get along with his father, a known womanizer and a drunk with a serious gambling problem.

At one point, things got so bad with Mario that he was forced to sell his tools to pay a gambling debt. Scarafile felt sorry for him, he said, and raised the cash at the clubhouse to buy him a new set of tools so he could go back to work. For his part, Musto made sure that any odd handyman jobs that came up at the city's school board be doled out to Mario Menendez.

Throughout his career, Menendez made few public statements about his father. In fact, he's been completely evasive about his entire family history. In an interview in 1980 at the beginning of his political career, he said his father had been a minister in the Cuban government—a statement that Eusebio "Chi Chi" Rodriguez—a Musto associate and powerful member of the Cuban Mafia in Union City who knew the Menendez family well—called "completely false."[8]

Rodriguez himself arrived in Union City from Cuba in 1956, he said, and became a power broker between city hall, the police, and the Cuban Mob. He was so powerful that when Deputy Police Chief Scarafile wanted to protect the teaching jobs of his son and daughter-in-law after a city hall shakeup, he went directly to Rodriguez, even though he personally knew the commissioners and members of the Union City Board of Education.

"If you want a job, call Chi Chi," said a grand jury report on corruption in Hudson County. "If you want to influence a commissioner, call Chi Chi. If you want the head of a national crime syndicate to influence a newspaper and affect an election, call Chi Chi. All of this is so, despite the fact that Chi Chi Rodriguez is not registered to vote."[9]

In subsequent retellings of Bob's family's journey to the United States, the story changed.

He described his parents as "average working people" in a 2014 interview with *The Jewish Standard*.[10] He told the reporter that his father ran the Havana branch of a tie factory owned by Jews in New York and described his mother as a housewife, although an extremely prescient one.

"My mother didn't like [Cuban President Fulgencio] Batista," Menendez told the outlet. "She didn't like what she saw in the mountains, with the cattle barons, and she didn't like what she was afraid was coming. She was the driving force behind our leaving Cuba. She said to my father, 'I don't want my kids to grow up here.'"

In Menendez's version of the family story, Evangelina implored his father to leave the country despite the fact that they had little money to travel.

"It took some convincing with my father," he wrote in his 2009 book, *Growing American Roots*. "He was working in a tie company and didn't want to leave, or to lose the little money and few possessions they had. But my mother was adamant. Life was tough, but she sensed worse times were coming. . . . My parents were hard workers; you could place them in the lower middle class. Life was hard, and work wasn't always available."[11]

≈

After a short stint in Puerto Rico, which did not suit his mother, according to Menendez, the family came to New York City in 1953. Some close to the family said that the harried mother of two traveled to the island seeking an abortion when she was pregnant with Menendez. But abortions were illegal throughout the United States in 1953 and safe ones were virtually impossible to get on the island of Puerto Rico. Even though New York City had also banned the procedure, it was known as a city where desperate pregnant women could safely obtain an abortion, provided they had the cash. It's not clear from publicly available documents when the family arrived in Puerto Rico or New York City, where Menendez said his family settled for a time. There are no passenger manifests listing Menendez's parents—Evangelina and Mario—with their two young children, Caridad and Reinaldo, arriving in the United States in the early 1950s. The only clue to their arrival in America is an application for an "Evangelina Menendez," born March 19, 1919, for a Social Security card issued in 1951. The date of death on the document corresponds to that of Menendez's mother, who died on October 23, 2009.

Menendez has repeatedly claimed his family left Cuba in 1953 during the first year of the Batista regime. At the third annual

Evangelina Menendez Trailblazer Award presentation, which he named to honor pioneering women after his mother's death, he told the audience that "my family arrived from Cuba in 1953." But in the same speech a few seconds later, he said, "So, in the fall of 1952, my family came to New York City, my mother then pregnant with her third child—me."

But during her testimony, under oath, at Menendez's trial in July 2024, Menendez's older sister, by then known as Caridad Gonzalez, said the family left Cuba a year before Batista came to power (1952–59). She told the court that the family left Cuba in 1951. In that year, the country was ruled by Carlos Prío Socarrás, an attorney, former senator of Pinar del Río Province, and former prime minister. Known as the "cordial president," he embraced freedom of expression and spearheaded the establishment of a national bank and public works projects.

But he proved a largely ineffectual leader who did little to stem the corruption or gang violence that marked the country as a haven for American and Corsican mobsters, such as Charles "Lucky" Luciano, Meyer Lansky, Santo Trafficante, and Amleto Battisti y Lora, known as the king of gambling in Havana. Beginning in the 1930s, Trafficante, who was born in Sicily, was in charge of cocaine distribution from Medellín, Colombia, through Havana—decades before the arrival of Pablo Escobar and the Medellín Cartel. Trafficante also had control of casinos and sex trafficking on the island.

Despite widespread crime and poverty in Cuba, the Menendez family was well off, according to Caridad Gonzalez's testimony. They had a chauffeur and were the first in their neighborhood to own a television set. But when a competitor in her father's tie business pressured him to join his company, things fell apart. After he refused, the competitor hired four police officers and two government officials to ransack their home, Gonzalez said. The family had no choice but to flee. They gathered up the cash they had stored in a secret compartment of a grandfather clock and left for the United States. She did not elaborate about what the journey was like. And neither the prosecutor nor the defense attorney thought to ask how the family traveled to America.

Although nailing down the exact year of their emigration from Cuba might seem a small point, in the fraught world of Cuban politics of the early 1950s, it makes a big difference. Were they fleeing organized crime and poverty on the island when the Mob controlled the country, or were they a political refugee family fleeing communism? Perhaps Mario had run afoul of the mobsters who controlled the island, had gambling debts he couldn't pay, and became a marked man in Havana. For years, Menendez said his parents feared "confiscation," which led many to believe that they were in fact fleeing the Communist regime of Fidel Castro, who came to power in 1959, years after the family was already in the United States.

The assertion was likely meant to appeal to Cuban American voters, tens of thousands of whom were in fact political exiles forced to flee the confiscatory regime, forced to watch helplessly as the government took over their businesses and homes on the island. Many arrived in the United States in the 1960s and 1970s, settling in Miami and in Union City, which has the highest concentration of Cuban immigrants in the United States outside of Florida. When he said that his mother "wisely sensed danger and instability in the air" after Fidel Castro attacked the Moncada Barracks in the summer of 1953, the implicit threat was that she sensed the arrival of communism on the island.

"The thing about Bob Menendez is that he uses the truth in a creative way that is just on the edge of a lie," said Paul Mulshine, a longtime columnist for New Jersey's *The Star-Ledger*, who has documented Menendez's career.[12]

"Bob Menendez never grew up a Cuban, and he could barely speak Spanish," said a former New Jersey lawmaker. "He never wanted to be Latino. The family was against Batista, and he used the Cuban issue for his own gain."[13]

Bob Hugin, who grew up in Union City and was on the school board as a nonvoting member representing Emerson High School when Menendez joined, said that Menendez refused to recognize his Hispanic heritage when he was in high school. "He was embarrassed about speaking Spanish in high school," he said. "It was only in his twenties when he realized that being Hispanic was good for his career and began to learn Spanish."[14]

Menendez was chosen by Jon Corzine to fill his US senate seat, left vacant after Corzine was elected governor of New Jersey in December 2005. Shortly after, Mulshine did an in-depth interview with Menendez, who refused to give him a straight answer when asked about his family history.

"He said 'my parents left Cuba fleeing' but when I asked who they were fleeing [from], he wouldn't give me a straight answer. He kept altering his history to say they were fleeing Batista in 1953, but it seems they actually came before. In his dodgy, greasy way, he manages to always dodge the question."

In *Growing American Roots*, his book about Hispanics in America, Menendez laid out his reason for not delving into his past.

"I knew what I did not want to do: Write a memoir of my life," he wrote. "I'll tell you in passing about myself by way of introduction, but it is a bit early in my life and career to be writing a memoir."

It's a strange statement given that he was already fifty-five years old when the book was published and had been in public life for thirty-six years—a time when most politicians of his stature would indeed have written about their lives.

So, "in passing," in the interview with *The Jewish Standard*, Menendez said that his family first settled with close friends—"soon to become my godparents"—in Midtown Manhattan, on East 33rd Street, according to public records and Menendez's own accounts. Menendez was born in Manhattan on January 1, 1954.

But his family was on the move. That same year, the unnamed and never identified "tie company" closed, and his father found work as an itinerant carpenter. The family moved across the Hudson River to Hoboken and then to Union City, a largely Italian immigrant enclave with a small Cuban community in the 1950s. His mother found a job in the machine embroidery factories that had been established by Swiss, German, and French artisans in the 1870s. By the early twentieth century, Union City had emerged as what the city proudly hailed in its promotional pamphlets as "the home of the American embroidery business," supplying New York City's Garment District across the river and companies around the world.

"They left New York when I was very young and came to New Jersey, first to Hoboken and then in Union City," Menendez told *The Jewish Standard*. "There was a nascent Cuban community—not from Havana, where my parents came from, and they didn't know anybody. What brought them over was the embroidery business. My mother started in the embroidery business in Hoboken. At one point, much later, I moved to a place called Clinton Mills. I told my sister about it, and she said, 'That's where Mom used to work.'"

By his own account, as a boy, he was doted on by his mother, who demanded that Caridad, who was nine years older than her little brother, monitor his homework, making sure that he completed it every night before he went to bed. As the only member of the family born in the United States, it was up to him to do well in school, go to college, and make something of his life.

"Growing up with Bob was average," said Caridad. "I was the typical big sister, but he was different. Always asking questions, loved to read, his favorite place to spend time was the library."[15]

The family settled in a tenement at 4607 Hudson Avenue, a few blocks from Bergenline Avenue, the main commercial hub, and walking distance to Roosevelt Elementary School, where a young Bob Menendez raced home every afternoon to eat a premade snack and do his homework before his parents and older siblings returned home. He was a self-confessed "chubby latchkey kid" and dutiful son.

"Much of my dad's life happened so young," Bob Menendez's daughter, Alicia, wrote in a 2024 letter to US District Judge Sidney Stein. "I had a long runway to adulthood and he did not. It's why, as a preteen, I'd find him up late at night playing my brother's Nintendo system. It's why, like an alien observing a different species, he once asked me why other people seem so happy and carefree."[16]

Menendez was the first in his family to do many things, she continued, and there was a lot of pressure placed on the young Menendez by his immigrant family.

"My mom and dad were very protective parents," Menendez wrote in his book, "and that was not unusual in the society we were part of. The whole Cuban-culture lifestyle was quite restricted. First things first: You had to do well in school. That meant there was no time to play until homework was done. . . . Even when I was allowed to go out to play, I was being watched."

In September 1968, Menendez became a freshman at Union Hill High School, where he would hone his leadership skills under the tutelage of a handful of teachers and forge important friendships that would last his entire life.

There was Manuel "Manny" Diaz who was senior class treasurer and a member of the history forum along with Menendez, a stellar history student who won numerous awards for his essays, including the American Legion Essay Award in 1969. Diaz would become Menendez's first law partner, contribute thousands to his political campaigns, and be invited to his Senate inauguration in 2006, even though by then Diaz was a convicted drug dealer. There was also Abraham Antun, who became student body president a year after Menendez held the title in his senior year in 1972. Antun remained so close to Menendez that the senator made him treasurer of his Senate political action committee decades later. Menendez was also best man at his wedding. And there was also Donald Scarinci, who ran Menendez's campaign for student body president and was the editor in chief of the *Midnight Hiller*, the newspaper that Menendez established at the school. Scarinci later followed him in Union City politics, becoming a lifelong best friend and calling him a "brother."

"We grew up together in Union City in the shadow of the Vietnam War and the Watergate scandal," Scarinci said, describing how they went door-to-door "with a vision and a plan to make life better for ordinary Americans."[17]

Among the teachers Menendez singled out for influencing him to pursue a political career was social studies teacher and academic adviser Tom Highton, who encouraged debate and discussion in class and was not afraid to ask his students provocative questions at the height of the Vietnam War, which raged throughout Menendez's years at Union Hill and didn't end until three years after his graduation in 1975.

In his book, Menendez recalls Highton asking students, "How can an eighteen-year-old be old enough to die for his or her country? But not old enough to vote?"

It was Highton's brother-in-law John Mielo, the school's director of student relations, who told Menendez he had "the capacity to be a leader" and encouraged him to run not only for student government but to get involved in local government at the Union City Board of Education.

Still, as a freshman, Menendez was painfully shy. He was also overweight and awkward, recalled Hugin.

"He was this wimpy kid, this fat, pudgy guy with glasses that were too big for him," said Hugin. "He was probably bullied. He was the last guy I would have been afraid of."

Back in high school, Menendez might have agreed with his assessment. "Speaking in public was a nightmare," Menendez wrote. "I was a good student, but a total introvert." He credited teacher Gail Harper with helping him overcome his fear of public speaking. Harper threatened him with failure if he didn't do a presentation in front of the class, and later in front of the entire student body. She coached him after school, asking him to read poetry and a short story aloud to her. She made him the narrator of the school's Christmas program, which would require him to speak in front of eight hundred people from ninth to twelfth grade. Menendez was up to the challenge, and later earned the praise of his teachers and fellow students for his public speaking skills.[18]

With his newfound confidence, Menendez flourished. He distinguished himself again and again in academics, sports, and student government. His political career began while he was still at Union City High School where he served in student government and headed a long list of clubs, including the school's history forum and debating team. He was also on the varsity bowling team—the Union Hill Keglers—when they won the state championship in his senior year. He was a valued player on the school's tennis team where he and the team's captain, Domingo Garcia, were praised as "the backbone" of the squad. "The desire, determination, and the will to win certainly proved to be true characteristics of both these fine athletes," according to the caption next to the team's photo in the 1972 Union Hill yearbook. Fellow students recalled little of the shy, overweight introvert, but remembered the bespectacled Menendez for his "golden voice over the PA system" and predicted that he was "one Hiller who will surely succeed."[19]

Still, when he qualified for the senior honors program, he was shocked to learn that he would have to pay $200 to buy his own books. He didn't have the funds, and protested to school administrators. "I created such a ruckus that the school administration got sick of arguing, told me to shut up, gave me the books and put me in the honors program," he recalled.[20]

But like so many of his origin stories, this one may not, in fact, be true. Two former teachers in Union City disputed his claim in letters to local newspapers. "It's a lie," said Paul Suriano, who taught high school in Union City from 1956 to 1990. "It's all fabrication," he told a reporter for *The Star-Ledger* in 2006. "Maybe kids paid for field trips. But books? Never."[21]

In retelling the story over the years, the figure has changed from $200 to $100. Either figure seems preposterous. The purchasing power of those amounts would translate to just under $2,000 today.

"It's my recollection of that time that it was collectively around $100," Menendez said during his 2006 campaign for senator. "I complained about it. I complained that girls had to pay for uniforms to be in clubs. I felt it was a public high school and no one should have to pay."

Once he found his public voice, there was no stopping Bob Menendez. He was one of eleven students from Union Hill to participate in Girls' and Boys' State, a program run by the American Legion that teaches high school students citizenship and leadership skills at the state government level. In the summer before his senior year, Menendez accompanied the other male members of his group to Rider College in Lawrence Township to learn about state government.

Menendez also traveled to the US capital to testify as a student representative before the House Education and Labor Committee at the invitation of New Jersey Congressman Dominick Daniels. The congressman wanted federal education aid for the tens of thousands of refugee children arriving on Freedom Flights from Cuba to the United States. The US and Cuban governments jointly transported some three hundred thousand political refugees, including thousands of children, out of the Communist country between 1965 and 1973. Arriving in Miami and Union City, they were overwhelming the local school systems, which needed so-called impact aid to address the situation. Bob Menendez was called upon to describe how the influx was affecting Union Hill, making the argument for more federal aid to local public schools to alleviate crowded conditions in schools in the South Florida and New Jersey communities where Cuban migrants were settling in the United States.[22]

In addition to Boys' State, Menendez was also part of a "specially selected group of students" who spent two weeks in Washington, DC, learning about the federal government. Menendez was one of four members of the school's Washington Workshop—part of eighty students selected from each state to live at Mount Vernon Junior College and attend daily lectures on Capitol Hill. Perhaps Menendez saw himself in the featured speakers during that Washington sojourn. The students attended lectures by Democratic US senators—Hubert Humphrey, a former vice president under Lyndon Johnson and the senator from Minnesota, as well as Birch Bayh, the US senator from Indiana.

"Who knows," reads the 1972 yearbook caption next to a black-and-white photo of the four budding politicians where Menendez stands slightly apart in a light, pin-striped suit and wide tie. "Maybe someday one of these four boys will be living in the White House!"

Bob Menendez graduated from Union Hill High School as an impressive student leader in the spring of 1972, one who had the power to inspire his fellow students. "Let us work towards the day when men will come to see more clearly, not that which divides them but that which unites them," he wrote in the 1972 Union Hill High School yearbook. "That the blessings of peace be ours, the peace to build and grow, to live in harmony and sympathy with others, and to plan and build for the future."

Bob Menendez was immersed in local politics even before leaving Union Hill High School. With the help of Mielo and Highton, he had already started volunteering at the Union City Board of Education and had met Bill Musto, the man who would be his most important political mentor and have an outsized influence on his career.

≈

William Vincent Musto was born in 1917 in what was then known as West Hoboken, which is now part of Union City. He came of age in a New Jersey where speakeasies and underground gin stills flourished during Prohibition, and decades later Italian mobsters aligned with the famous Five Families ruled hand in hand with their paid stooges in local government. His father, Patrick Edmund Musto, a labor union delegate and member of the International Association of Machinists, had served as an aide to Samuel Gompers, the founder of the American Federation of Labor, who died in 1924. Patrick Musto fought for affordable housing in New Jersey in the 1920s and presided over the Union City Board of Education for forty years.

William Musto attended Emerson High School. By the time he was drafted into the US Army as a twenty-three-year-old, he had already earned his law degree after six years of night school at John Marshall Law School in Newark. He listed his father as the "person who will always know your address" on his yellow draft card.

Musto was a patriot and a war hero, who served for more than four years in the US Army during World War II. He served in Europe, helping to liberate France and then Luxembourg during the Battle of the Bulge. He earned a Bronze Star "for meritorious service . . . in connection with military operations against an enemy of the United States" in January 1945 and was promoted from first lieutenant to captain.

Before he shipped off to Europe, he met his future wife, Rhyta Palmerini, in 1941 at Fort Dix where he was an artillery officer. She worked as a medical technician at a Trenton hospital, and the two fell in love in letters they sent each other during Musto's deployment.

The Mustos were married in January 1946, the same year that he was elected to the state assembly. Eight years later, in 1954, he was elected as one of five commissioners who govern Union City. In 1962, that chamber chose him as the mayor, and three years later he was elected as a state senator. He served in both the senate and the mayor's office at the same time.

Musto looked up to New Jersey's original Democratic Party boss, Francis "Frank" Hague, who was mayor of Jersey City from 1917 to 1947. Hague, the son of Irish immigrants, despite being expelled from grade school, was a canny political operator who started his career as a prizefight manager. He avoided numerous federal and state investigations because he took his bribes in cash. Although his salary never topped $8,000, he was a millionaire with a lavish apartment on Park Avenue in Manhattan, a mansion in Miami Beach, and he spent vacations in Paris.

Boss Hague, as he was known, was a longtime vice chair of the Democratic National Committee and political ally of Franklin Delano Roosevelt. He bankrolled public works projects in Jersey City, which enabled him to stay in power, offering free medical care and food during the Depression.

"I am the law!" he famously declared during a talk on city government before nearly one thousand members and guests of the Emory Methodist Episcopal Church in Jersey City in 1937. Although he was beloved by many of his constituents, he was branded the "Führer of Union City" in the national press. When he left city government, he installed his nephew Frank Hague Eggers in his seat, but retained the chairmanship of the state and county Democratic Parties as well as the vice chairmanship of the Democratic National Committee.

"He was known for doing whatever it took to get his way, and the joke was the governor had on his desk a direct line to Hague," wrote Bob Ingle and Sandy McClure in *The Soprano State: New Jersey's Culture of Corruption*. "He got his strength from patronage, corruption, and public jobs doled out to supporters."

Hague supported Musto for state assembly in 1946, and Musto followed his example in his own pursuit of power. Unlike Hague, Musto began cementing his hold on power in state elections before taking control of the Union City mayor's office in 1962. With Hague's backing, Musto was elected to the state assembly, and by 1953 became the Democratic minority leader. Two years later, he was elected to the state senate, occupying the seat while he also served as mayor of Union City. Ultimately, it was Musto's control of the mayor's office and the Board of Education where he amassed a great deal of his power, following Boss Hague's example of providing social services and doling out jobs to his constituents. Musto is credited with spearheading programs to help Cuban refugees, propping up small businesses and pushing to legalize gambling throughout a long and storied political career, but a good deal of his power came from his close association with the city's unions.

"You couldn't get a job as a teacher in Union City without buying a ticket to a Musto fundraiser," said one observer, adding that cash collected by the Musto machine was only done with music blaring in the background at the Italian Cultural Center in Union City. The loud music made it impossible for anyone wearing a wire to get a good recording, he said.[23]

Alan Jay Weiss, a writer and business consultant who grew up in Union City in the 1960s, came face-to-face with the Musto machine as a student at Emerson High School. Weiss had taken part in a student exchange with Finland in 1963. When he returned to Union City, Musto summoned him to the mayor's office to congratulate him for doing his hometown proud.

"He said to me, 'Is there anything I can do for you?'" said Weiss. "I told him that I wanted a job in the post office, because I knew they paid $6 an hour, and I needed to make money to pay for an engagement ring and my college tuition."[24]

Musto said he was glad to help, but told him he had to do things according to the rules. Weiss would have to take a civil service exam first, Musto said. Weiss took the exam, but was certain he failed it. Two weeks later, he was surprised when he received his results in the mail. He had scored 100 percent, and he was approved for a part-time job with the post office.

"What mattered was that I took the test and followed the rules," said Weiss. "This was Musto at work."

Weiss proved so good at his job that his supervisors promoted him to a truck route, which he was able to finish in just three hours every day.

But his work ethic and diligence were not appreciated by the union and the full-time post office employees. "At eleven thirty in the morning, I would be walking down Bergenline Avenue and see the postal inspectors drinking, and I was told that if I came back before 5:00 p.m., they'd break my legs," he said.

So, after he finished his route, Weiss drove around searching for a place he could park the postal truck to wait out his eight-hour day. "I read a lot of books," he said. "These guys may have been breaking the law, but they were always enforcing the rules."

When Weiss's mother needed a secretarial job, she also went to Musto, who found her one at the local school board. In exchange, she showed up at rallies to support him. Musto could always count on her vote, Weiss said.

"He was a pretty sharp political operator, and a master of patronage politics," Weiss said. "It wasn't just the school principals and the police chiefs. It went right down to the janitors and the street sweepers. Every job in the city flowed through city hall, and Bill Musto personally approved everything."

But in 1970, Musto lost his reelection to the city commission, and his most important base of power in the mayor's office.

"I was at the rally in the Italian wedding hall in 1970 when he lost," said Weiss. "He had all of his supporters there, and runners would come in, and it quickly became apparent he was going to lose, which was unthinkable."

His nemesis Paul Lombardo, a former Union City police chief who headed the reform slate Project 70, won the race. Two years later, Musto believed that Lombardo had a hand in his father's conviction after a four-week trial in 1972 on federal kickback charges along with two other defendants. Patrick Musto, at seventy-nine, was sentenced to two and a half years in prison plus a $20,000 fine. School board architect Joseph D. Lugosch was also convicted and sentenced to two and a half years and an $11,000 fine. A third defendant, board member John J. Powers, a key Bill Musto crony, was acquitted of all charges. Musto Sr. died three years later.

Musto never forgave Lombardo, who was himself indicted in 1972 while he served as commissioner of Union City's police department for awarding $24,000 in repair contracts without undergoing a public bidding process.

Bob Menendez waded into the Union City quagmire in 1972 while he was still in high school. At the time, Musto chaired the Senate Judiciary Committee and was pushing for the creation of the state lottery. Like his father before him, Musto was active on the school board through members who had been loyal to the entire Musto family, including John Powers.

"He [Menendez] learned everything about politics at age eighteen," said a longtime New Jersey political observer. "You take care of yours and the government is a profit-making operation."[25]

In Bob Menendez, Musto had found a fledgling leader whom he could mold into a politician who could help him appeal to the scores of Cuban refugees who were settling in Union City and Hudson County. For his part, Menendez had found the father figure he was so sorely lacking—the Democratic power broker, who was willing to take him under his wing and teach him everything he knew.

"Bill gave him everything," said Libero Marotta, a Union City attorney. "Anything he wanted, he got. He was the darling of Bill Musto and his organization, no question about it."

According to Rhyta Musto, her husband instantly took a shine to the boyish and rather awkward Cuban American student. "He came to the house almost every day," she recalled. "He literally had papers in his shoes to cover the holes."

By the time he was a freshman majoring in political science at St. Peter's College in Jersey City, Menendez and some of his friends were hired as aides to Musto. Part of the job was speaking to constituents, who queued up to meet Musto at the Italian Cultural Center where he liked to hold court. They came seeking the don's help with myriad problems—including health care, housing, and immigration, among other issues.

"It was every range of personal pain," said Scarinci, who began working for Musto in 1978, becoming Union City's public information officer while still in law school at Seton Hall University. "They were down on their luck and they were looking for someone to help them. It was always conducted as counseling. He was always empathetic."

Musto was beloved among many of the sixty thousand residents of Union City. In addition to government jobs, Musto helped voters pay medical bills and found them homes. "He's concerned about us," said Patricia Evans, a Union City resident. She went to Musto after her daughter was injured in two separate accidents and said he reached into his own pocket to help with the medical bills. "You don't see that too often."[26]

Menendez had that same sense of idealism, at least as a student leader.

"Bob said, 'You change the world one community at a time, and you change the community one person at a time,'" Scarinci said.[27]

Menendez was laser focused on a career in politics. "I can't remember Bob Menendez sitting in front of the TV with a bowl of chips," Scarinci said.[28]

"I remember one day when he was on Bergenline [Avenue] and I saw him across the street," said Abraham Antun, who attended high school with Menendez. "I rushed over to him, and he had just gotten elected student council president, and I said I wanted to help him. As we got to . . . peel the onion, we got to see that we needed to get more involved in government because government influences a lot of lives."

Antun became a student delegate to the Union City Board of Education, where he joined Menendez who was given his seat on the board by Musto shortly after he graduated from high school. The friends started Citizens for Community Action, a civic organization that began campaigning for an elected school board rather than one in which representatives were appointed. The petition passed in 1973, paving the way for elections a year later. The nonprofit awarded Menendez a prize "for his efforts in putting the elected school board form on the November ballot."

"He sucked up to the party machine," said Paul Mulshine of *The Star-Ledger*.

In the winter of 1974, twenty-year-old Bob Menendez ran on a slate with a doctor, a teacher, a police officer, and an undertaker to take over the Union City Board of Education—a chance for the Musto machine to regain its footing after he'd lost the mayor's race in 1970.

"In crass political terms, the machine needed a Cuban on the ticket to attract votes and support from what was then the city's emerging ethnic groups," said journalist Fred Snowflack, who attended a candidates' night. "Menendez certainly fit the bill."[29]

Still, he had a lot to learn, recalled one of his confidants. When Menendez showed up to a speech on José Marti Day, commemorating a Cuban national hero and freedom fighter, he sported a black and red tie. "I said, 'Bob, you can't do that, people will see that and think of the [26th of July Movement] Cuban flag and think you're pro-Castro,'" said José Manuel Alvarez. "I had to tell him not to mention the Kennedys and things like that."[30]

Menendez and his slate won the election in February 1974, and his mentor was reelected in May of the same year. Musto made sure that Menendez rapidly moved from school board member to secretary of administration on the board—a paid position.

"Menendez was a prince," said a New Jersey political operative. "Everything was taken care of for him by the Mustos."

Not only was Menendez dining at the Musto home several times a week, but the Mustos took it upon themselves to arrange his marriage.

Jane Jacobsen was a year older than Menendez, and, like him, she was a student at St. Peter's College. Like him, she grew up in Union City where she was captain of the marching band's majorettes at Emerson High School. Her father was the captain of the local fire department, who was keen to do anything to make Musto happy, even if it meant marrying off his tall, blonde daughter to the Democratic boss's nerdy protégé.

They met in 1974 when they were both campaigning for the Union City school board. Both would later go on to Rutgers University, where Jane studied for a master's degree in education and Menendez went to law school. By this time, Menendez knew he had to embrace his Latino background if he were to succeed in a political landscape carved up by racial and cultural identities. He joined Lambda Theta Phi, a Latino fraternity founded in Union, New Jersey, in 1975.

"Musto called all of his associates, and said this is the kid that we have to build," said Chi Chi Rodriguez. "He told them that he wanted Bob to marry Jane because she would be good for his career."

Jane was striking, with a Norwegian background and a love of Latino culture. To Menendez, she must have seemed a statuesque Amazon, who was much taller than the young politician. Rhyta Musto knew her family, and soon Janie, as she was known to her friends, was also a regular at the Musto dinner table. The couple married in 1976 after Menendez finished his undergraduate degree at St. Peter's.

Menendez did not invite his father to his wedding, said Rodriguez. In 1978, Mario Menendez was found dead under a nearby viaduct in his car, where carbon monoxide had seeped through the exhaust and gassed him to death.

It's not clear what Menendez's reaction was to his father's suicide. Likely he was shocked even as he was deeply ashamed over the kind of man he was. Still, neighbors in Union City were disgusted when he waited more than ten days to pick up his father's body at the morgue.

—

By the time he was twenty-four, Menendez was a married man and secretary of the school board. He began to have conflicts with school

board president John Powers, who had narrowly escaped conviction for taking kickbacks in 1973. Powers was handing over checks
to Rudolph Orlandini, a contractor working on new annexes to two
schools in Union City without Menendez's signature. Despite $746,000
in overruns, the annexes were not getting built. Menendez complained
to Powers.

Those who were close to Menendez at the time said he was not
comfortable with Powers's shenanigans at the school board. In those
days, he was still the idealistic student leader that Scarinci and Antun
had come to know when they were all in high school.

In addition to Powers's shady behavior, there had been rumors
for years that Musto himself was involved in corruption, supporting
underground gambling. There were whispers in Union City that a federal grand jury had been convened after a raid on one such operation
organized by Musto and his cronies.

Later, Menendez worked up the courage to confront Musto about
the rumors and some of the newspaper accounts of wrongdoing. By
November 1977, Musto had been indicted on a charge of conspiring to
assist an illegal gambling operation run out of a tavern on Bergenline
Avenue. The bar where an underground baccarat game was going
on was owned by the wife of Lombardo, the former police chief and
Musto's sworn political enemy. Frank Scarafile, the deputy police chief
who had spoken to Mario Menendez years earlier, was also indicted
along with three other police officers.

"I'm absolutely, completely innocent of anything whatsoever," said
Bill Musto, who was attending a convention in Atlantic City when the
indictment was unsealed. "I'm amazed and shocked."[31]

Musto was likely telling the truth. Nathan Lemler, a chiroprac-
tor and former police informant, testified in federal court in 1978
that he had heard of a police plot to frame Musto. Lemler was in
prison for taking thousands of dollars in bribes to get students into
medical and dental schools. He found himself in the same prison as
Lombardo, who confessed to him that he was being forced by the

US attorney's office to lie about Musto's involvement in the baccarat scheme. Musto was alleged to have urged Jack Prizzia, a Union City municipal court judge, to acquit several men who had been arrested in the 1975 raid on the tavern, and to warn the players before the arrival of law enforcement.[32]

Celin Valdivia, the brother-in-law of one of Musto's top aides, initially sought police protection for the baccarat game. Later, Lombardo and his family were reportedly placed in protective custody by federal authorities outside New Jersey.

A year after the raid, in January 1976, Prizzia was killed when he was shot several times on the way into his law office on Bergenline Avenue. The assassination came weeks after he had testified before the federal grand jury. He was later revealed to be an unindicted coconspirator in the scheme to protect the gambling operation. The charges against Valdivia and Musto were eventually dropped after federal authorities failed to bring forward the informant they claimed they had.

Prizzia's murder remains unsolved.

Musto smelled a rat and immediately suspected Lombardo, whose testimony had landed his elderly father in prison. There was "no question" that the United States attorney's office in Newark "is out to get me," he told reporters. "I am not guilty. Ask the people of Union City."

With his political mentor in the news on corruption charges and shady dealings going on at the school board, Menendez began to worry. Menendez wasn't happy with the picture that was emerging, especially after he spoke to Musto.

"He was on a tirade," Menendez recalled. "He'd look at you and tell you, 'These hands are clean,' and suggest that anything of disagreement or whatnot was disloyal."

CHAPTER TWO

Little Havana on the Hudson

E ulalio José Negrin might not have ever known what hit him as he attempted to step into his car on the morning of November 25, 1979. Perhaps the thirty-seven-year-old Cuban American community leader caught a glimpse of the two men wearing ski masks and pointing their MAC-10 submachine guns in his direction as they came to a screeching halt in a silver car with a red top next to his own vehicle, which was parked on 10th Street in front of his girlfriend's home in downtown Union City. It's likely he didn't have time to process that he would probably be dead in the split second that it took him to crumple to the pavement in what a reporter later described as a "fusillade of semi-automatic weapons fire."[33]

As his father hit the ground, Richard Negrin, age thirteen, who was poised to enter the passenger side of the car, rushed to his side.

"Without any regard for me or anybody else on the streets, [they] just sprayed the whole street, bullets everywhere," Richard said years after the shooting. "My dad never made it into the car. I went around to the back of the car and saw him and held him as he died."[34]

Reports said that Eulalio Negrin had been struck in the upper body by five bullets, one of which entered the left side of his neck and lodged in his left shoulder. He died before the ambulance pulled in at Riverside General Hospital in nearby Secaucus—the latest victim in a vicious campaign of terror unleashed by Cuban exiles determined to bring down Communist leader Fidel Castro, who had already been in power for two decades. Members of the Cuban Nationalist Movement, popularly known as Omega 7, had already planted more than a dozen bombs in New York and New Jersey since the early 1970s and had participated in a handful of high-profile assassinations in Puerto Rico and Washington, DC.

"We will continue these executions until we have eliminated all of the traitors living in this country," said the anonymous caller who spoke in what an Associated Press reporter later described as a "Hispanic accent." The call came into the newsroom more than ten hours after the hit on Eulalio Negrin, which seemed an aberration for the members of the radical right-wing group who were usually quick to publicize their terrorist acts.

≈

Omega 7 allied itself with a host of other militants in Miami as well as with operatives in the CIA working to assassinate Castro. In Union City, the headquarters of their "northern zone" of operations, they forged strong ties with the Italian Mafia, extorted fees from local merchants, and enjoyed the support of members of the Musto machine.

Julia Valdivia, the top Cuban American aide to the mayor, known widely as the *alcaldesa*, or the "lady mayor," frequented their fundraising events and was among their most loyal supporters. It was thanks to the "lady mayor" that Union City financed radical Cuban exile newspapers, spending more than $30,000 in one year alone to advertise in *Avance*, a paper published by Bill Musto ally René Avila, and *Guerra*, the mouthpiece of the Association of the Bay of Pigs Veterans, also known as Brigade 2506.

A bleached blonde with an imposing manner, Valdivia was officially an aide to Mayor Musto, a member of the powerful school board, and unofficially "the head of Hispanic affairs" for Union City where

Cuban immigration had exploded since Menendez's parents settled there in the early 1950s. By the 1960s and 1970s, tens of thousands of exiled Cubans were finding their way to what became known as Little Havana on the Hudson. To cement his hold on power, Musto and his cronies on the local school board knew they needed their support.

"The Cuban people have enabled Union City to hold its own, to tread water when all other cities are sinking," said Union City's school board president John Powers in an interview with *The Hudson Dispatch* in 1977.

Valdivia had arrived in Union City with her husband, Luis, in the mid-1950s, about the same time as the Menendez family. She had come to rule the lower level of city hall where a large, gilt-framed portrait of a decidedly younger Valdivia as a beaming brunette in a white dress and clutching a bouquet of flowers hung behind her cluttered desk. Cuban immigrants lined up to seek her help with all manner of government bureaucracy, from immigration issues to school registration. Musto, who had lost the mayoral election in 1970, recognized the importance of his tough-talking Cuban aide and even created a no-show city job for her husband to keep her happy. Valdivia, after all, was his entrée into the Cuban community. The Cubans she helped returned the favor by voting in the Musto machine. Valdivia knew how important she was to the veteran politician and was fond of saying to anyone who would listen that Musto's political fortunes were in her hands.

"When Musto lost in 1970, he came to know white rice, black beans, and chunks of fried pork for the first time," she said.

"Julia Valdivia has the reputation of being a very powerful figure in Union City, a dispenser of favors or a roadblock to those she doesn't like," according to a 1979 article in *New York Magazine*, which also noted that, like many of the Cuban émigrés who sought her out, she practiced Santeria, an Afro-Cuban religion that relies on animal sacrifice to appease the Orishas or Yoruba gods.[35]

"The Cubans call her up for anything, because they don't know any better," a local reporter told the magazine. "Say somebody needs a dog license. They come into Valdivia's office and ask for help. She makes a big deal out of it. 'Give so-and-so a dog license, I'm sending them over,' she'll say into the telephone. The poor person thinks he's getting a dog license because Mrs. Valdivia used her influence."

The Cuban patronage mill at city hall masked a dark underworld. Mob violence permeated Union City where murders and firebombings of local shops that did not support Omega 7 and the Musto machine made the city into a modern-day Wild West. In the early days, Omega 7's members included veterans from the Bay of Pigs invasion in 1961, who were angry at President Kennedy and the US government for not providing the promised air cover to shore up the brigade. Later, Kennedy made a deal with the Russians to end the Cuban Missile Crisis, and promised not to invade Cuba, further angering anti-Castro militants throughout the United States.

The violence spilled across the Hudson River to Manhattan when Omega 7 leader Armando Santana planted a bomb at the door of the Academy of Music Theater on 14th Street where a celebration of the Cuban Revolution was scheduled to take place in 1976.

In addition to Santana, other ruthless Omega 7 militants included Ignacio Novo Sampol and his younger brother, Guillermo—known as Bill in Union City. Both were notorious radicals behind some of the most outrageous acts of violence in the anti-Castro cause. The brothers once fired a bazooka at the United Nations headquarters in 1964 during a speech by Che Guevara, the Argentine-born Cuban revolutionary leader and minister of industry in the Castro government.

"They could have hit the United Nations headquarters, but purposely didn't," said Stanley Ross, editor of *El Tiempo*, a Manhattan-based Spanish language newspaper, who brokered the surrender of the brothers and one other suspect.[36] The missile, fired from Long Island City, landed in the East River, about two hundred yards from the UN. Ross said their sole purpose was to take the spotlight away from Guevara and start a demonstration against Cuba outside the United Nations. The brothers confessed to the crime, but the case against them was eventually tossed after it was revealed that police failed to read them their Miranda rights.

The Novo brothers, along with Union City resident Alvin Ross Diaz, were arrested and initially found guilty of the 1976 assassination of Orlando Letelier and researcher Ronni Moffitt in Washington, DC. Letelier, a former ambassador to the United States and minister of foreign affairs in the government of Chilean leader Salvador Allende, was arrested and tortured after the US-backed coup that brought General Augusto Pinochet to power in the country in 1973. In 1975, Letelier moved to Washington where he continued his opposition against the Pinochet government, working as a professor at American University and writing anti-Pinochet articles for a think tank. He and Moffitt were killed after a bomb strapped to their Chevelle exploded as they were driving in Sheridan Circle in the city's Embassy Row on the morning of September 21. The Novo brothers and Ross Diaz had met with Chilean secret police and helped construct the bomb, according to the federal indictment against them.

Forty years after the murders, in 2016, the CIA released classified documents to the Chilean government, noting that "A review of our files on the Letelier assassination has provided what we regard as convincing evidence that President Pinochet personally ordered his intelligence chief to carry out the murder." The assessment added that Pinochet later "decided to stonewall on the case to hide his involvement and, ultimately, to protect his hold on the presidency."[37]

When the Novo brothers and Ross Diaz were indicted for the murders of Letelier and Moffitt in 1978, Valdivia and other members of the Musto administration proudly rose to their defense. They organized local events to help raise money for them. Supporters lined Bergenline Avenue and demanded that merchants shut down for one day in protest.

"It was Capone-style," one resident told *New York Magazine* at the time. "They put their stickers on my store window. I told them they had no right. They came back the next day and smashed my window. . . . Later, I sold my shop."[38]

Valdivia herself appeared at several rallies for the Novo brothers and encouraged fellow members of the school board, including a young Bob Menendez—the promising Cuban American board secretary who was in law school at Rutgers University—to do the same. In the 1970s, he needed the support of Valdivia and did her bidding by backing the anti-Castro cause and showing up at rallies and fundraisers for these extremists.

Local businessmen such as Abel Hernandez, owner of Mi Bandera restaurant and grocery, as well as Arnaldo Monzón, a banker and member of the Cuban American National Foundation, a fervidly anti-Castro group, all lined up to finance Omega 7, according to federal authorities. Both men continued to support Menendez throughout his career and were among his biggest benefactors.[39]

Like Valdivia, Menendez supported the hardcore anti-Castro Cubans and would later campaign for the defense of Eduardo Arocena, a former longshoreman convicted of several bombings, including one at the TWA terminal at the John F. Kennedy International Airport.

"I endorse the fact that there are times when what one looks at as a law at a given time has to be broken," Menendez said.[40]

In addition to the TWA bombing, Arocena was found guilty in November 1984 of organizing the murder of a Cuban diplomat in Queens and organizing the bombings of Cuban, Soviet, Venezuelan, Mexican, and Nicaraguan missions in New York and Miami, as well as at Madison Square Garden in Manhattan.

Valdivia had no qualms about supporting the growing violence.

"I have known him so many years," Valdivia said of Ignacio Novo, an unemployed shoe salesman and high-ranking member of Omega 7. "He was a friend and I respected his opinions. He believed in what he was doing, and I respected what he did."

When asked about the frequent bombings in Union City, Valdivia shrugged: "I don't see any violence to worry about."[41]

Eulalio Negrin worried every day about the violence. On March 25, 1979, his office in Weehawken—the New Jersey Cuban Refugee Program—had been demolished by a bomb planted by Omega 7. The bomb exploded the same day that the group blew up the TWA terminal at JFK airport in Queens as well as a building in Union City that housed the Almacen El Espanol, a supermarket and community group that shipped medicines and other supplies to Cuba.

Negrin, who had run a losing campaign as a Republican against William Musto in the state senate and had once campaigned for Richard Nixon, was a member of the Committee of 75, a group of Cuban-born pastors, academics, and other community leaders who lobbied for "dialogue" with the island's hardcore leaders. They had met with Castro on a trip to the island in 1978 and had lobbied for an end to the American trade embargo. Working from his Weehawken storefront, Negrin arranged for the reunification of families, charging between $2,000 to $5,000 to bring Cubans to the United States. Perennially hard-pressed for cash, the Cuban government assessed each request individually and based its recommendations on how much property it could confiscate from Cubans desperate to leave the island.

Negrin, who sneaked out of Cuba disguised as a priest when he immigrated to the United States, later became so trusted by the Cuban regime that he was the only person Castro would deal with in northern New Jersey, his bodyguard Rudolf Benitez told reporters. For this reason, Negrin was branded a traitor by Omega 7 and became a marked man, even as his efforts resulted in the release of some three thousand political prisoners from the island. In April 1979, months before Negrin was killed in Union City, the terrorist group took credit for the assassination of Carlos Muñiz Varela, a fellow Committee of 75 member who ran a similar travel agency in San Juan, Puerto Rico.

At the time of the bombing at his agency, Negrin and Reverend Andres Reyes of the Holy Family Church in Union City convened a press conference amid the rubble of his destroyed offices. The two men told reporters that the FBI and local authorities knew the identity of the Omega 7 terrorists who had carried out the bombing but had "done nothing."[42]

Reyes, a fellow participant in the "dialogue" with Cuba, was forced to leave his post at the Holy Family Church in Union City and move to Newark because of death threats to blow up the church-affiliated high school in May.

"Terrorism here is worse than in the era of McCarthy," said Reverend Eduardo de Mayas who replaced Father Reyes at the Holy Family Church. "The accusation of Communism comes against anyone who moves towards peace."

Negrin knew he was a marked man. He regularly received death threats. In late October, weeks before his assassination, he started getting telephone calls at three in the morning. There would be nothing coming from the receiver "except the metallic tick-tick-tick of an alarm clock," reported *The Village Voice*. "And so he would lie there in the darkness with the telephone to his ear, listening to the tick-tick-tick. His time was running out." In early November he bought a casket and made his will.

Days before his death, he asked for help, according to Union City Police Chief Herman Bolte, adding that Negrin had "often" come to his office to ask for police protection.[43] He employed a bodyguard and carried a fully loaded .38 caliber revolver, for which he did not have a permit. But on the day he was killed, he never had an opportunity to reach for his weapon, and the bodyguard was not with him during the lightning ambush.

"Omega 7 has directed their bombing activities to diplomatic consulates belonging to Cuba and Venezuela . . . to installations that sponsor pro-Castro meetings as well as merchants who are currently sending medical supplies to Cuba in addition to travel agencies and airlines who sponsor flights to Cuba," said the FBI in a March 25, 1979, press handout.

The group had little regard for the collateral damage it caused or whether innocent bystanders were caught in its line of fire. Two months later, in June 1976, Omega 7 bombed the Cuban Mission to the United Nations just as seven young children passed by the agency's doorway, an FBI investigation revealed. A year earlier, in October 1978, Omega 7 bombed *El Diario* newspaper's offices in New York, nearly killing a professor from North Carolina as he walked past. The unidentified professor was thrown into a parked car, although he was not badly injured. The attack on *El Diario* was aimed at Manuel de Dios Unanue, its dogged investigative reporter whose beat was right-wing Cuban exile groups. And had the TWA explosion taken place while the airplane was in the air or while passengers were on board, "the possibility exists that 155 persons, including the crew, may have been killed because Omega 7 disagrees with TWA sponsoring flights to Cuba," the FBI report said.

Days after his death, Negrin was buried outside Union City in a secret ceremony so as not to attract radicals. The family did not invite any of his friends to the funeral.

A week after the shooting, moderates in the Cuban American community urged federal authorities to establish a task force to investigate terrorist acts by the militant Cuban groups.

Negrin's murder ushered in even more violence and repression in Union City where Bob Menendez and a group of fellow school board trustees were poised to launch a coup d'état against their longtime mentor, Bill Musto.

In 1979, Menendez and Bruce Walter, deputy public works director for the city, formed the Alliance Civic Association and began to consolidate their own power. They enlisted Julia Valdivia, the high priestess of city hall who continued to practice Santeria, especially against her political enemies.

"Musto better pray to all the saints that she never turns on him," said one former city hall staffer. "When that day comes, he'll be through."

CHAPTER THREE

Feet of Clay

Six years after graduating high school, an earnest twenty-four-year-old Menendez began to lose some of his youthful idealism when he saw what a little bit of corruption could do for his friends and family. By then, the young law student and secretary of the Board of Education must have known how the Musto patronage machine worked and, like everyone else around him, took advantage of the perks that came with his office. He found jobs for his beloved mother and sister, who appeared on the city hall payroll—his mother as a part-time janitor with a $6,000-a-year salary (the equivalent of nearly $30,000 today). His father also did contract work for the city. Later, his young wife, Jane, would also find herself working for Union City.

In his role as school board secretary, Menendez also gained the title of chief financial officer, and his signature was necessary on any purchase agreement. In 1977, Union City and its Board of Education applied for federal funding to make improvements to two high schools. Grants totaling more than $4.4 million were doled out to the city to complete renovations on Menendez's own alma mater as well as Emerson High School, where Bill Musto had gone to school years earlier.

But nearly $1 million went missing.[44] Menendez said he first became aware of the missing cash when he caught school board president John Powers, a close Musto confidant, writing inflated checks to Orlando Construction Company, a firm owned by local contractor and former carpenter Rudolph Orlandini, age fifty, who was rumored to have connections to the Italian Mob. The outflow of cash was not going through the proper approvals and not being cosigned by board secretary Menendez, who was required to sign off on all expenditures.

Menendez claimed he confronted Powers. Menendez never did get along with the school board boss, who was constantly running scams behind the board's back, even if he was also one of Musto's handpicked protégés. He may have also confronted his mentor and surrogate father Musto himself about Powers's inflated payments to Orlandini. Years later, he said that he tried to warn Musto of the corruption on the school board, but perhaps he was simply upset about being kept in the dark or that he wasn't getting a share of the kickbacks.

"He had gone to his mentor, the mayor . . . and pleaded with him to get rid of the crooks," wrote a columnist for *The New York Times* in 2006, a few days into Menendez's campaign for the US Senate, and after his Republican rival Thomas Kean began to question Menendez's past dealings with Musto. "Nothing happened; it seemed that Mr. Musto was a captive of his loyalties to the corrupt people he had put in positions of power."[45]

One of those people was surely Menendez himself. It could not have been a revelation to the studious law student that Musto ran a dirty patronage mill, even as he himself was taking advantage of the machine to help his family. It's hard to believe that Menendez, for all his accomplishments, was little more than a naive dupe, even as an idealistic young man. He must have been aware that Musto had been indicted in 1974 for illegal gambling with respect to the underground baccarat games in Union City. Perhaps he believed his mentor when he said that the charges against him were fabricated by his political enemies. Could his beloved surrogate father be guilty of corruption?

The knowledge might surely have been difficult to take in all at once, but Bob Menendez likely knew it to be true.

Whatever his reasoning for exposing Powers and Musto, who was in his sixth term as mayor of Union City, Menendez soon saw an important role for himself, and immediately took on the mantle of anti-corruption crusader after he was subpoenaed to testify before a federal grand jury.

By his own account, he played it magnificently, wearing a bullet-proof vest for protection in the run-up to his testimony in open court against the various Mafia organizations—Cuban, Italian, the local Democratic Party—that he must have known controlled Union City. The assassination of the town judge Jack Prizzia, who was shot dead after giving testimony to a federal grand jury, was surely an ominous sign that snitches were simply not tolerated in Union City.

"Bobby Menendez was starting to put the pieces of the puzzle together," Orlandini later said at the landmark Musto trial in Newark federal court, describing how Menendez was scrutinizing the false paperwork that Powers put in place to cover up the bribes.[46]

"I started to see serious trouble," wrote Menendez in his book.

"Coming back from a vacation trip, I found that a series of checks had been issued for a particular contract without my approval," he wrote. "I protested, asking how checks could be issued without my authorization and without confirmation from the architect involved that the work would be completed. There was no satisfactory answer. It became evident that the president of the school board was working on shady projects with the mayor."

In 1978, after Musto was reelected mayor, he continued, he had other plans up his sleeve, such as attempting to sell the city's most popular park to a developer to make way for a department store across the street from St. Michael's Monastery Church (its full name is the Monastery and Church of St. Michael the Archangel). Menendez said he continued to protest, saying that the park was crucial to the residents of Union City, which had become one of the most densely populated cities in the country.

When he didn't receive answers to his questions from members of the school board and Musto, he raised his concerns in public and went to the local newspapers. He also began working on an anti-corruption campaign at the City Commission and the school board.

The extortion scheme eventually fell apart when the school board ran out of cash before Orlandini's company could complete the renovations on the high schools. Under a cash crunch and facing years in prison on bribery charges himself, Orlandini agreed in 1980 to cooperate with authorities to wiretap Powers, Musto, and others discussing the bribes, which amounted to nearly $400,000. The short, stocky builder struck a deal with prosecutors. He claimed there was a $250,000 bounty for him in the Union City underworld, largely because a Mafia partner in his company thought he had stolen some of the cash that they had set aside for bribes. So, to protect himself, Orlandini confessed how fake invoices were approved for construction work at the two school sites so that cash could be used for bribes. He pleaded guilty to a single conspiracy charge and became a protected federal witness.

Orlandini taped Musto at the Monmouth Park racetrack on August 2, 1980. But he didn't get much out of the mayor or any of the other defendants he tried to wiretap. When he told Musto that he had given Scarafile $400,000 in bribes, Musto denied knowing anything about it. Throughout the investigation and the subsequent trial, Musto fiercely maintained his innocence.

"You gave him what?" Musto said on the recording. "You'd have to tell me that in front of him. I trust Frank like a brother."[47]

Adding to the charged atmosphere, federal prosecutor Richard Friedman called Musto's cronies, including Menendez, who began helping the prosecution in 1979 and testified in secret several times before a grand jury. "Richard was relentless," Menendez said. "He would call and call and call, and whenever he had a factoid that he wanted verification of, he would call."

Among those factoids was the fact that it was Musto himself who insisted on hiring Orlandini's company for the construction work on the schools despite rumors of the firm's Mob involvement, and he authorized them for dozens of construction projects in Union City beginning in 1974. Under Musto, the city was processing phony claims for hundreds of thousands of dollars for excavations that never took place.

"I said to myself, 'well, he's clearly part of this,'" Menendez recalled of his mentor.

Still, he continued to socialize with Musto and his family, going over with Jane for frequent dinners.

"He was like a member of the family," recalled Rhyta Musto. "Bill really, really liked him. I liked him too, but he turned out to be feet of clay."

The comment might seem rich coming from the wife of Union City's most famous Democratic Party boss, but Musto was never seen as a corrupt politician to his supporters. He was beloved, even years after he left power and was convicted of public corruption.

For Rhyta Musto and other Musto acolytes, it was Menendez who had the biggest character flaw: He turned out to be a rat. And he turned against the man who had believed in him the most, who had groomed him for a successful career in politics, who had treated him like a son.

When Menendez was subpoenaed to testify in front of a grand jury investigating Union City corruption, there is little doubt that he threw Musto and his cronies under the bus at the secret hearings. The idealistic law student may have wanted to release Union City from the corrupt stranglehold of William Musto, but he also wanted to promote himself.

He may have even needed to save himself.

Chi Chi Rodriguez, Union City's fixer, said that federal agents had threatened to prosecute Menendez and fellow school board member Bruce Walter for their roles in the widening corruption scheme—an assertion that prosecutors and defense lawyers involved in the Musto trial vigorously denied years later. Rodriguez claimed that in addition to the inflated construction costs, cash for supplies, such as plastic garbage bags and toilet paper, had gone astray, ending up in banks in Puerto Rico.

"Bob and Bruce had no choice but to cooperate with the feds," Rodriguez said. "They were threatened with arrest, and they cooperated."[48]

By the end of 1979, Menendez and Walter had openly broken with Powers and Musto, and in January 1981, they held an extraordinary meeting at the Italian Cultural Center—pointedly on Musto's own stomping grounds—that solidified their opposition against the Union City Democratic Party bosses.

"A son who sees his father continuously drinking in excess is much more loyal when he disobeys his request to go to the liquor store and buy more alcohol," Menendez said at the meeting, perhaps conflating his own father with his political surrogate. "True loyalty is not what is convenient, but what is right. True loyalty can direct, correct, and protect an individual from a dangerous course."[49]

Menendez was now charting his own, bold course, forming the Alliance Civic Association with Walter, Julia Valdivia, and Karen Highton, whose husband, Tom, a former city commissioner and high school teacher, had been fired by Musto as superintendent. The progressive slate was led by incumbent commissioner Ronald Dario. Like many others on the ticket, Dario had broken ties with Musto after he was indicted on corruption charges. Dario had been removed from his position as parks commissioner soon after he began to oppose his boss. "After his thirty-five years of expertise, he's showing signs of weakness," Dario told a New Jersey news program. "I never thought that Bill would stoop that low to fire people off the bat, to intimidate people."

Valdivia had a similar reason for joining. Despite her loyalty as Musto's Hispanic affairs aide, she felt she had been pushed aside when she wanted to run for city commissioner. "Musto told her 'no,' and so she joined Menendez's team," said a political observer who was close to the Musto machine.[50]

"When you travel outside of this immediate area, everybody does think that Union City is a laughingstock," Menendez said.

But few were laughing in Union City. Months later, in April 1981, indictments were finally handed down for Musto, Powers, Union City deputy police chief and school board trustee Frank Scarafile, and four others, charging them with thirty-six counts of racketeering, fraud, and extortion. Musto faced up to 235 years in prison and fines of up to $120,000.

The epic trial began in November, shortly after Musto was overwhelmingly reelected to a sixth term as a state senator from Hudson County. It was the first time that federal prosecutors used the Racketeer Influenced and Corrupt Organizations Act (RICO), a federal law passed in 1970 to crack down on organized crime, against elected officials.

Confident of his stranglehold on power, the charismatic Musto, then sixty-four, had managed to retain his chairmanship of the Senate Judiciary Committee and was greeted by supporters every day when he entered the packed Newark federal courtroom. Proceedings went on for five months—the longest criminal trial in New Jersey history. But despite the serious charges against him, Musto continued to campaign for mayor in that year's election, which was scheduled for May.

In an "only in New Jersey" scenario, the mayor attended his trial during the day, and at night headed to his clubhouse with Scarafile to party with his supporters and continue his campaign—known as "Your Operation Uplift"—for reelection.

"The optics were bad, but he was beloved in Union City," said Joe Hayden, a defense attorney for Powers. "And the thing about Billy Musto is that he was courteous to the end. People loved him."[51]

Musto was adored in Union City, and for many of those who worked as tireless volunteers on his campaigns, he could do no wrong. Among them was Brian Stack, a sixteen-year-old campaign volunteer who attended Musto's trial in Newark and remained faithful to the political boss until his death, writing him letters while he served out his sentence in federal prison. Stack would later follow in his idol's footsteps and become mayor of Union City.

Orlandini, the construction boss from Bayonne, was the star witness at the trial. He testified that he never made payments directly to the mayor, and instead gave the cash to Scarafile to be split between Musto and Powers. The prosecution said the payments were made between July 1974 and September 1980, at a time when Orlandini was involved in the renovations of the two high schools as well as the construction of a twenty-four-story housing complex for senior citizens.

Orlandini told the court that he kept a list of illegal payments worth hundreds of thousands of dollars that he had made to city officials. He said he paid bribes for tax abatements on housing projects and for help in processing fake claims for excavation work that never took place.

He gave Scarafile a total of $396,500 for distribution to officials in Union City and nearby towns. "He picked up money for various people and saw to it that my paperwork got processed and everything fell into place," Orlandini said of the former deputy police chief.

Orlandini said Scarafile told him that he was going to distribute the cash to Musto, Powers, and others. He said he also gave Powers an extra $34,000 from 1974 to 1979 to "make sure my work got done."

Defense attorneys ripped Orlandini apart, calling him "a paranoid liar" and a thief who forged documents. They said he had only been motivated to testify because he faced a long jail sentence.

Orlandini may have been the star prosecution witness, but Menendez's betrayal of his political father on the witness stand made for gripping theater.

Hayden remembered a hushed silence when Menendez took the stand against Musto and the other defendants. "The courtroom was packed when Menendez testified," Hayden recalled. "Musto didn't move a muscle. He [Menendez] was this young, earnest-looking man. He was smart and verbally very effective—tough and ambitious."[52]

Richard Friedman, the lead prosecutor on the Musto case who questioned Menendez before the grand jury and in court, denied that Menendez had been pressured to testify against Musto by federal authorities.

"I thought he was very gutsy and courageous because he stood up to Musto," Friedman told *The New York Times* more than two decades after the trial in 2006. "There certainly was never any deal or any need for a deal. Menendez just testified truthfully."[53]

Hayden had a similar recollection. "It was a huge risk to go after Billy Musto, and Menendez did it," he said.

Prosecutor James Plaisted, who was in the courtroom when Menendez testified, recalled that Irving Anolik, Musto's defense attorney, attacked Menendez mercilessly during cross-examination. "The irony is that if you look at his testimony, it's difficult to find anything of evidential consequence," Plaisted said, adding that much of the evidence against Musto was circumstantial.[54]

"But Menendez had been told not to cooperate [with the authorities] by Musto and this was significant because he was asking him to cover up a crime and obstructing justice," he continued.

Other observers put it more plainly.

"Was he a rat who turned on his father? Or a true reformer trying to clean up this mess?" said Rudy Garcia, a Cuban American politician and Union Hill High School football star, who led the team to three state championships. Garcia was a protégé of Bruce Walter, and had once been close to Menendez, but they later became rivals after Garcia became mayor of Union City in 1993. "That was always the question."[55]

For his part, Musto vigorously maintained his innocence, and his fans believed him. Musto took the stand in his own defense, and endured three days of brutal cross-examination, denying all the charges against him. At one point, he stood up and declared in a raspy voice, "I never violated a public trust and I never will."

"There is no way in the world," he said when asked in court about the bribes paid by Orlandini through Scarafile. "You know how I think of Frank Scarafile. I trust him with my life. He may have made a mistake with some miscalculation."

Other defendants backed him up. Anthony Genovese, the architect for the Board of Education who worked on the school projects, said the only payments he had received from Orlandini were for legitimate building fees on other projects. Orlandini had claimed that Genovese had received $80,000 for signing fake documents, adding that the cash was also meant to ensure that "my work had no problems."

"I never received a dime from Orlandini that I didn't earn as an architect, in creating with these two hands," Genovese told the court during cross-examination by Plaisted, who noted that the renovation costs on the two high schools had doubled from the original estimate of $2.2 million to more than $4 million.

For his part, Powers testified that Orlandini had tried to set him up by tricking him into making incriminating statements when he was secretly taping him. He told the court that Orlandini was "completely paranoid and had gone completely out of his head" when he said that he had doled out the bribes.

Musto seemed to agree and said that the wiretapped conversation he'd had with Orlandini at Monmouth Park in August 1980 was confusing. Orlandini was clearly nervous that Musto would guess that he was a snitch during the secret taping, and it showed in the convoluted way he asked his questions.

"I didn't have any idea what he was talking about at all," Musto said, adding that Orlandini had mentioned $25,000, which he said he mistook for a campaign contribution. He later found out that Scarafile had borrowed the cash from an Orlandini associate.

During the course of the trial, Orlandini admitted that he had no records of the bribes he paid. He said he could not recall how and where the bribe payments to Union City officials had been made, and spent two days at the home of a friend burning his company's records in a fireplace.

—

On March 26, 1982, the crowd of spectators in the courtroom seemed to collectively hold their breath when Judge H. Lee Sarokin announced that a verdict had been reached.

As the three men and nine women of the jury took their seats, the crowd in the courtroom was on the edge of their collective seat. The jurors looked harried; an observer later noted they hadn't eaten all day. A distraught Rhyta Musto held onto her husband and sobbed loudly. During the reading of the guilty verdicts of the thirty-six counts that included racketeering, conspiracy, and mail and wire fraud, several of the jurors couldn't contain themselves and were sobbing uncontrollably. Musto was convicted on twenty-eight counts to loud gasps from the crowd. Although prosecutors could not link him directly to the bribes, Musto was convicted on multiple public corruption charges.

Later, each juror was polled and asked whether they had reached their decisions in a "free and unpressured" way. Josephine Melnick, age forty-three, of Secaucus, was juror number four, and when the judge asked her the questions, she blurted out, "No."

"Pandemonium doesn't do it justice," said Hayden more than forty years after the trial. "The crowd stormed the court cheering as if we'd won. If you saw it in a Hollywood movie, you'd think it was contrived."[56]

According to a news report, "many supporters of the defendants who were present leapt to their feet screaming. People pounded on the benches of the courtroom and some of the defense attorneys pounded on their desks and shouted."

A reporter for United Press International, who was in the courtroom, described the scene as "instant bedlam." John Powers's wife, Barbara, shot up from her seat and waved her fists in the air, signaling a triumphant victory.[57]

But the euphoric moment was short-lived. Plaisted asked that the jury return to deliberate, while Anolik demanded that the polling of the jurors continue. "There is no question that she is emotional and upset, as any juror would blunder these kinds of circumstances," he said.

Judge Sarokin ordered the jury back into deliberations, agreeing with Plaisted that the tense atmosphere in the courtroom had clearly upset many.

"When the jury first came out and began announcing its verdict there was tremendous emotional outbreak, particularly and certainly understandably from Mrs. Musto, [and] while the jury was being polled, she was visibly crying and holding on to her husband and standing," Judge Sarokin noted. "Although I took a moment in an effort to see if she could regain her composure and have somebody assist her, she refused, again understandably, to leave the side of her husband."[58]

Judge Sarokin later said there was no question "that the very dramatic moment had a tremendous impact upon the jury." At 7:45 p.m., the jurors sent the judge another note, indicating that they had reached a unanimous decision.

When they walked back into the courtroom and took their seats, Judge Sarokin polled them a second time, Melnick threw her hands up in the air and was visibly crying when she said "yes" to the guilty verdicts, with an air of resignation, noted Robert Baime, a defense attorney.

"I really did not have the impression that [it] represented her free will," Baime said.[59]

Another juror—identified as Mrs. Steidl—was so distraught that she was unable to stand when she was polled. She remained seated and crying when she answered "yes" to the judge.

Despite the emotional scenes and protests from the defense attorneys, Judge Sarokin accepted the guilty verdicts. "Insofar as the jury is concerned that certainly includes Mrs. Steidl and Mrs. Melnick, you have to be inhumane not to react emotionally to the rendering of the verdict in this courtroom, particularly to the reaction of Mrs. Musto and others."

Musto did not allow his conviction to get in the way of his campaign and continued to run for mayor of Union City. On May 11, a day after he was sentenced to seven years in prison, he was reelected, with his supporters capturing three of the four Board of Education seats.

"*This* is the real jury," Musto said after the votes were counted. "This is my jury."

Menendez's Alliance Civic Association did not fare so well on his "housecleaning campaign to wipe out corruption."

"I ran against the mayor's commission ticket and lost by several hundred votes, the only election I have ever lost," he wrote. "It was a well-oiled machine—we lost by very little, but we lost."[60]

As a result of supporting Menendez, many who worked for the city lost their jobs. Menendez prepared wrongful dismissal cases in court, charging that Union City had violated the rights of civil servants. "And those cases started to be won," he said in his book, adding that he considered leaving politics at that point and concentrate his efforts "to challenge injustice and corruption where I found it."

Meanwhile, Musto had every intention of resuming his old office, but his municipal career was over. The court ruled that he had to give up his elected positions in the state senate and city hall. Undaunted, Musto enlisted his sixty-year-old wife to run for his old seat.

For her part, Rhyta Musto played the shy, retiring homemaker, who was ready to make the ultimate sacrifice and step in for her powerful husband. "I'm just a little housewife, I haven't decided yet what to do, but if the organization wants me to run, I guess I will," she told *The New York Times.*[61]

"The organization needs a Musto, and I say that modestly," said Bill Musto. "I seem to have been their guiding force. If they can follow me for thirty years, I owe it to them to comply with what they want."

Rhyta Musto won her husband's old seat on the board of commissioners in the special election that was called when Musto was ousted. She defeated Joseph Bonacci, an insurance broker, by 508 votes. "They put me in the lion's den and I won," she said.

Then, at the direction of her still powerful husband, Rhyta Musto backed Robert Botti, Union City's public works commissioner and a loyal supporter of Musto, for mayor of Union City. It was not a good choice. Seven weeks after taking office, Botti himself was indicted on eighteen corruption charges, including mail fraud, income tax evasion, and conspiracy in a bid-rigging scheme in Hudson County. According to prosecutors, the charges stemmed from the continuing probe into corruption in the county. The jury of seven men and five women took only two hours to find him guilty in December 1982. Botti was convicted of conspiring to steal $50,000 worth of contracts for janitorial supplies for the Hudson County Vocational and Technical School to Eastern Supply and Equipment Company, where he worked as a salesman.

During the trial, forty-two-year-old Botti was accused of conspiring with Powers as well as Milton Reid, owner of the Eastern Supply and Equipment Company, to have company employees submit fake bids. At the trial, company employees said that they typed letters quoting prices for supplies and mailed them to school officials. Botti was also found guilty of skimming off $15,000 in commissions from the deals and then failing to record the cash on his tax returns in 1978 and 1979. The cash was paid to him through Puerto Rican banks.

Botti was sentenced to eighteen months in prison and was removed from office as mayor.

With Botti out of the picture, Musto, who continued to maintain his innocence, was losing his grip on city hall. For him, it was all part of a vast conspiracy. He blamed the feds for his conviction, and accused the US attorney's office in Newark of targeting him with "malicious" intent.

"I have never been investigated by the Hudson County prosecutor's office or the attorney general of this state," he said. "They want to smear me and smear me and smear me. They want to break me."

"There's no one that can come in here and say they ever gave Bill Musto two cents," he continued in an interview with *The New York Times* a few days after his sentencing. "This case was so orchestrated. I can't believe this. Words can't explain it. It's terrible but I am innocent. The only things that keep me going through all these trials and tribulations that I have right now are my innocence, my love for my family, and my devotion to the people who have been good to me."[62]

Musto was so beloved in Union City that when he was finally released from prison in Indiana on December 4, 1987, he returned to a hero's welcome, including a sumptuous banquet prepared by his supporters at the Italian Cultural Center.

It's unclear whether Musto ever spoke to Bob Menendez again.

"They hated his guts," said a Union City political observer with reference to Musto and his old cronies. "They were convinced he was a rat. They all went down, and he skated."[63]

Musto himself said the same thing when he left the federal courthouse after his trial. "He's the biggest mistake I ever made," said Musto, speaking of an aide who had turned against him. "Other than Bob Menendez."[64]

Menendez may have lost his first go at his mentor's old seat, but once Musto disappeared into the background, there was no stopping him.

As Paul Mulshine, the New Jersey *Star-Ledger* columnist, noted, "After Musto left the scene, you could never get rid of Bob Menendez."

CHAPTER FOUR

Hudson County Boss

B ob Menendez was determined to bury the Musto machine once and for all. He already saw himself as Union City's first Cuban American mayor and, like his mentor, took on the mantle of Hudson County political boss.

Menendez surrounded himself with friends from high school, college, and law school to begin creating his own political movement in Union City and secure his hold on local and national politics. With the help of his friends and his wife, Jane, Menendez also began to build a mini real estate empire in his hometown in the late 1970s and early 1980s. By age thirty-three, he owned three properties in Union City.

The couple purchased their first building—a three-story walk-up at 1806 West Street—in 1977, while Menendez was still a full-time law student, aide to Musto, and a member of the Union City Board of Education where Jane worked. He was also reportedly collecting a paycheck from the North Hudson Community Action Corporation, a local nonprofit that would come to play an important role in his political rise.

In 1983, the couple purchased a second property, a row house at 535 41st Street in Union City, for $92,000. They received a loan from the Pamrapo Savings Bank in Bayonne for $74,000.

Those properties were in addition to one that Menendez had briefly owned in the city's commercial district. Menendez, who failed the bar exam twice before passing on his third attempt, opened a law firm a year later with his friend Manny Diaz, also a newly minted lawyer. In December 1981, the two bought a property at 512 42nd Street in Union City for $61,500 to use as their law office.

Menendez and Diaz took out a $48,000 mortgage with a 15 percent interest rate and a twenty-year term from the Pan American National Bank in Union City, the state's first Hispanic bank. It was declared insolvent a year later after an audit revealed numerous loan irregularities. The bank's director, Luis Perez Vega, was indicted on fraud charges, and cofounder Arnaldo Monzón, a member of Menendez's mayoral campaign's steering committee in the 1982 race, pleaded guilty to a misdemeanor charge of laundering $100,000 through the bank.

The Menendez/Diaz law office building purchase took place when Musto was on trial and Menendez was still secretary to the Union City Board of Education, one of the highest paid positions in municipal government. But the firm was short-lived. Perhaps Menendez's plan to testify against his mentor threw a wrench in his business plans with Diaz and affected their friendship. The firm survived for little more than a month. On January 28, 1982, one of the days that Menendez was in a Newark federal courtroom testifying at the historic corruption trial, Diaz bought out Menendez's interest in their building for $6,150.

While Menendez broke with Musto, Diaz remained loyal to the disgraced mayor. In what must have been an uncomfortable development in their friendship, Diaz was part of the slate that defeated Menendez in the 1982 municipal elections. Diaz was elected a city commissioner along with Rhyta Musto, with the authority to return Musto, or at least his handpicked successor, to power.

Menendez may have lost his 1982 campaign for Union City mayor, but he and his wife celebrated milestones at home. Their daughter, Alicia, was born in 1983, and their son, Robert Jr., was born two years later.

Menendez wasn't exactly a hands-on father. Growing up, his daughter described their dinners at a local pizzeria "inevitably punctuated by constituents seeking help. The heat not working in public housing or a stolen trash can elicited the same 'fix it' spirit."[65] And his son later complained that Menendez was largely absent for a good part of his childhood. Menendez was "away for many of those small moments that make a life," said Rob Menendez

"It took me a long time to appreciate why those decisions were made having experienced first-hand the challenges they caused."[66]

≈

Menendez was obsessed with power. He desperately wanted to be mayor of Union City. And to get there, he was prepared to make a deal with the devil.

He continued to gather support among the city's shady Cuban business leaders by stressing his anti-Castro bona fides. He also agreed to work with his rivals in the Republican Party.

Buoyed by the success of Ronald Reagan in the 1984 presidential election and a Republican sweep in Hudson County a year later, the Republican Party poured resources into local politics in the state. In 1985, moderate Republican Tom Kean was reelected governor in a landslide, with 70 percent of the vote. With Bill Musto in prison, the GOP focused on taking Union City and dismantling the Democratic machine, but they still faced the old political boss's loyal supporters who were determined to continue his legacy. Unfazed, GOP operatives set about creating an anti-Musto alliance of Republicans and Democrats. The Alliance Civic Association was led by Republican Assemblyman Ronald Dario, the former parks commissioner who slammed Musto, along with Republican Manny Alcober and Charles Velli, an Independent who became a Democrat and ended up a Republican. Menendez and Bruce Walter were the only two Democrats on the ticket. The understanding was that Dario would become mayor of Union City if the ACA won the 1986 elections.

"I had sworn off politics, but was persuaded by my friends and colleagues to run again for the Commission," wrote Menendez in his book, one of many disingenuous comments about his rise to power.

The ACA swept Union City elections with 57 percent of the vote, beating out the Musto-backed Together Party that included Rhyta Musto in her reelection bid for commissioner. With the Musto machine out of the way, Bob Menendez prepared to seize the top job for himself, turning the tables on his Republican benefactors.

Taking advantage of the confusion that came after the poll while Dario returned to Trenton to resume his duties in the assembly, Menendez teamed up with Walter to convince Alcober, now a Union City commissioner along with Velli, to support Menendez for mayor. Dario only found out about the switch when he showed up on July 1 to take the oath of office for mayor. He quickly realized that it was Menendez on the dais, poised to take the top job.

For his part, Alcober said he had no idea that he was supposed to back Dario for mayor. Republican campaign managers never told him, he said. The coup de grace for Dario came the following year when Menendez and a fellow Democrat won the 33rd Assembly district that Dario and Republican Jose Arango had flipped to the Republicans in 1985. Like many of his predecessors, Menendez would simultaneously occupy two elected positions in New Jersey.

Among Menendez's first acts as mayor was to throw out "the remains of the machine" and create his own political dynasty. He surrounded himself with his faithful comrades. He hired his old friend Donald Scarinci—"my lifetime friend"—as city attorney and forged alliances with political strategists Steve DeMicco and his partner Brad Lawrence, who would go on to advise him throughout his political career. DeMicco was two years ahead of Menendez at Rutgers Law School.

Among his proudest achievements in those early days was recruiting grandmothers in the community to help in a citywide daycare initiative, bolstering Little League teams, and building a city park. He also began officially observing the birthday of José Martí, Cuba's national hero, to win even more favor with his Cuban American constituents.

Politically and financially, Menendez began to strengthen his ties to Walter, who would succeed him as mayor when he resigned and went to Congress in 1993.

Shortly after Menendez took office as Union City's first Cuban American mayor, a sweetheart real estate deal, arranged through Menendez's law firm, helped both Menendez and Walter.

On October 30, 1986, Walter bought property at 910 Summit Avenue in Union City for $170,000 from Isabel Mirasola, whose husband, Carl, served on the Union City Board of Education. On the same day, Walter received a $32,660 mortgage from Menendez's law firm. The mortgage instrument noted that "this is a second mortgage, not assumable." Walter also received a $125,000 mortgage from the Mirasolas. Less than a year later—on June 24, 1987—Walter sold the property to Efren Ferrer, a Union City contractor and owner of Cecil's Limousine Corporation for $225,000—an inflated price, allowing Walter to pocket $55,000 in profit. By October 2002, fifteen years after Walter flipped the building—the property sold to a local developer for just $160,000.

Less than a month after Menendez discharged his $32,660 mortgage with Walter, he and his wife, Jane, bought another property at 517 15th Street in Union City on July 21, 1987, from the estate of Helen Smith for $165,000. The sprawling single-family residence became the family home. The couple received a $132,000 mortgage from First Northern Mortgage Corporation in Garden City, New York, which was $33,000 less than the price of the property.

In addition to the lucrative real estate speculation, it didn't take long for Menendez's city hall administration to have its first major brush with corruption. In 1987, the same year that Menendez was running for a seat in the New Jersey State Assembly, his municipal administration gave DeMicco and Lawrence no-bid contracts worth $80,000 to do public relations for the city's Community Development Agency, which received its funding from the federal government.

In fact, the US Department of Housing and Urban Development found that Menendez's administration had "wasted" $600,000 in federal cash that was supposed to help renovate affordable housing and provide services to the poor in Union City. Much of that money ended up squandered on administrative expenses, the federal agency found.

"The federal government has demanded that it be reimbursed by the city for nearly $600,000 worth of improper expenditures of urban aid that was intended to benefit poor and moderate-income families, federal authorities say," wrote *The Jersey Journal* in 1992 when the waste was exposed.[67]

From August 1987 through July 1991, Union City's Community Development Agency spent "far too much" of its federal grants on administration, a category that included consultants, occupancy, and other costs, HUD said, adding that the agency doled out the $80,000 to DeMicco and Lawrence's firm as well as $30,000 to a part-time media consultant who worked on Menendez's campaigns. CDA, which was overseen by Menendez, who approved the agency's budget and spending, also blew $153,000 on office rent. HUD rules required that no more than 20 percent of grants were to be spent on administrative costs.

HUD noted CDA's "inadequate financial management system" as well as "a lack of internal fiscal controls and a lack of efficient city oversight."

"They have wonderful public relations, but how many housing units did they rehab? Not that many," said Richard Kotuski, the director of HUD's Program Support Branch in Newark. "Part of the problem was they were living too luxuriously."

Spending was approved by Union City's board of commissioners, which was chaired by Menendez. Commissioners Walter and Alcober voted to approve the spending, while Velli, the Republican commissioner, voted against it in 1989.

The HUD scandal may have made headlines in New Jersey, but it did nothing to dampen Menendez's rising political fortunes. Nor did a curious contribution to his campaign for state assembly.

On April 28, 1987, Virginia Jacobsen, Menendez's mother-in-law, made a $15,000 contribution to Menendez's assembly campaign committee—the largest individual donation, according to New Jersey Election Law Enforcement Commission records. On June 9, Menendez's assembly campaign made a $12,000 "loan" to Virginia Jacobsen, according to ELEC records. There was no evidence that the loan was paid back.

And, a month before the assembly election, which took place in November 1987, Menendez worked hard to solidify his support among Cuban American voters and donors in his district.

In October 1987, during his second year as mayor of Union City, Menendez made a contribution to a fundraiser for Eduardo Arocena's criminal defense. Menendez attended the event, spending $200 for a table of ten to help the former New Jersey longshoreman and Omega 7 kingpin, who had been convicted on multiple counts of murder, conspiracy, and a spate of bombings from Manhattan to Miami three years earlier. Federal prosecutors said Arocena had financed his terror campaigns, including bombings at JFK International Airport and Madison Square Garden, through extortion and the drug trade.[68]

Arocena was convicted of two murders, including the shooting in broad daylight that killed Eulalio Negrin, the Cuban American activist who had negotiated with Fidel Castro for the release of political prisoners.

Whether Menendez recalled the grisly Mafia-style hit on a street in Union City is unclear, but eight years later he had firmly sided with Arocena's supporters, who were, in turn, backing his political fortunes.

Menendez repeated his allegiance to the anti-Castro radicals to a local reporter, adding that the fight should be carried out "wherever the enemy may be."[69]

When *The Hudson Dispatch* reporter pressed Menendez on his support for Arocena, he replied, "I don't look at it that I am support-ing 'a murderer.' I look on it that I am supporting a goal, which is the liberation of Cuba."

Menendez later said that he had been misquoted.

In addition to Arocena, Menendez, like the rest of the prominent anti-Castro Cubans in Union City, also supported Hudson County residents Alvin Ross and the Novo Sampol brothers—Guillermo and Ignacio—who had been found guilty of the 1976 murder of former Chilean diplomat Orlando Letelier in Washington, DC. Ross and the Novo brothers were eventually acquitted of the murder.

On the eve of the assembly election, Menendez pulled out all the stops to rally his supporters, continuing to work for the anti-Castro underworld. In one memorable case, he advocated removing a court-appointed trustee from a Mob-controlled labor union. According to local reports, he attended a Teamsters Local 560 rally and gave a speech supporting members of the union, who demanded the removal of the federal court–appointed trusteeship. The Department of Justice insisted the union had been infiltrated by the Cuban and Italian Mob, but Menendez disagreed and said he planned to attend a Teamsters rally to demand that federal courts allow for an election of new union officers.[70]

Among the moneyed anti-Castro Cuban Americans who threw their support behind the Teamsters, Arocena, and the other Cuban extremists was Abel Hernandez and his assistant, Lourdes Lopez. Hernandez was the owner of Mi Bandera restaurant and grocery store in Union City—an important hub of anti-Castro activity. Both

Hernandez and Lopez would go on to become among Menendez's biggest supporters.

In 1992, Menendez steered a special low-interest-rate state loan through Union City's CDA to Hernandez's business. At the time, Menendez was settling into his role as a state senator, a position he assumed in 1991 following the death of Democrat Christopher Jackman. This marked the beginning of Menendez's rise in political influence, as he cultivated relationships with key figures in his community.

Years later, when Menendez was a rising star in Congress, Lopez paid an inflated price for Menendez's 41st Street property in Union City. The row house that Menendez bought with his wife for $92,000 sold to Lourdes and Mario Lopez for a whopping $450,000 on May 19, 2003, even though the assessed value was just $203,000. According to the sale prices for comparable properties on the same block, Lourdes and Mario Lopez seemed to have overpaid by more than $200,000. Menendez was not at the closing and completed the transaction through a power of attorney.

To sell the property, Menendez said that he managed to change the zoning from residential to commercial-office use, even though it was located in the middle of a one-way residential street and not on busy Bergenline Avenue where most businesses are located in Union City. Commercial properties rent for about four times as much as residential ones, which was reflected in the sale price as well, noted *Star-Ledger* columnist Paul Mulshine. But Mulshine found out that Menendez had never switched the zoning designation when he searched public documents. When Mulshine confronted Menendez about the commercial designation, Menendez said it was up to the buyer to switch it over.

"No, it's not," wrote Mulshine. "The application form on the city website makes it clear that the owner has to get the C.O. [Certificate of Occupancy]."[71]

Menendez, who was mayor of Union City when he bought the property as well as an attorney with plenty of experience in real estate transactions, claimed he did not recall the details of how the zoning got switched from residential to commercial during the interview with Mulshine.

But the 41st Street property is significant for other reasons. For years, the Menendez couple rented out part of the property to the North Hudson Community Action Corporation, a local nonprofit that once employed Menendez. Since its founding in 1965, the group has provided health and social services to the local community. The couple rented out the building for $3,100 a month and raked in more than $300,000 in rent from the group during their ownership of the property. The rent was astronomically high for Union City, where a four-thousand-square-foot commercial property on New York Avenue was available for $1,600.

It's not clear why the organization would want to rent office space on a quiet residential street in Union City. "It was a dump," wrote Mulshine, who visited the property. "Air conditioners sprouted from worn-out windows. It was only twenty-five-feet wide, and it was crammed into a narrow lot."

Later, Menendez secured a special designation for the nonprofit that permitted it to receive federal health grants. Menendez steered $4 million in federal funds to the group during his time in Congress. For years, he collected thousands in contributions to his political campaigns from the nonprofit's employees. He also hired one of the group's board members to work for his congressional office. Maria Almeida simultaneously chaired the group's board and also worked for Menendez's Newark Senate office.

≈

Like many of his campaigns, Menendez's run for Congress came about almost by accident following New Jersey Congressman Frank Guarini's decision to retire amid redistricting in 1992. That same year, Guarini's Fourteenth Congressional District was divided in half and renumbered as the Thirteenth Congressional District, where 43 percent of registered voters were of Hispanic origin. For Menendez it was an opportunity to become New Jersey's first Latino in the House of Representatives.

In the Democratic primary, Menendez beat Robert Haney Jr., a corporate lawyer with an office in Manhattan who had never held elected office. He campaigned on a promise to dismantle the machine politics that had made Menendez a star.

"Mr. Menendez is basically a person who worked his way through the machine and then took it over," Haney told *The New York Times*. "There's an undue awe for the machine. People think it can't be beat."[72]

And he was right. In what Menendez later described as "a bizarre democratic primary race," Haney played the ethnic card against him, putting word out on the street that Menendez couldn't speak English, especially in heavily Irish American enclaves of Bayonne and Jersey City. Menendez says that his opponent put out a campaign flyer showing him with a burning cigar and a warning: "we need to stop this!"[73]

"It sounds funny, but at the time, it was potentially effective negative campaigning," Menendez wrote in his book, adding that he went to Bayonne to meet members of the Irish community. Following a campaign speech, he was approached by a woman who spoke with an Irish accent. When she thanked him for coming, Menendez asked what impressed her about his speech. She replied "It's not so much what you said, but the fact that you can speak English. I'm going to vote for you."

"I didn't know how to respond, but smiled and thanked her again," he wrote. "Take the votes any way you can."

Menendez went on to beat Republican rival Fred Theemling Jr. in the general election by a 64 percent to 31 percent margin. Menendez proved so wildly popular that in subsequent House elections until he was appointed to the US Senate in 2005, he would rake in more than 70 percent of the vote. He won his third term in Congress with 79 percent of the vote.

Menendez was the first Hispanic member of the House from New Jersey and the first Cuban American congressman who was a member of the Democratic Party. For his first speech on the House floor, he sided with fellow Democrat and Committee Chairman Charles Rangel, imploring the body to support a resolution to continue the Select Committee on Narcotics Abuse and Control. The committee was established as a temporary committee in 1977 and had thirty-five members, eighteen staffers, and cost $750,000 a year, even though it could only advise members of the House and had no ability to draft legislation. It was deemed by many to be redundant and unnecessary, though Rangel and other Democrats felt otherwise.

"I recognize that select committees are not intended to continue indefinitely [but] unfortunately, the drug problem is not about to go away," said Menendez, taking to the floor like a seasoned veteran of the House in a navy suit and matching diamond patterned tie.

"At a time when drug abuse and crime are costing our society an estimated $300 billion a year in lost productivity, lost revenues, and increased health care and criminal justice expenditures, terminating the select committee in the name of congressional reform would send the wrong message, the wrong signal to the American people that Congress is not serious about this enormous problem," he said in his long-winded address.

"And as someone who was a former mayor for over six years and a state senator dealing with community groups, law enforcement on these issues, terminating the select committee would send the wrong signal to local police officers, to community activists, to DEA agents, to treatment providers and residents of inner-city communities who are putting their lives on the line every day in the war against drugs," he continued. "The problems associated with substance abuse, violent crime, lost productivity, escalating health care, and criminal justice costs are no longer just an inner-city problem; they've reached the suburbs and small-town America, and we should support its reestablishment."

The members of the House weren't persuaded by Menendez's impassioned soliloquy and ultimately voted to scrap the committee by a 237–180 margin.

Still, Menendez continued to distinguish himself in foreign relations in Congress. He immediately joined the Congressional Hispanic Caucus, which was dominated by Mexican Americans at that time. And for a Democrat, his views were markedly Republican. As a member of the House International Relations Committee, he inserted himself into negotiations to bring peace to Northern Ireland and sort out the tensions between India and Pakistan over the disputed territory of Kashmir. And he continued his hard-line policies against Cuba, in many cases siding with Republicans to maintain his support among the powerful anti-Castro lobby in his own state and in South Florida. Supporters in the Sunshine State contributed more than $1 million to his campaigns between 1992 and 2006.

At home in Union City, his campaign doled out tens of thousands of dollars to place ads in *Avance*, René Avila's anti-Castro newspaper. The ads promoted Menendez's campaign as well as those of like-minded Democrats in his district.

~

But helping anti-Castro radicals was having dire consequences on the Communist island. In 1997, the country's hotels and bars in Havana and Varadero endured a spate of violence orchestrated and financed by militants in South Florida and New Jersey—some of them benefactors of Bob Menendez.

In the late morning of September 4, 1997, Italian businessman Fabio di Celmo and his father, Giustino, emerged from a series of sales meetings with Cuban state authorities in Havana, and made their way back to the beachfront Miramar neighborhood where they were staying at the Copacabana Hotel. The father and son business partners had been traveling to the Communist island since 1992 and had forged important relationships with state officials for their company, Rime S. A., an import-export concern that was involved in everything from helping to renovate the city's historic Hotel Nacional to importing critical supplies, such as sewing machine needles, to the island after the devastating loss of aid from the Soviet Union, which collapsed in December 1991. According to his older brother, Livio, Fabio, thirty-two, was obsessed with Fidel Castro, and in his free time, he listened to the Cuban leader's lengthy speeches and read about the history of the 1959 revolution.[74] Fabio spent four months of the year on the island since the import-export business had taken off, splitting the rest of his time between Montreal and Genoa.

He also urged his friends in Italy to vacation in Cuba and was on his way to meet newlyweds Francesca and Enrico Gallo Argelia for one final lunch in the Copacabana Hotel's lobby bar before they returned to Italy later that day. Fabio had postponed a business meeting in order to meet them. Earlier, Enrico had told Fabio that his new wife was obsessed with the thought that something bad would happen to them in Cuba. Fabio was determined to set her at ease.

Fabio himself was on top of the world. For the first time in his partnership with his father, Fabio was feeling good about himself, he told his brother two days earlier. He had just negotiated two contracts completely on his own, and he had a Cuban girlfriend. There was talk of buying an apartment in the Monte Carlo Palace, a proposed condo development for foreigners in Miramar.

Fabio glimpsed Francesca and Enrico at the glassed-in lobby bar as he passed the high-backed wicker chairs and tan-colored couches to meet his friends. He never made it. The bomb that had been planted by anti-Castro terrorists in a nearby standing crystal ashtray exploded as he was walking. He died instantly when a shard of glass hit him in the throat, slicing through a major artery.

The Copacabana Hotel bombing was part of a wave of hotel attacks in Cuba orchestrated by Cuban mobsters led by Cuban-born CIA agent and anti-Castro terrorist Luis Posada Carriles, who wanted to thwart the country's booming tourist industry and remove Castro from power. Posada Carriles seemed to confess to the hotel bombings that left a dozen people injured and resulted in di Celmo's death in a 1998 interview with *The New York Times*. "It is sad that someone is dead," he told reporter Ann Louise Bardach. "But we can't stop. That Italian was . . . in the wrong place at the wrong time."[75] He later said he had been misquoted, and that all he had done was publicize the bombings.

But the complicated story of terrorism that tore apart hotels in Havana and Varadero didn't end there. It led, in a circuitous route, to Union City and to the door of some of Bob Menendez's biggest donors.

The New Jersey angle had been rumored for years, but was finally confirmed at a federal trial in Texas, more than fourteen years after the string of hotel bombings. At an extradition trial for Posada Carriles in El Paso, Texas, an elderly accountant from New Jersey was granted immunity to testify about the financing for the terrorist attacks, and he told the court that he had done it at the behest of his boss, Arnaldo Monzón, who had backed Menendez in Union City, served on his first campaign for mayor, and whose long-shuttered Pan American National Bank had given him one of his first mortgages to purchase property in Union City.

The accountant, Oscar de Rojas, then seventy-four, testified that he had wired money to Posada Carriles at his bases of operation in El Salvador and Guatemala for the hotel bombings in 1997. Salvadoran mercenary Raúl Ernesto Cruz León was convicted of setting the bomb at the Copacabana Hotel that killed di Celmo and spent thirty years in a Cuban prison. He was released in 2024.

Prosecutors at Posada Carriles's extradition trial in 2011 said the cash was used to fund the string of bombings at hotels and bars throughout the island and to pay Cruz León and other Salvadoran mercenaries who made $2,000 each. After a career of destabilizing Latin American Communist governments for the CIA, Posada Carriles had returned to the United States in 2005, but lied to US authorities about his shady past. He was wanted by the governments of Cuba and Venezuela, where he was a naturalized citizen, to stand trial for the bombings.

De Rojas, who attended the same Jesuit school in Havana where Fidel Castro had been a student and studied accounting at the Universidad Católica de Santo Tomás de Villanueva, left Cuba in 1967 and fled to Spain before finally settling in New Jersey. There, he worked as the bookkeeper for Arnold Fashion, a women's clothing store chain owned by Monzón, for more than twenty-three years. Monzón and Posada Carriles had been friends since their childhood in Cuba, according to the *Miami Herald*, and the Cuban government had provided the Clinton administration with evidence in 1998 that Monzón was the "money man" for Posada Carriles.

De Rojas testified that he sent between ten and twelve transfers of $800 each to Ramón Medína in El Salvador on the orders of Arnaldo Monzón. The name was one of the aliases used by Posada Carriles while he was in Central America. The cash was sent between March and September 1997, during the wave of terrorist bombings in Cuba. Special FBI Agent Omar Vega, who headed the investigation into Posada Carriles, testified that a total of twenty-one electronic transfers of cash were made between New Jersey and Ramón Medína between 1996 and 1997 for a total of $18.9 million.

Posada Carriles was eventually acquitted of US immigration charges in April 2011, angering Cuba and Venezuela. Cuba, which regarded Posada Carriles among its biggest enemies, called his trial "a farce," and Venezuela accused the United States of harboring a terrorist. They called the trial "an act of theater" designed "to protect the terrorist Luis Posada Carriles." But he was also a CIA agent. Declassified documents showed that he worked for the spy agency between 1965 and 1976.[76] After the trial, Posada Carriles moved to Miami where he participated in protests against the Cuban government. He died in 2018—two years after the death of his biggest rival, Fidel Castro—at a home for veterans.

In other testimony at Posada Carriles's trial, de Rojas also provided evidence of another New Jersey link to Bob Menendez. According to the accountant, both he and Monzón were members of the Cuban American National Foundation, and Jorge Mas Canosa, the radical anti-Castro group's founder, was a regular at Arnold Fashion in New Jersey. Both Monzón and Canosa were two of the biggest contributors to Menendez's first run for the House of Representatives in 1992.

The massive support Menendez received from Canosa and Monzón propelled him into the highest levels of national politics. In his first race for Congress in 1992, he outspent his Republican rival Fred J. Theemling by nearly 18-to-1, canvassing the state in eighteen-hour days and spending more than $200,000 compared to his opponent's $11,000.

Menendez acknowledged his benefactor through a spokesperson in 1998, praising Monzón's "work for the community and his struggle for peace, freedom, and a democratic transition in Cuba."[77] The Cuban American National Foundation vigorously denied allegations that they had anything to do with the Cuban bombings. Monzón died of prostate cancer in 2000. Menendez was one of the most prominent mourners at his funeral.

Another recipient of Monzón and Canosa contributions was another Bob—Bob Torricelli, a Democratic congressman from New Jersey, who became a senator in 1997 and dated Bianca Jagger, a Nicaraguan activist and former wife of Rolling Stones front man Mick Jagger. Menendez, Torricelli, and Bill Clinton teamed up for the Torricelli Act in 1992 to pressure President George H. W. Bush to further strengthen the US blockade against Cuba.

"I've never had a Democrat to work with the way I do with Governor Clinton," Menendez told *The New York Times* during his run for the House of Representatives in 1992. "For instance, Bill Clinton spoke out before President Bush did in support of a bill sponsored by . . . Torricelli that would, among other things, tighten an embargo against Cuba. In fact, Clinton forced Bush's hand, and he is not seen as a traditional liberal by a lot of the Republicans, which is a plus."[78]

But in 1993, Menendez opposed the Clinton administration's proposal to return migrants to Cuba who had committed crimes in the United States. A year later, as desperate Cubans poured into South Florida on rafts to escape the economic downturn on the island caused by the end of Soviet support, Menendez called for a military blockade to force Castro from power, and tougher sanctions, including cutting off all travel and remittances from Cuban Americans to their loved ones on the island. That same year, he introduced the Free and Independent Cuba Assistance Act, which prohibited the president from lifting the 1962 trade embargo against the island until it became a democratic country and adopted a free market economy. Although the bill didn't pass the House, it paved the way for the Cuban Liberty and Democratic Solidarity Act in 1996, known as the controversial Helms-Burton Act, which penalized foreign companies doing business with Cuba. Named for Republican Senator Jesse Helms of North Carolina and Representative Dan Burton from Indiana, also a Republican, the law stipulated that principals of non-US companies doing business with Cuba could be barred from entering the United States and would be prohibited from doing business with US companies. It also opposed Cuban membership in international financial institutions and prohibited television broadcasts from the United States to Cuba, among other sanctions.

≂

Monzón and Canosa were not the only anti-Castro financiers backing Bob Menendez and other politicians in New Jersey. In Union City, as Menendez was rising through the ranks of state and local politics, Cuban American mobsters dominated the numbers racket and threw their cash behind the politicians who would do their bidding in Cuba. Among them was José Miguel Battle Sr., a Bay of Pigs veteran and former Havana vice cop under the corrupt regime of Fulgencio Batista.

Battle Sr., whose underworld monikers were Don Miguel, El Gordo (the Fat One), and El Padrino (the Godfather), presided over a gambling empire that stretched from Union City to Miami and beyond. He controlled a vast criminal enterprise known as La Corporación that numbered more than 2,500 members and at its height raked in millions a week in an illegal lottery known in Spanish as *la bolita*. From 1977 to 2002, La Corporación made $1.4 billion in proceeds from the numbers game in New Jersey, New York, and Florida, with much of that cash going to offshore accounts in Panama and the British Virgin Islands.

"In twentieth-century America, gambling in general, and the numbers racket in particular, was the third most profitable criminal activity for the Mob after illegal booze and narcotics," wrote T. J. English in *The Corporation*, a biography of the Battle crime family.[79]

According to a federal commission on organized crime in 1985, the empire run by Battle Sr. stretched beyond gambling to control mortgage and finance companies, banks, and real estate agencies.

For years, Battle Sr. had a relationship with the Italian Mob in Union City and ran his enterprise through fear. A ruthless leader, he was also a war hero who had risked his life saving comrades during the ill-fated Bay of Pigs invasion. He spent nearly two years in Castro's infamous Isle of Pines prison. He emerged bent on revenge against the Cuban leader and President John F. Kennedy, who had withdrawn air support for the Bay of Pigs rebels just five minutes before they had reached their beachhead in Cuba. But he was also a shrewd businessman and criminal who had no compunction about using arson, torture, and assassination against his enemies and those who betrayed him. He did not oppose personally participating in a hit against a traitor to his organization. In 1976, he flew to Miami to kill Ernesto Torres, a hit man for La Corporación whom he considered a prodigal son, aiming the final bullet in the middle of the man's forehead—right between the eyes.

It was over a rumored assassination threat in Union City that federal prosecutors along with a host of FBI agents interviewed an unnamed cooperating witness at "a secure location" in Saddle Brook, New Jersey, in 1998.[80] The never named witness meticulously outlined the connections between Battle Sr. and Cuban American underworld figures, including Chi Chi Rodriguez, the Union City power broker, well-connected *bolitero*, and close personal friend of the Battle family. As a 1986 Hudson County report on corruption put it, "Chi Chi Rodriguez could not have attained and maintained this position of importance in the community by himself. He had, and still has, the help of public officials and employees who have become far too cozy with individuals in organized crime. . . . The picture is frightening."

Rodriguez was so loyal to both the Musto machine and the Corporation that he refused to testify against them in front of a federal grand jury in 1976.

"I went to jail for eighteen months because I refused to testify," said an eighty-six-year-old Rodriguez, who still lives in Union City. "When I finished my time, I still had everyone's respect."[81]

Other comrades included René Abreu and René Avila, publisher of the anti-Castro weekly newspaper *Avance*. Monzón, the moneyman for Posada Carriles, was also among the group.

All were involved with La Corporación, and many were political benefactors of Bob Menendez. They generously supported the young Cuban American's political aspirations, financing his rise from Union City school board secretary to US senator. For years, they contributed to his election campaigns in exchange for his hard-line political stance against the Castro government.

In fact, years later, when Menendez was poised to replace Jon Corzine in the federal Senate, many New Jersey political insiders working for his Republican rivals suspected that Menendez himself had been the unnamed cooperating witness who showed up in the secure location in Saddle Brook, and whose information about La Corporación and its members led to their arrests years later on a slew of corruption and racketeering charges.

"Once you cooperate with the FBI, you always cooperate with the FBI," said Rodriguez recalling Menendez's fateful decision to rat out Musto to federal authorities in the early 1980s. "Menendez had no scruples about throwing anyone under the bus."[82]

During the 1998 interview with the FBI, prosecutors described a meeting between Battle Sr. and the cooperating witness at a gas station in Hudson County. "Battle was eager to meet with the CW because the CW treated the Spanish people well," noted the FBI document, perhaps suggesting that the cooperating witness was, in fact, a politician. At the time, Menendez was already in his second term representing New Jersey's Thirteenth Congressional District.

For years, Menendez counted Battle's son José Miguel "Miguelito" Battle Jr. among his friends. They both attended St. Peter's University in Jersey City, and both graduated with degrees in political science. Miguelito was part of a band that played rock n' roll tunes with a Cuban flair. He and Menendez organized block parties throughout Hudson County and dances at St. Rocco and St. Brigid Church in Union City in the 1970s.

Unlike his father, Battle Jr. was uninterested in joining the *bolita* business. In Union City, many described him as a young Michael Corleone, the college-educated son of Vito Corleone in Francis Ford Coppola's *The Godfather*, who is reluctant to join the illicit family business. Battle Jr. was spoiled and drove a red sports car while his family lived in hiding in Madrid in the early 1970s. Battle Sr. fled to the Spanish capital months after he was hit with an indictment on gambling charges in New Jersey and soon after he was charged with assault while trying to defend his son. El Padrino had snapped when he saw a Mob rival, Alejandro Lagos, fighting with Miguelito at a block party in Jersey City in 1970. "He pulled out a gun and began pistol-whipping [Alejandro] Lagos, putting him in the hospital," wrote T. J. English. "Later that day, Senior was arrested by officers from the North Bergen Police Department, charged with aggravated assault and released on his own recognizance."

Battle Jr. returned from Spain with his parents after nineteen months to attend St. Peter's and had every intention of following his friend Bob Menendez through law school. But after a few weeks, he dropped out and agreed to be groomed by his father to join the family business.

In addition to his links to Cuban militants, Menendez found himself associated with a drug trafficker when his high school buddy and former law partner Manny Diaz descended into the criminal underworld. Beginning in 1997, Diaz worked with one of his immigration clients, Juan Carlos Huertas, a Colombian national, to create a cocaine pipeline from Colombia to the United States. Together with another partner—Juan Vega of Union City—they conspired to sell nearly a hundred pounds of cocaine valued at $2 million. Diaz was arrested on October 24, 1997, along with Vega and Huertas.

"Warrants were issued for Diaz, Vega, and Huertas . . . and the three were arrested," according to *The Jersey Journal*. "But sources say both Diaz and Vega were walking the streets until recently. He was routinely tested for drugs and forced to undergo rehabilitation treatment only months following his arrest, when a court officer found traces of cocaine in his system."[83]

Diaz was defended by Joseph Hayden, the defense attorney for John Powers, the former head of the Union City school board convicted of corruption along with Musto. Menendez had had a rocky relationship with Powers, but befriended his lawyer after the trial. Later, Hayden became a loyal supporter of Menendez and donated to his campaigns.

Diaz pleaded guilty in 1999 and was sentenced to two years in federal prison. That same year, in September, Diaz was disbarred by the New Jersey State Bar Association. The Office of Attorney Ethics, which had been investigating claims that he had misappropriated client funds in 1997, ruled that Diaz had improperly entered into a business relationship with a client, misappropriated clients' money in four different cases to pay personal debts, and presented altered bank statements to federal authorities during a probe.

"Manny's situation is a tragic one," Hayden told *The Jersey Journal* in November 1999. "He was a respected lawyer who helped a lot of people in his time. He has accepted responsibility by pleading guilty."[84]

Menendez veered from his hard-line stance against Cuba only once, when he reluctantly backed his party's decision on Elián González, a Cuban boy rescued by a fisherman in the Florida Straits on Thanksgiving Day in 1999. Initially, Menendez led the charge against the Castro regime. The father of two young children, he was nevertheless at the forefront of efforts to keep the six-year-old from returning to his biological father who had remained in Cuba after the boy's mother and her partner drowned on a raft as they tried to flee to the United States with Elián and several others.

In the United States, the Immigration and Naturalization Service granted Elián temporary permission to stay with his great-uncle Lazaro González in Miami. The boy's father, Juan Miguel González, filed a complaint with the United Nations, seeking global attention in his bid for custody of his son. On top of that, Castro demanded Elián's immediate return to Cuba. In Miami, Cuban Americans took to the streets to protest the child's return to the Communist island. In Cuba, the Castro government organized mass rallies demanding that the US government return Elián home.

The emotional tug-of-war for Elián played out between his family in Miami and Cuba and in US courts for more than six months, with Menendez introducing a bill in Congress—"For the Relief of Elián"—to grant Elián permanent residency in the United States. Menendez could not muster a cosponsor, and the bill went nowhere.

But it put Menendez in the national, and even international, spotlight. When US Attorney General Janet Reno ordered Elián returned to Cuba in April, the Miami relatives refused to comply. In June, more than a hundred federal agents, some dressed in riot gear and wielding assault rifles, broke into his great-uncle's modest bungalow at dawn and whisked Elián out of the home amid violent street battles with anti-Castro activists who stood vigil at the property. Elián was later reunited with his father who had been allowed to travel to Andrews Air Force Base in Maryland.

"The decision to return Elián González to Cuba is one that we will regret for a long time," Menendez said in a statement. "We have subverted our own laws and our own legal precedent to satisfy the Cuban dictator. This case should have been determined in a court of law and not through blackmail. We still do not know what Elián's father truly wants in this matter because there is no freedom of speech in Cuba."

Again, the statement is shocking coming from the father of two children. But Menendez didn't seem to care about the consequences of keeping a young boy from his biological father. For him it was all about being in the national spotlight and appealing to his benefactors in the Cuban community. Once he had achieved power on the national stage, he was desperate to hang onto it and grab even more.

At the same time that Menendez was working to prevent the reunion of the young child with his father and drafting legislation to make him a US citizen, he was being seriously considered as the vice presidential candidate for Al Gore's second presidential run in 2000. Gore's campaign advisers likely felt that as the only Cuban American Democrat in Congress, Menendez could help him win votes in the

Cuban American community in Florida. In the end, Gore chose Connecticut Senator Joe Lieberman instead, but Menendez continued to work on Gore's campaign for president. He also became an indefatigable fundraiser for other Democratic candidates, successfully marshaling his Cuban American supporters to their cause.

But the Elián González case proved too much for him to overcome among his Democratic power base. Bob Menendez tried and utterly failed to sway a Cuban "revenge vote" against Gore because of the Clinton administration's handling of the Elián situation.

The Elián González saga created a protest or "punishment" vote— "*el voto de castigo*"—against the Democrats. George W. Bush, the Republican candidate in the 2000 election, ultimately received fifty thousand more Cuban votes than Republican presidential candidate Bob Dole did in the previous election in 1996. As a result, Florida's twenty-five electoral votes went to Bush, giving him the state and the presidency in a Supreme Court–contested recount by a margin of 537 votes.

In fact, many political analysts would come to refer to the 2000 poll as the "Elián election." In 2020, *537 Votes*, an HBO documentary by a Miami-based filmmaker, revisited the importance of Elián González to the Cuban American vote.

"In Miami, we have long had a subset of the Cuban American community—this small, vocal, fanatical, right-wing, extremist group—that has effectively held us hostage politically," said the filmmaker Billy Corben. "The Republicans learned early on that they could weaponize the Cuba issue by using the C-word, 'communists.'"[85]

While Bob Menendez may have held sway over the machinations of US government foreign policy to hammer away at the Castro regime, the Elián saga proved he didn't have the wherewithal to help steer the Clinton administration toward a winning political strategy or the gravitas in the Cuban community on the ground in Miami to assuage an angry protest vote that ultimately led to the demise of his party in a pivotal election that changed the course of history.

Despite the loss, Menendez continued to forge lasting relationships with Bill and Hillary Clinton, which had begun during the darkest days of the Clinton administration, when the president faced impeachment for his corrupt business dealings and his affair with an intern in the White House.

As some fellow Democrats abandoned the president after he admitted during grand jury testimony in August 1998 that he had, in fact, engaged in an "improper physical relationship" with White House intern Monica Lewinsky, Menendez was one of the few who publicly came to his defense. Clinton began his sexual relationship with Lewinsky in 1995 when she was twenty-two and he was forty-nine years old. The relationship ended two years later. Clinton had previously lied about Lewinsky in televised remarks after the scandal broke in 1998. "I did not have sexual relations with that woman, Ms. Lewinsky," he said.

Weeks after his grand jury testimony in the summer of 1998, Clinton tried to repair relations with his own party. Following a breakfast meeting of congressional Democratic leaders at the White House in September just as a federal report was released, Menendez told reporters that the president had engaged in some serious soul searching.

"The scene was both emotional and straightforward," Menendez said. "No punches were pulled. I saw a president who was clearly, unlike at his televised appearance about Monica Lewinsky, contrite. . . . He accepted constructive criticism and was sincere and remorseful, taking responsibility as it affected his family, Democrats, and the country."[86]

He went on to say that he had begged Clinton to make his case to the American people, and to spare Democrats any further "surprises" just as the federal government report on corruption and the affair, conducted over four years by independent counsel Ken Starr, was made public.

"I may forgive him for the position that he has put us in," Menendez continued. "I am in no position to forgive him for anything else until I see the report."

But he was ready to support Clinton no matter what. During a debate in Congress on whether Clinton should be censured or impeached, Menendez showed little patience with his moralistic colleagues.

"I warn my colleagues that you will reap the bitter harvest of the unfair partisan seeds that you sow today. Monica Lewinsky is not Watergate," he said. "Let he who has no sin in this chamber cast the first vote."[87]

The sentiment fell on mainly deaf ears. Clinton was impeached by Congress, which adopted two articles of impeachment against him—lying under oath and obstruction of justice. Clinton was acquitted by the Senate two months later.

The Clintons never forgot Menendez's unwavering support during the dark days of the Starr inquiry and the impeachment. Years later, when Menendez took his seat in the Senate, it was New York Senator Hillary Clinton who became his best friend in the chamber.

"After the impeachment, Hillary Clinton turned into Bob's political godmother," said a New Jersey lawmaker.[88]

Still, there were dark days ahead for the crusading congressman. In February 2003, Menendez separated from Jane after twenty-seven years of marriage amid rumors that he was having an affair with a former intern who worked in his congressional office.

In January 1998, at the same time that Bill Clinton's relationship was publicly exposed, Kay LiCausi, a twenty-six-year-old Rutgers University graduate, took a job as a scheduler in Menendez's office, "sorting through invitations, checking Amtrak timetables, and fetching breakfast," according to *The New York Times*. Less than three years later, LiCausi was promoted to director of Menendez's New Jersey headquarters where she helped Menendez win a third term in Congress. By 2002, she left the staff and became a high-level lobbyist virtually overnight. Menendez's campaign paid her more than $200,000 in political consulting and fundraising fees.[89]

"But what has struck many seasoned politicians and consultants in New Jersey is the speed of Ms. LiCausi's ascent and the scope of her work, even in the state's forgiving political culture," said *The New York Times* article. "She had little experience on Capitol Hill or in Trenton. In her highest position, she supervised a half-dozen members of Mr. Menendez's Jersey City staff."

Neither Menendez nor LiCausi ever addressed the rumors of a romantic relationship. Menendez moved out of the family home, and he and Jane began the difficult process of dividing up their assets.

And at the federal courthouse in Newark, US Attorney Chris Christie, newly appointed by George W. Bush in 2002, began to take notice. Did LiCausi's meteoric rise have anything to do with the New Jersey congressman? What about Menendez's relationship with the North Hudson Community Action Corporation and the millions in federal cash he had steered to the group that was renting space in one of the Union City buildings he owned with his wife?

For prosecutors in Christie's office, there was something about the crusading congressman that didn't quite smell right, and they were determined to get to the bottom of it.

CHAPTER FIVE

I Ain't No Fortunate One

Bob Menendez stepped out onto the podium at his East Brunswick campaign headquarters, his right arm raised in triumph. He stood beaming in front of a giant US flag as a raucous crowd of supporters clapped and shouted his name amid the jangly opening electric guitar riffs of "Fortunate Son." He drew New Jersey Governor Jon Corzine in a bear hug when he stepped onto the stage to greet him before embracing his son and daughter, and his new mentor Frank Lautenberg, the senior US senator from New Jersey. Supporters waving red, white, and blue "US Senator Bob Menendez" signs cheered as the rock classic blasted over the speakers. The 1969 anti-war anthem by Creedence Clearwater Revival was the perfect message for the hero myth that Menendez had created for himself since running for student body president at Union Hill High School.

Unlike his Republican rival Tom Kean, the son of the popular former New Jersey governor and chairman of the 9/11 Commission, Menendez was no child of privilege or scion of a powerful political dynasty. To drive home the point that he was a self-made success, he launched his senate campaign in the gymnasium of his high school in Union City surrounded by five hundred cheering Hillers, underlining the message that this son of hardworking immigrants and a product of public education rose through struggle and sheer perseverance to reach the pinnacle of power in America.

It was November 7, 2006, and Menendez had beaten Kean by three points in a hard-fought election. A year earlier, Menendez had been handpicked by Corzine to fill in the remainder of his Senate term when he decided to run for governor of New Jersey.

For Corzine, Menendez was a logical pick because the seven-term congressman had become one of the most important Democrats in the House of Representatives. As chair of the Democratic Caucus, he was the third-ranking Democrat with the ability to raise millions for his colleagues and marshal the Hispanic vote, campaigning for fellow Democrats in Latino communities across the country.

"We're fortunate to have a candidate of the skill and knowledge that Bob Menendez has," said Lautenberg in his speech to his fellow senators during Menendez's appointment for the partial Senate term.

Lautenberg trotted out all the iconic stories about the Cuban American lawmaker, emphasizing Menendez's courageous decision to testify against Musto, wearing a bulletproof vest, the success of his children. Robert Jr. was a student at the University of North Carolina, and Alicia had recently graduated from Harvard where she was voted class valedictorian.

"He was born in America of parents who had immigrated from Cuba," Lautenberg continued in the address to his fellow senators. "So, when I look at our future, I am so pleased to have someone who understands New Jersey fully, who has lived the dream from very modest hardworking parents. . . . He's worked his way through the system very, very well."

Perhaps too well. As he promised to defend the US Constitution in his oath of office, Menendez remained dogged by allegations of corruption surrounded by his shady friends. At his historic investiture in the United States Capitol building, Menendez invited his most beloved supporters, including his mother, Evangelina; his children; and longtime allies Abraham Antun and Donald Scarinci. Manny

Diaz, the convicted drug trafficker and Menendez's first law partner, was also there. He had completed his prison term and was working at the North Hudson Community Action Corporation after Menendez intervened with his favorite nonprofit to get both him and his wife no-show jobs. In turn, Diaz became a loyal campaign contributor. He and his second wife, Gina Miranda, donated more than $13,000 to his friend's campaigns between 2004 and 2006.

"I admire him greatly," said Diaz. "It's sad that my support has become a campaign issue when there are much more important issues to focus on."[90]

In fact, over the years, Menendez's campaigns raked in nearly $500,000 from donors with criminal backgrounds. René Abreu, a Union City mortgage broker, who was convicted on several counts of fraud in 2004, doled out more than $7,600 with his wife, Lourdes Abreu, while Menendez was in Congress. Joseph Auriemma and his family gave $1,000. Auriemma, the North Bergen township administrator and director of the North Bergen Municipal Utilities Authority, pleaded guilty to mail fraud in 2003 and spent thirty-six months in federal prison.

René Avila, the publisher of the radical anti-Castro *Avance* newspaper who benefited from thousands spent on ads by the Menendez campaign, was also a loyal supporter. He donated $8,600 to Menendez campaigns along with his wife, Amanda Avila, from 1995 to 2006. Avila arrived in Union City from Cuba in 1961 with nothing and built a mini media empire, using his newspaper to promote city commissioners and influence county elections. Fond of fur coats and flamboyant hats, he often drove around Union City in a Rolls-Royce crowded with beautiful young women. In 2004, Avila was sentenced to twelve months and one day in prison after he pleaded guilty to tax evasion. He admitted that he failed to pay taxes on more than $400,000 in revenue to *Avance* and concealed the income by cashing business receipts at a check-cashing outfit rather than depositing the funds into *Avance*'s business accounts.

Avila portrayed himself as an upstanding citizen and serious businessman, but he was not above helping the Corporation when José Miguel Battle needed his services. At one point, Battle was listed as an employee of Avila's newspaper, a fellow Cuban American whom Amanda and René Avila considered to be a friend.

"I deal with a lot of people," Amanda Avila said in a 1986 interview with *Asbury Park Press*. Amanda worked closely with her husband from the newspaper's basement office. "I talk to a lot of people. But none on a deep and personal level. Battle is a friend."

Avila and his wife were also close to Battle enforcer Chi Chi Rodriguez and fiercely loyal to disgraced former Mayor William Musto. "When the Cuban community started to grow, when most of the Cubans were not citizens and therefore did not have a right to vote, [Musto] was the only mayor in Hudson County to name Cuban Americans, not to cleaning positions, not to sweep the streets, but to important posts in Union City government," Amanda Avila said.

Another Musto stalwart who supported Menendez was Christopher "Butchie" Crispino, a Union City fireman and boyfriend of Bruce Walter, who succeeded Menendez as mayor of Union City and donated $2,250 to Menendez. Crispino was convicted on a state drug charge in 1997, the same year Walter died of cancer.

Among the largest shady contributors to Menendez's campaign coffers were New Jersey developers, including Charles Kushner, the father of Jared Kushner, who is married to President Trump's daughter Ivanka. Charles Kushner donated more than $159,000 to Menendez and was involved in "one of the most loathsome, disgusting crimes" that Chris Christie said he had ever prosecuted in his role as US attorney in New Jersey. After he discovered that William Schulder, his brother-in-law, was working with federal agents in a probe against the developer, Charles Kushner sought revenge. He hired a prostitute to lure his brother-in-law to a motel room equipped with a hidden camera and arranged to have the recording sent to his own sister, Esther.[91]

The scheme failed, and on August 18, 2004, Charles Kushner pleaded guilty to eighteen counts, including tax evasion, witness tampering, and making illegal campaign contributions. Menendez ended up returning $6,000 of Kushner's contributions to charity—the amount the Federal Election Commission determined had been contributed illegally.

In 2004, Kushner was fined more than $500,000 by the FEC for contributing to Democratic campaigns in the names of his various companies when he did not have the authorization to do so. Charles Kushner received a pardon from Trump in 2020 with the White House citing Kushner's devotion to philanthropy after he completed his two-year sentence in 2006.

Another donor, developer Joseph Barry, cofounder of Applied Housing Companies, contributed more than $130,000 over the years, along with members of his family, to Menendez campaigns. Barry was charged with paying Robert Janiszewski, the former Hudson County executive and the county Democratic leader, more than $140,000 in bribes between 1996 and 2001 in exchange for $9 million in county, state, and federal grants for his residential projects along Hoboken and Jersey City's "Gold Coast." During the investigation, Janiszewski, who pleaded guilty to accepting bribes, agreed to cooperate with federal authorities and wear a wire in his dealings with Barry and his bagman. Barry pleaded guilty to bribery in 2004 and was sentenced to twenty-five months in prison. His attorney was Joseph Hayden, who was also a big supporter of Menendez and had defended Musto crony John Powers, the former head of the Union City school board. Years later, Barry's company, which was taken over by his two sons, gave generously to Menendez's legal defense fund after he was charged with public corruption in 2015. The fund received $10,000 from Barry's wife and $130,000 from executives of the development company.

During the campaign for the full-time Senate seat, Tom Kean's campaign tried to capitalize on some of the shadier aspects of Menendez's rise—including his experience with Bill Musto, who died in February 2006 from complications of Alzheimer's disease one month after Menendez was sworn in to fill Corzine's spot. It's not clear what the eighty-eight-year-old disgraced lawmaker thought about his old protégé's meteoric rise to the marbled halls of the US Senate. After his corruption trial, Musto never spoke to Menendez again.

Kean also ran a campaign ad featuring a garbled tape recording of Scarinci speaking with Oscar Sandoval, an FBI informant and government doctor with $1 million in Hudson County contracts. On the call, Scarinci seems to pressure him to hire one of Menendez's cronies or risk losing the contracts. Even though the tapes were more than seven years old, they proved a liability in the close race, and Scarinci stepped aside as a top adviser to Menendez's Senate campaign. For his part, Menendez denied any participation in the alleged Scarinci shakedown.[92]

But perhaps most important, prosecutors in Chris Christie's office began to issue subpoenas in their ongoing probe of Menendez and his relationship with the North Hudson Community Action Corporation, the group that paid Menendez more than $300,000 in rent payments and received $4 million in federal grants and now employed Manny Diaz and his wife. A subpoena was delivered to the nonprofit, and the investigation was leaked to the press two months before the election. For his part, Menendez said he had sought and obtained approval for the rental arrangement from a congressional ethics panel.

"This transaction was already approved by the House Ethics Committee, and the US attorney will find that Bob Menendez did nothing but support a well-respected agency in the exact same manner that he has supported other nonprofits in the state," said Matthew Miller, Menendez's spokesman, in a statement. "We're troubled by the timing of this subpoena in the middle of a political campaign, but the facts are that the NHCAC has received federal funds for over thirty-five years because they provide education and health care services to New Jerseyans who need it the most."

In addition, there were many unanswered questions about Kay LiCausi, which came to haunt the campaign and were also part of the Christie probe. Federal investigators had examined LiCausi's work as a lobbyist, trying to determine whether her influence with Menendez might have improperly helped her win contracts or helped her clients win public funding.[93]

The former scheduler in Menendez's office maintained a close relationship with the senator who helped her snag lobbying work for "campaign committees over which he controlled or had strong influence," according to *The New York Times*. While Menendez acknowledged that he had helped her win hundreds of thousands in contracts from the Democratic Congressional Campaign Committee, he denied helping LiCausi obtain any work with private businesses. LiCausi set up her lobbying business in 2003, and in three years had earned more than $1 million in contracts.[94]

Nevertheless, in August 2004, a deal with a cruise line seemed to benefit them both. Months after Royal Caribbean hired LiCausi as their lobbyist, Menendez announced the first of two appropriations totaling $9.5 million to repair the shoreline and extend a berth for the company's cruise ships. Royal Caribbean paid LiCausi $180,000 between 2004 and 2006.

Neither Menendez nor LiCausi have ever commented publicly on their relationship, although the timing of Menendez's separation from his first wife and LiCausi's employment in his office seems to suggest that things between the lawmaker and the former intern might have turned very personal very quickly. After leaving his wife, Menendez took up residence at Clinton Mills, a luxury renovation of a former lace factory in Hoboken where his mother once worked as a lacemaker after immigrating to the United States. The property at 1034 Clinton Avenue was owned by Pegasus Group, one of the developers who had donated to his campaigns. Executives at the company had contributed $18,600 to Menendez's campaigns between 2001 and 2006. "We are completely confident, as we have been all along, that the US attorney will come to the same conclusion that we have: that Senator Menendez has scrupulously abided by all laws and rules," said attorney Marc Elias in a press statement in 2007.

For their part, prosecutors in Christie's office denied that they had leaked any information to the press about their Menendez probe.

The Kean campaign wouldn't let up on the federal probe against Menendez, and spread the rumor that the Democrats would kick Menendez off the ballot in the same way that Senator Robert Torricelli, who had been mired in his own corruption scandal, was replaced by Lautenberg in 2002.

The shady arrangement with the 41st Street property caught the attention of the US Attorney Chris Christie, who issued a subpoena to Menendez and the nonprofit requesting all documents related to the federal grants the organization had received as well as records related to rent payments to Menendez. The Republicans jumped on the issue, with a spokesperson for the Republican National Committee condemning Menendez for "links to corruption." This forced the Democrats to come to the defense of Menendez, creating an unnecessary distraction during a time when the party was having great success focusing on criticisms over the Iraq War.

"As far as I know, the only thing that's been unfair so far is public revealing of subpoenas sixty days in front of an election," Governor Corzine quipped to members of the media who were pressing him for answers over why he was appointing Menendez to the seat to begin with.

"Such cozy relationships are typical for Hudson County," wrote Mulshine, as Menendez went on to win by eight points one of the nastiest campaigns New Jersey had seen in years.

Menendez shrugged off the federal probe as a political smear job by his Republican opponents on the eve of what was turning out to be a very close election. Democrats said the investigation was likely the Bush administration's continuing weaponization of the Department of Justice against his political rivals. The corruption case that Chris

Christie was preparing against Menendez ultimately closed a year after Christie became governor of New Jersey in 2011.

"There was an actual grand jury in place, so how did this just disappear?" said Mulshine.[95] "There's no reporting out there questioning where this grand jury went."

For his part, Mulshine believed that a backroom political deal had been struck between Christie, a Republican, and the New Jersey Democrats.

But if Menendez himself wasn't guilty of corruption, he was guilty of surrounding himself with criminals and dubious state officials.

One of those officials was Zulima Farber, the Cuban-born New Jersey attorney general who was a major campaign supporter and honored guest at his first inauguration in the Capitol Building in January 2006.

Farber, who had donated $19,000 to Menendez since 1992, was forced to resign in disgrace months later. A former member of Corzine's ethics advisory group during his pre-inauguration transition as governor, Farber tried to help her live-in boyfriend Hamlet Goore when Bergen County police stopped him in Fairview for driving with a suspended license and an expired registration in late May 2006. Farber was taken to the Fairview traffic stop in her official state car, driven by a trooper. Although she claimed that she did not intervene with the police investigation and simply showed up at the scene to retrieve items from the vehicle, her appearance raised "serious ethical questions" according to a report that cited three violations of the Department of Law and Public Safety's code of ethics that prevents authorities from accepting favors or using the influence of their office.

"Coming to the scene of a traffic stop where you have a personal interest in the outcome of police decisions made at the scene creates a serious risk of raising public suspicion about the legitimacy of those decisions," said Richard Williams, the former New Jersey state appeals court judge from Atlantic County who led the ethics investigation against the attorney general. Farber resigned in August, three months before the election. Her own driving record was less than stellar and raised serious questions about whether she was an appropriate candidate for the top cop job in New Jersey. At the time of her investiture, Farber had twelve speeding tickets, four bench warrants, and three license suspensions.[96]

In the press conference announcing her resignation, a defiant Farber stood next to her boss, Governor Jon Corzine, for whom the behavior of his attorney general was the first crisis of his administration. "I am steadfast in my conviction that the findings do not compel my resignation, and no one has asked for it," Farber said, adding that she was stepping down because she did not want to cause a "disruption" that would prevent her from serving effectively.

There were other ethics issues that dogged Menendez during the campaign, including his holdings in the Spanish Broadcasting System, Inc., the sole stock listed on his federal disclosures, worth between $15,000 and $50,000. He purchased the stock in 1999 when SBS conducted its initial public offering. At the time, the stock was worth $20 a share. In 2002, the radio company had opposed the merger of its competitor, the Hispanic Broadcasting Corporation, with Univision—a $3.5 billion deal that would create a Spanish-language media behemoth. To thwart the move, SBS filed a federal anti-trust lawsuit against HBC. A year later, Menendez got involved and cosponsored legislation as a member of the House to halt mergers that would create monopolies of Spanish-language broadcast companies. Menendez's Preservation of Localism, Program Diversity, and Competition in Television Broadcast Service Act of 2003 was introduced in May of that year. He also lobbied the Federal Communications Commission and the US Senate on SBS's behalf. The FCC approved the merger months later, in September 2003. After the bill failed in the 108th Congress, Menendez reintroduced it in 2005.

During the campaign, New Jersey state Republicans filed a complaint with the Senate Ethics Committee over an alleged quid pro quo between the congressman and SBS. SBS's chairman Raúl Alarcón

Jr. had given Menendez more than $145,000 in campaign contributions throughout his federal career, which was 40 percent of the total amount that the company had given to federal candidates between 1991 and January 1, 2006. Menendez's Senate campaign alone received $24,500 from the broadcaster.[97]

Menendez hit back at his critics during the race. "Nobody has bought me, no one," he told Univision during the campaign. "Never, in twenty years that I have been in Congress, never has this been suggested that this has been possible. Never in forty years of public life."

Still, there were so many allegations of shady dealings with Menendez that in the early days of the race for the Senate, Kean's campaign even floated the idea of making a film documenting Menendez's relationship with Musto and the culture of corruption in Union City. They hired a producer, but soon abandoned the project. The Kean campaign never disclosed why they scuttled the project, although New York Times reporter Jim Dwyer, who had covered Menendez for decades, said he had been approached by an opposition researcher for Kean who did not disclose his affiliation when he asked him to be part of the film. When the newspaper learned of the affiliation, discussion of the film project abruptly ended.[98]

During that election campaign, Bob Menendez was made of Teflon—nothing seemed to stick. Lawyer Joe Hayden could have been describing Menendez's unique ability to avoid prosecution when he told New Jersey Lawyer magazine in 2003 that some of his greatest victories involved "prominent clients" who were investigated but never charged.

"I won't give you names of people who weren't charged, but I can tell you there were half a dozen grand jury investigations that never got any further."[99]

For his part, Menendez forged ahead, aided by his glamorous brunette daughter and Democratic power players. Alicia Menendez, who was named one of the fifteen most interesting members of the Harvard class of 2005 by The Harvard Crimson, took to the campaign trail to stump for her father. At Harvard, the women's studies major distinguished herself as head of the oldest women's final club on campus—The Bee Club—and as a political organizer, working on two campaigns for student leaders—Rohit Chopra in 2004 and Tracy Ty Moore in 2006 for Undergraduate Council presidents—and later on Corzine's campaign for governor of New Jersey.

"She really could sell a pork chop to a rabbi," said Rohit Chopra,[100] who would go on to become a commissioner of the Federal Trade Commission and director of the Consumer Financial Protection Bureau.

In addition to Alicia Menendez, former President Bill Clinton came out twice to support his old pal Menendez, who had stood up for him during the Monica Lewinsky scandal. In one instance, Clinton headlined a political fundraiser at the home of New Jersey State Senator Raymond Lesniak in Elizabeth, while another former president—George H. W. Bush—stumped for Kean at a hotel in Bridgewater on the same day and only miles apart.

Menendez drew on other Democratic star power, including Edward Kennedy of Massachusetts who made return appearances at rallies for the New Jersey lawmaker. Other fellow Democratic senators Hillary Clinton, Joe Biden, and Barack Obama also hit the campaign trail for Menendez. At one campaign event, Obama told a crowd of about two hundred supporters: "I need Menendez back, because otherwise I'll just have Lautenberg." The folk singer Carole King was also tapped to appear at an event.

By June 2007, Menendez began the task of thanking those who had been particularly useful to him during his rise. On June 12, he endorsed fellow Senator Hillary Clinton for president of the United States and became cochair of her campaign.

"Senator Hillary Clinton is uniquely prepared and unquestionably ready to lead this country and inspire each of us to be our best," Menendez said in a press release from the Clinton campaign. "Senator Clinton stands out for the richness of her experience, the depth of her intelligence, and the strength of her ideals. She is clearly the right leader, ready to chart a new course for America."

In a joint news conference, Menendez promised to deliver the Hispanic vote. Hillary called her Senate pal "the embodiment of the American dream" and stressed the importance of Latino voters to her campaign.

"The support of Latin Americans is especially important to me because these days require us to bring our country together," Clinton said.

But it wasn't enough. Hillary Clinton lost the Democratic primary to fellow Senator Obama, who would go on to win the presidency in 2008.

During his own campaign, Menendez focused a great deal of his rallies on his opposition to the war in Iraq. At the campaign kickoff in the Union Hill gymnasium, he referred to the war seven times in his speech and called himself "an agent of change"—someone who was willing to follow his conscience rather than simply follow the party line.

"New Jersey cannot afford to send to Washington a senator who will blindly follow the president as he marches our country further and further down the road to dangerous insolvency at home and reckless entanglements abroad," Menendez said.

The message resonated with voters who had endured more than three years of a military campaign in Iraq that had no end in sight. They propelled the lawmaker to victory.

"This victory is rooted in the simple idea that faith trumps fear, that creating opportunity is more noble than protecting the powerful," Menendez said in his speech to supporters after his win. For those at the East Brunswick campaign headquarters, the speech was an obvious reference to his testimony against Musto and perhaps even a swipe at President George W. Bush's ongoing war.

In Congress, Menendez proved prescient about the ill-fated war, voting against sending troops to Iraq on what was later revealed to be the false premise that Iraqi leader Saddam Hussein had worked with Al-Qaeda terrorists and was developing weapons of mass destruction.

"I know who I had to stand up to because I know who I stand up for," he told the cheering crowd during his victory speech.

He was also standing up for himself. Days after his historic win, columnist Mike Kelly of the Bergen *Record* reported that Menendez had been the guest of honor at a private party hosted by Michael Hutton, Menendez's former chief of staff who had opened a new lobbying firm. Guests, most of whom were Hutton's clients, donated $5,000 apiece for the soiree. Despite the fee, most maintained that the party was not a political event. Among the guests were Scarinci and Joseph Simunovich, chairman of the New Jersey Turnpike Authority, who resigned as Menendez's finance director in the wake of an ethics probe into alleged favors provided to a contractor. Simunovich and his wife contributed nearly $15,000 to Menendez's political committees.[101]

But Menendez had other things on his mind. In February 2007, weeks after he took his seat in the Senate, Menendez was off on a romantic trip to Puerto Rico with his married lover, a Mexican-born former church secretary and publisher of *Nosotros*, a Spanish-language newspaper founded in 2002 that served the Hispanic immigrant community in Freehold, New Jersey. Cecilia Reynolds was a sexy brunette stunner who later appeared nude on the beach at the governor's beach house in photos circulated in a bombshell thirteen-page dossier obtained by the *New York Post*, *The New York Times*, and the National Legal and Policy Center, a conservative ethics watchdog group in Virginia in 2013.

According to the explosive document, Menendez had "seduced" Reynolds in 2005 and later showed her "bundles of cash" stuffed in "hidden places." The document also claimed that Menendez boasted about "kickbacks from contractors and influence-seeking people" while they conducted a torrid affair that included sex on a private jet provided by one of his benefactors and closest friends, a shady Palm

Beach ophthalmologist named Salomon Melgen, and on a bed that the senator said had been used by President John F. Kennedy.

In February 2007, the couple embarked on a seven-day getaway to Puerto Rico where they stayed at the official residence of Governor Aníbal Acevedo Vilá, according to the dossier, which featured photos of the couple at different tourist sites on the trip.

Reynolds boasted about the senator's piles of cash to friends in 2007—fifteen years before the FBI discovered bags, jackets, and even boots stuffed with banknotes at his Bergen County home, as well as a cache of gold bars.

"She knows a lot of intimate stuff about Menendez and even knows federal and state secrets and all about his kickback schemes, etc.," the document claimed. "She was told by him that he has kickbacks from contractors and influence-seeking people."

After their sojourn in Puerto Rico, Menendez wrote to Monmouth University—for which he secured $7 million in federal grants—calling Reynolds "extraordinary," which went a long way to helping her secure a spot in a highly competitive business incubator program where she was mentored in setting up the Nosotros Center for Immigration Services in Asbury Park. Reynolds had no experience in social services. Still, the opening ceremony for the center took place in May 2010. Menendez even dispatched his deputy chief of staff to deliver a proclamation in Spanish declaring the center an important community asset.

He also lavished praise on the small community newspaper, whose name translates to "Us" in English. "One of the most substantive newspapers in either English or Spanish that I have read," said Menendez, after he was glowingly portrayed in *Nosotros*. During his race for the Senate, Menendez's campaign took out a full-page ad in the newspaper.

Despite all of his work to help Reynolds get the center up and running, it did not prosper. Critics said that instead of providing free legal help for newly arrived immigrants, it directed them to private attorneys who charged them fees. It was eventually evicted for not paying rent, and the state revoked its nonprofit status in 2013.

Menendez continued to back Reynolds and posed with her in a group photo that appeared on *Nosotros*'s front page in 2011. Reynolds contributed $2,500 to Menendez's campaign that year, even though the couple had already broken up.

Reynolds eventually returned to her husband. The couple had been separated and contemplating a divorce while she was dating Menendez. The senator didn't seem very distraught. He quickly moved on to a striking blonde paramour and a far darker set of circumstances that would cost him nearly everything he had built during his entire political career.

A year after their romantic Puerto Rican sojourn, Menendez found himself enmeshed in another scandal, involving his old friend Acevedo Vilá. In March 2008, the Puerto Rican politician was indicted on nineteen counts in a campaign finance probe involving a Philadelphia dentist and nearly $80,000 in allegedly illegal campaign contributions intended to help him pay off debts from his 2000 race. Moneyed interests backing Acevedo Vilá were at war politically with proponents of Puerto Rico becoming the fifty-first state. Menendez was on the side of the fat-cat donors, who wanted special nation-state status for the US territory, allowing it to become a tax-free haven. These donors feted Menendez at swanky Caribbean fundraisers while Acevedo Vilá continued to give him free access to his beach house. Menendez raised hundreds of thousands of dollars at these fundraisers. In the process he secured Acevedo Vilá's support to become chair of the Democratic Caucus in 2003. Before that, from 1999 to 2003, Menendez was vice chair of the powerful group.

To help his friend Acevedo Vila, one of his first moves as a newly minted senator was to place a secret hold on the confirmation of Rosa Emilia Rodríguez-Velez, the acting US attorney, who was investigating the governor. This was a rare and bold move for a junior senator to use against the president of the United States, not to mention against the Department of Justice. Rodríguez-Velez was appointed by President George W. Bush and had the support of most of the Senate but could only stay in office 120 days if she was not officially confirmed. The hold was seen as a politically motivated move that would have allowed the District Court in Puerto Rico to choose a replacement for Rodríguez-Velez as acting US attorney.

In the end, the tactic didn't work, and Rodríguez-Velez was confirmed as US attorney in 2007. However, her investigation failed, and a year later, most of the charges against Acevedo Vilá were dropped. After a trial in 2009, he was found not guilty of the remaining charges.

—

Despite his success in politics, Menendez was confronted with the decline of his beloved mother, who was suffering from Alzheimer's. His older sister, Caridad, was Evangelina Menendez's caregiver during her long illness. Evangelina died in October 2009 and a former girlfriend said he was so grief-stricken, "he would go to the gravesite on Mother's Day to visit her every year."

Menendez set out to honor his mother's memory by setting up the Evangelina Menendez Trailblazer Award for enterprising and courageous women in 2011. Menendez's friend and political godmother Hillary Clinton would be among the first recipients of the distinction.

He also dedicated his 2009 book to Evangelina, as well as his sister and his two children. In *Growing American Roots: Why Our Nation Will Thrive as Our Largest Minority Flourishes*, Menendez spends 256 pages celebrating Latinos in the United States. A chapter on famous Hispanics listed astronauts of Latino heritage as well as Nobel Prize–winning scientists and labor leader Cesar Chavez. But he also mentioned his pal with the private jet. In his book, Menendez referred to Salomon Melgen as a "prominent, well-respected" Dominican Republic–born eye doctor who set up a lucrative practice in Palm Beach, Florida.

"Sal," as he was known to his friends, was the son of a Lebanese father and Palestinian mother. He was already a physician in Santo Domingo before he immigrated to the United States in 1979. Although he barely spoke English, he went on to study at Yale and Harvard. A year after his arrival, he was interning at Yale New Haven Hospital, and within five years Melgen worked in residency at the University of Missouri, becoming a chief fellow at Massachusetts Eye and Ear, a hospital connected to Harvard Medical School.

"Perseverance and internal fortitude paid off in the face of insults," wrote Menendez, who met Melgen at a fundraiser in South Florida in 1993 where Melgen contributed $500 to Menendez's first congressional reelection campaign—the doctor's first contribution to a political candidate.

"Especially before he could speak English well, other doctors in training even 'laughed at me, treated me like nothing.' Dr. Melgen said that the insults somehow didn't distract him from his goal," wrote Menendez about the man who would prove to be one of his greatest friends and benefactors. "'I had the inner feeling that I was going to do whatever I had to do to make it.'"

Melgen not only "made it," he gained entrance to important government circles in Florida. His clients included Lawton Chiles, the governor of Florida between 1991 and 1998.

Melgen also considered Menendez a close friend. He rushed to the senator's side in Union City after his mother's death in 2009 and held a fundraiser for him in May 2010 after Menendez became head of the Democratic Senatorial Campaign Committee. At that particular event, Melgen and his wife donated $60,000 to the committee. And later Melgen began donating to a political action committee to help with Menendez's reelection bid in 2012. Melgen's company donated more than $700,000 to the Majority PAC, which went a long way to helping Menendez rise to victory with 58 percent of the vote.

Including Melgen in a worthy list of high-achieving, popular Hispanic celebrities and professionals might have raised eyebrows in 2009 when *Growing American Roots* was published. In addition to outlining Melgen's accomplishments, Menendez made sure to thank him in his acknowledgments at the end of the book.

Years later, when Menendez was charged for the first time with public corruption, it suddenly became clear why the doctor was so important.

Menendez may have thought he had dodged a bullet when the Christie probe closed, but the US attorney for the District of New Jersey wasn't done with him. As Menendez inched closer and closer to his ophthalmologist pal, federal investigators followed their every move. It was soon clear that Melgen was Menendez's biggest benefactor, but he would also prove the catalyst for his precipitous downfall.

CHAPTER SIX

The Dark Side

Hillary Clinton's motorcade sped through the bucolic woods near her Chappaqua estate en route to the forty-two-story Goldman Sachs Tower, the second tallest building in Jersey City, overlooking the Hudson River and Lower Manhattan. It took the secretary of state a little more than an hour—a trip that would normally take almost double that time even on a Saturday in summertime for anyone else.

For Menendez, who waited with anticipation and some anxiety for his political godmother's arrival on the afternoon of June 23, 2012, Clinton couldn't arrive soon enough. He was eager to introduce her to the international power players he had gathered in New Jersey with the help of a former congressional aide. They were an illustrious group that included the crown prince of Spain and the "well-respected" Palm Beach eye doctor Salomon Melgen, who had earned a glowing passage in *Growing American Roots.*

Emails between Clinton and her staff show that she was more than happy to take time out of her busy schedule to give one of the keynote speeches at the weekend meeting of the United States Spain Council, the group Menendez chaired. Still, her staff squabbled over setting a time limit on her participation. One staffer suggested avoiding the banquet dinner that was scheduled to take place at the Great Hall on Ellis Island that evening at all costs as royal protocol would force attendees to stay seated until the prince of Asturias and his wife, Letizia, had finished their meal. Clinton had already indicated that she was more than willing to stay as long as she was needed, although she would be returning from a United Nations conference in Rio de Janeiro on that same day. She was so eager to support Menendez that she admitted in an email that she couldn't quite remember why exactly he had asked her to be there in the first place.

"I'm ok w [sic] the later hour," wrote Clinton to her aides Huma Abedin and Lona Valmoro on June 15. "I just can't remember what it is!"[102]

Menendez wanted to show off his deep ties to the secretary of state during the weekend of business meetings and bilateral discussions to cement his own meteoric rise on the global stage.

The international conference was also a culmination of the years that Menendez spent lobbying and preparing his global bona fides to launch himself into the vaunted role of chairman of the Senate Foreign Relations Committee. He had spent the previous decade cultivating ties to members of Congress, especially those in the Hispanic Caucus, while sparring with the Bush administration over the Iraq War.

But he stumbled along the way. Even though he had been considered a running mate for Al Gore's presidential campaign, he simply didn't have enough juice with the Cuban American lobby at the time to convince them to back the Democratic candidate for president. He suffered a serious defeat with the anti-Castro lobby in 2000 when he backed the Clinton administration's decision to send Elián González back to his father in Cuba, even though he had once campaigned to keep the boy in America. The Elián factor ultimately contributed to Gore's loss at the polls and paved the way for George W. Bush to take the White House.

Menendez didn't allow the defeat to get in the way of his political ambitions. He shrugged it off as he began to position himself as an important national fundraiser for the Democratic Party.

In one of his early attempts to gain favor with the party, he partnered with a controversial Puerto Rican Democrat, who used his friendship with Menendez to score his own political points and lobby to change the status of Puerto Rico as a territory of the United States into an independent entity—a situation that would have been counter to American interests.

Even though Menendez did not support the movement for the independence of Puerto Rico, he believed that Aníbal Acevedo Vilá, the island's resident commissioner and later its governor, could be useful to him and the Democrats in marshaling the Puerto Rican vote in New York State for both of Hillary Clinton's Senate campaigns in 2000 and 2006 as well as her run for president in 2008.

But the relationship with Acevedo Vilá would backfire on Menendez. For one thing, Acevedo Vilá was fond of hyperbole, and he annoyed high-ranking Democrats because he couldn't keep his stories straight.

In 2003, Menendez partnered with Acevedo Vilá on a weekend fundraiser for the Democratic National Committee on the island. Events were centered on the guest of honor, former President Clinton, who was paid $125,000 to talk about international relations and participate in a round of golf with donors. The cash for the speaking fee came from the Caribbean Council on World Affairs, an obscure group that later seemed to disappear without a trace.[103]

Acevedo Vilá had hoped that by partnering with Menendez, he would get valuable face time with Clinton. But neither politician got very close to the former president. Menendez was relegated to a side table, far away from Clinton during his speech and gala dinner, as was Azevedo Vilá.

That didn't stop Azevedo Vilá from bragging to the local press that he had played a round of golf with Clinton and sat at the main table. He told anyone who would listen that he had spoken to Clinton about Puerto Rico becoming an independent state, and also laid out a case against the island's then Governor Pedro Rosselló, who Acevedo Vilá claimed was corrupt.

A local newspaper revealed the truth that Clinton couldn't even remember what Azevedo Vilá's job in the government entailed, and praised Rosselló.

"Although Clinton only mentioned Acevedo Vilá speaking to him about Puerto Rico's status issue and his job, Acevedo Vilá said he also spoke about the corruption to which he tried to link Rosselló," said the article in *The Puerto Rico Herald*, which also noted that Clinton never played golf with Azevedo Vilá and actually left the island without fulfilling his obligations to the hosts to play a few rounds with donors.[104]

The relationship with Acevedo Vilá also led to Menendez getting involved with an investigation by the Bush-influenced Department of Justice into allegations that the Puerto Rican politician was using straw donors in his campaign—a charge that was later dismissed.

Still, the fundraisers for the Democratic National Committee and for Hillary Clinton's campaigns continued, helping to cement Menendez's role as a leader in the Congressional Hispanic Caucus and proving himself indispensable to his political godmother.

By 2012, Menendez was primed to become the next chairman of the Senate Foreign Relations Committee. The New Jersey Democrat was also in his second year of heading up the US Spain Council, a nonprofit that worked to encourage stronger corporate, educational, and cultural ties between Spain and the United States. Founded by former US Vice President Al Gore and former Spanish President José Maria Aznar in 1996, the United States Spain Council was presided over by a former Menendez staffer with a glowing reputation in Washington and strong ties to anti-Castro Cubans in Miami where he grew up.

Pedro Pablo Permuy, who worked for Menendez when he was in Congress in the early to mid-1990s and then again in the early aughts, was now a leading Washington, DC, lobbyist and business partner of the Spanish royals. Permuy was himself a minor aristocrat descended from Galician nobility on his father's side. His grandparents settled in Cuba to escape political turmoil in Spain in the 1920s. The family later fled the island shortly after Fidel Castro came to power. Both Permuy's mother and his father had worked in the student resistance to the Castro regime. The couple fled to Venezuela in 1962 but eventually settled in Miami where Permuy's father, Jesus Permuy, became a distinguished architect and urban planner as well as an important patron of the arts and human rights activist. He worked to expose human rights violations in Cuba. In 2020, the city of Miami named a street in his honor. Permuy's mother, Marta Permuy, was a leading art dealer in South Florida, the first to introduce Cuban artists to the United States. She was also the aunt of Jorge Mas Canosa, the Miami businessman who launched the Cuban American National Foundation, the most influential anti-Castro lobby group in the United States.

Pedro Pablo Permuy, one of the couple's seven children, continued the family's legacy of public service. By the time he organized the weekend conference in Jersey City, he had already worked as a senior adviser to Madeleine Albright, the former secretary of state, and been appointed by Bill Clinton to serve as the assistant secretary of defense during his second term in office.

Permuy tapped Melgen as well as Alan Solomont, who had been appointed ambassador to Spain in 2009 by then-President Barack Obama, as speakers at the weekend conference. Solomont had made his fortune running nursing homes and other elder-care facilities and was a Democratic fundraising powerhouse, well known to the Clintons. Solomont, who served as national finance chairman of the Democratic National Committee, raised more than $40 million for the Democrats. For his efforts on behalf of the Democratic Party, he was among an elite group of donors who were invited to spend a night in the Lincoln bedroom at the White House—a situation that raised a storm of controversy when it was revealed in 1996. The Clintons had invited more than eight hundred celebrities and financiers to sleep in the historic room.

The weekend also featured panel discussions with Ramón Gil-Casares, Spain's ambassador to the United States, and Ana Pastor, the country's minister of public works and infrastructure development. The Assistant Secretary of State for Economic, Energy, and Business Affairs for the US Department of State Jose Fernandez was the moderator for a panel on "Opportunities in Transportation and Infrastructure Development" that included Rafael Del Pino, the chairman of Ferrovial, a multinational Spanish corporation that specializes in transportation and infrastructure projects around the globe.

The conference was a success, with Clinton making a brief speech, followed by Felipe VI. Princess Letizia was present for the remarks, but because she does not involve herself in anything political, she asked to greet Clinton in the hall on the way to the main dining hall with Pedro Pablo Permuy only after Clinton's closed-door meeting with the crown prince and Bob Menendez.

Although Clinton was only present for a little more than an hour, the event was a major success, and Permuy was praised for a job well done. Menendez always knew that his former staffer was a rising star even as a junior aide in his congressional office in 1991. Permuy, who graduated with a master's degree in international relations from Johns Hopkins University in 1990, began his government career as a legislative staffer for Florida Senator Robert Graham, a Democrat. It culminated with his role as foreign policy adviser to Menendez, who was chair of the Democratic Caucus until his appointment to the Senate in 2006. His key responsibilities for Menendez included working as an adviser on intelligence and international trade.

In 2003, when Permuy left the House Democratic Caucus to become director of government affairs at Greenberg Traurig, a global law firm, Menendez noted, "[Permuy's] now going to the dark side. . . . We're going to miss him, but we want to congratulate him and thank him for all of the tremendous service that he has given the committee."

But the lawmaker didn't miss Permuy for very long. Despite his career change, Permuy, then forty-seven years old, became even closer to Menendez.

In his new career, Permuy used the connections he made in the hallowed halls of Congress for thirteen years. He created a lobbying and business empire that stretched from the United States to the Dominican Republic, Panama, and Spain. He became business partners with Spain's royal family in a Panamanian gold mining corporation while heading up a port security company in the Dominican Republic that had been linked to the family of Panamanian dictator Manuel Noriega and both Melgen and Menendez.

Emboldened by his bond with Hillary Clinton and his brush with Spanish royalty during the conference he organized with Permuy in New Jersey, Bob Menendez might have considered himself an important player on the world stage.

Menendez already held sway in Europe and the Caribbean as chair of the Senate Subcommittee on the Western Hemisphere. He was so powerful that he often blocked the nominations of ambassadors. In June 2011, he was hell bent on not allowing Jonathan Farrar, appointed by Obama as the chief of mission at the US Interests Section in Havana, to become ambassador to Nicaragua, even though Farrar's long experience as a career diplomat in Latin America made him an obvious pick. In a leaked WikiLeaks cable that came to light in December 2010, Farrar had been critical of Cuban dissidents.

"We see very little evidence that the mainline dissident organizations have much resonance among ordinary Cubans," Farrar said. Without changes, he said, "The traditional dissident movement is not likely to supplant the Cuban government."

Both Menendez and fellow Cuban American Senator Marco Rubio were displeased with Farrar's handling of Cuba during his three-year tenure. They felt he hadn't been hard enough against the Castro regime, and they didn't want him heading up US interests in Nicaragua, which was ruled by Daniel Ortega, a Cuban ally.

"Senator Menendez is intent on blocking his nomination," said Miguel Rodriguez, the deputy assistant secretary for senate affairs in the State Department in a July 25, 2011, email to Cheryl Mills, Clinton's chief of staff.[105]

Months later, Menendez was on the warpath, flexing his political muscle over the selection of key ambassadorial positions in the Western Hemisphere where his ire was directed at any appointee who hadn't kissed his ring.

In a December 19, 2011, email, Rodriguez informed Mills that "as suspected Senator Menendez is quite furious on the heels of this piece." Menendez didn't like anyone attempting to skirt direct communication with him while going through the nomination process to become an ambassador, making it clear to Hillary Clinton's staff that any avoidance of his direct influence would be met with seething hostility. One such nominee attempted to make a public case through the writing of an op-ed for positions that were counter to Menendez and his interests. This didn't go over well as "his staff explained that [he] did himself a 'great disservice' and dug himself a 'deeper hole.' They explained that Menendez is insisting that [he] meet with him personally before he's ever considered for another posting."

Mills forwarded the email to Clinton a few hours later with the words "Your boy," referring to Menendez.

Six months after his successful Jersey City conference, Clinton's "boy" won reelection to the Senate and became the chairman of the Senate Committee on Foreign Relations, one of the most powerful groups in Congress. Established in 1816, the twenty-one-member committee has enormous influence on US foreign policy. It has authority over border disputes, international treaties, and can approve foreign aid and arms sales to foreign countries. The committee's members also have authority over foreign loans and the US diplomatic service. It rules over the acquisition of land and buildings for US embassies in foreign countries and approves diplomatic appointments.

"Senator Menendez constantly dealt with the most critical geo-political issues of the day," said Danny O'Brien, Menendez's former chief of staff. "He led congressional delegations abroad, and he had profoundly strong views on supporting the issue of democracy in Cuba, Israel's right to exist, the rights of the Cypriots to exist securely without Turkish occupation, and so many other issues."

As his international ambitions soared, Menendez drew closer and closer to Permuy and Melgen—relationships that would later shock many of his constituents and his fellow senators, ultimately endangering his own political future.

Sal Melgen, a portly playboy from the Dominican Republic, nearly ended the career of Bob Menendez.

Fond of cigars, expensive cars, and fast women, Melgen split his time between Palm Beach, where he ran his successful ophthalmology practice, and a sprawling seaside villa in Casa de Campo, which backs onto a lush golf course designed by renowned course architect Pete Dye. Menendez enjoyed several trips to the resort in La Romana, where celebrities such as Oscar de la Renta were among Melgen's neighbors. Menendez was often a guest at Melgen's villa and on a few occasions flew to the Dominican Republic on the doctor's private jet.

Among the women Menendez brought to La Romana was Gwendolyn Beck, an investment banker and associate of billionaire pedophile Jeffrey Epstein. Menendez needed help wooing the sultry blonde and prevailed upon Melgen, who cashed in 650,000 American Express points to secure an executive suite at the Park Hyatt Paris-Vendome—valued at more than $5,000—for the New Jersey Democrat. Menendez asked Melgen to pay for the hotel after searching for a discount. In an email, he promised the doctor he would repay him when he accumulated enough American Express points of his own. Instead, he redeemed his accumulated points three years later, in 2013, using 134,328 points to buy a Weber Genesis barbecue grill.

According to prosecutors in a 2015 indictment, Menendez traveled to Paris to spend three nights with a girlfriend—he was dating Beck at the time—sending Melgen an email describing the setup of the luxury suite he wanted: "King bed, work area with internet, limestone bath with soaking tub and enclosed rain shower, [and] views of courtyard or streets. . . . You call American Express Rewards and they will book it for you. It would need to be in my name."

A month later, Beck, in a green, sleeveless dress and dangly earrings, was photographed next to a smiling and very bronzed Menendez at Melgen's dinner table in La Romana. The color photograph, which also features Flor Melgen and the couple's two children and a friend, was later used as evidence for the defense in Menendez's first corruption indictment. A lawyer for the senator showed jurors a collection of snaps from the Dominican Republic to prove that it was simply "a family home."

In many ways, Menendez did indeed become part of the Melgen family. Over the years, Menendez became so close to Melgen and his wife that he called Flor every year to sing happy birthday to her over the phone.

Despite his friendship with the US senator, the married eye doctor was a controversial figure in Florida. Several malpractice lawsuits accused him of experimenting on inmates in the state's prisons while developing procedures to treat macular degeneration, which often causes blindness in elderly patients. In one instance, an elderly woman who was undergoing a special retinal treatment designed by Melgen died on the operating table after he refused to allow nurses to run a heart monitor, because he said the sound distracted him during surgery. A nurse was ultimately blamed for the woman's death.[106]

He was also overbilling Medicare, at one point charging more than any other doctor in the country. In 2012, he received $20.8 million in connection with treatments at his clinics in Florida. Most of the bills were for procedures involving Lucentis, a drug that costs about $2,000 per dose. Melgen would typically squeeze three doses out of a single container of the drug, but bill the government for the individual doses.[107]

At one point, a contractor for Medicare demanded Melgen repay nearly $9 million in overbilling. Unfazed, Melgen relied on his friend to get him out of a jam with the federal government. Menendez pressured the secretary of health and human services to get Melgen off the hook for the cash. Louis Jacques, a former Medicare official, said that a group of staffers in the senator's office pressured him to allow Melgen to continue to overbill.[108]

Jacques recalled a striking conversation with a Menendez aide, who emphasized the senator's personal interest in the matter, saying: "The issue is very important to the senator. Dr. Melgen is a personal friend of the senator. Bad medicine is not illegal. Medicare should pay these claims." The dispute centered on $8.9 million that Medicare contractor First Coast Service Options had flagged as overbilling.

The aide's justification left Jacques unsettled. "It was literally when the person said, 'Bad medicine is not illegal. Medicare should pay for it,' that I felt I should stand up and just stretch, clear my head," Jacques recounted.

Senator Tom Harkin, an Iowa Democrat who was then chairman of the Senate Committee on Medicare, agreed to a 2011 meeting with Melgen and Menendez, but decided to take no action.

"Two things stick out in my mind," recalled Harkin years later. The first, he said, was a medical company manufacturing a vial of eye medicine with enough for three doses, even though the Food and Drug Administration had approved only a single dose per container for the medicine.

"I wondered about that," said Harkin, who retired from the Senate in 2015. He said he also wondered about Melgen's billing practices. "If he's treating three people and he's charging three people for three but he's only paying for one vial, that doesn't sound right to me, either." He said he instructed his staff to "keep tabs on it," but didn't do much else.

Undaunted, Menendez appealed to then–Senate Majority Leader Harry Reid, who reached out to the White House deputy chief of staff to inform her that Menendez was upset. Reid later brokered a meeting in his Senate office with Health and Human Services (HHS) Secretary Kathleen Sebelius in which Menendez pressured her to approve Melgen's overbilling.

Melgen's doses were split at Franck's Pharmacy, a drug compounding facility in central Florida that was cited by the Federal Drug Administration for filthy conditions that led to dangerous drug contamination. In 2009, the facility said that the medication it prepared for twenty-one elite polo horses contained incorrect dosages of a drug that killed the animals. The horses, from Venezuela's Lechuza Caracas Polo Club, began collapsing shortly after arriving at the International Polo Club Palm Beach in Wellington, Florida, where they were scheduled to play in the US Polo Open.[109]

In total, Melgen received more than $90 million from the Medicare program between January 2008 and 2013.

In addition to the Medicare fraud, Melgen was also a womanizer with a harem of sexy, young women from around the world. When he needed help arranging visas for his girlfriends, he called on Menendez, for whom no favor for his doctor benefactor was too minor.

In fact, Menendez directed six members of his Senate staff, including his senior policy adviser Mark Lopes, to email a high-ranking official at the State Department to give "careful consideration" to the visa application of a Brazilian woman, who had once posed nude on the cover of Brazil's *Sexy* magazine. The girlfriend, Juliana Lopes Leite, was applying for a student visa in the summer of 2008 to study law at the University of Miami. Lopes wrote that Lopes "(no relation to me) has her visa application appointment in Brasilia, Brazil, tomorrow. . . . Sen [sic] Menendez would like to advocate unconditionally for Dr. Melgen and encourage careful consideration of [her] visa application." The State Department responded within hours. Lopes got her visa the next day and went on to travel to Florida. Her tuition at the university was paid by the Sal Melgen Foundation in West Palm Beach.

Around the same time that Menendez advocated for Lopes, he also instructed his staff to help secure a visa for a twenty-year-old Ukrainian actress living in Spain. Svitlana Buchyk, a TV anchor, needed to "undergo medical evaluation for plastic surgery," and visit Melgen, said the letter sent by the senator to the State Department.

"Dr. Melgen is a person of the highest caliber," Menendez wrote in the February 2007 appeal. "He is a fine citizen and held in high esteem by his peers." A week later, the unidentified woman got her visa and traveled to Florida, where she stayed in one of Melgen's apartments in Palm Beach. She joined Melgen and Menendez for dinner at Azul, a restaurant in Miami's Mandarin Hotel. Melgen introduced his lover to the senator and told her Menendez helped to get her visa.

Later, a mysterious tipster mentioned a woman named "Svetlana B," a Russian national who lived in Miami and was a frequent guest at Melgen's homes in Casa de Campo. "This girl is one of the most regular participants in the activities the Doctor arranges for the Senator," the tipster wrote. "She has traveled with them in the jet, sailed with them in the yacht, and has repeatedly visited the Doctor's house."[110] A woman named Svitlana Buchyk suffered a minor accident while driving a Chevrolet Impala in Coral Gables in 2010. The car was in the name of Melgen's wife, Flor. Buchyk gave the eye doctor's North Palm Beach address to the police as her own.

Buchyk was living in a condo rented by Melgen on Singer Island north of Palm Beach in 2009 when she became embroiled in a dispute because her name wasn't on the lease. Buchyk also listed her address as Melgen's West Palm Beach office, according to a traffic ticket she received a year earlier for driving with windows that were tinted too dark.

Menendez and his staff also helped secure visas for Rosiell Polanco, a twenty-two-year-old Dominican woman, another Melgen girlfriend, and her eighteen-year-old sister, redoubling his efforts after their visas were denied because neither was gainfully employed in the Dominican Republic.

"Call ambassador ASAP," wrote Menendez to his staff in an email. Menendez wrote to a high-ranking State Department official and, within a few weeks, the women were granted US visas. In an email to a colleague, Lopes, the foreign policy aide, wrote, "ONLY DUE to the fact that RM intervened."

Polanco admitted that she had reached out to Melgen to help with her visa. "Hello, my love," she wrote in an email to the eye doctor. "I write to remind you that you need to send me a copy of what Senator Bob Menendez's office sent you, which I need for the embassy. . . . Thank you. A kiss."

Polanco later said that she received much more favorable treatment at the US Embassy in Santo Domingo when she went for her appointment armed with the senator's letter.

Menendez seemed to work on autopilot for Melgen, probably because he had been doing it since they met in 1993. In the early aughts, when he helped Melgen end a particularly messy tryst, he very nearly created a diplomatic incident.

Yudehiris (Judy) Dorrejo was a twenty-eight-year-old Dominican entrepreneur when she met Melgen, then forty-five, at the Jaragua Hotel and Casino in 1998. Built in 1942 at the behest of dictator Rafael Trujillo, the modernist five-star hotel on George Washington Avenue in Santo Domingo overlooked the Caribbean Sea and was the center of the city's moneyed social scene for decades until it was largely destroyed by protestors in 1985. During the early years of the Cold War, Trujillo used the hotel to lure international investors and US politicians to the fiercely anti-Communist Caribbean country. It was also said to be staffed by Dominican intelligence agents who would set up US lawmakers in compromising positions with local prostitutes and later bribe them with surveillance of their trysts to "encourage" their backing for US investment on the island. Dorrejo's relationship with the prominent eye doctor started at the refurbished hotel but it also ended there when she sat for a deposition nearly two years later, after Melgen sued her for fraud.

At the beginning of their love affair, Melgen put Dorrejo up in a lavish apartment he owned in Santo Domingo, and gave her nearly $1 million to help establish a clothing franchise. He flew her and her sister to Palm Beach and paid for their stays at the Ritz-Carlton on Singer Island and at Mar-a-Lago. He also gave her access to one of his corporate bank accounts linked to his medical practice.

"He wanted me to live like royalty, to have no problems of any kind," she said.

Dorrejo, who was born into an Orthodox Jewish family, had an on-again, off-again relationship with Melgen, which she ended after discovering he was still married.

"He had told me that he was single, but then I found out that he was married," Dorrejo testified in a 2001 deposition taken in a conference room of the storied hotel. She added, "When I went there he showed me divorce papers, which were falsified I later found out."

Shortly after they got back together in the first days of 1999, Melgen discovered that Dorrejo had another lover—a notorious drug trafficker—when he called his Santo Domingo apartment and a man answered the phone. Melgen's jealousy seemed to get the better of him, and he started to demand an accounting of the cash that Dorrejo had withdrawn from his company's account, harassing her and at one point threatening to kill her and her son. Melgen moved quickly to evict Dorrejo from his apartment and convinced a Dominican judge to issue a travel ban against her and prevent her from leaving the country. Melgen said that Dorrejo's boyfriend threatened his life. Eventually, in the fall of 2001, Vitreo-Retinal Consultants, Inc., which was wholly owned by Melgen, sued her for fraud in Palm Beach County court, claiming that she stole money from the medical practice even though Melgen had given her signing authority on the company's bank account and a credit card. Dorrejo admitted that she used the account to pay for furniture for Melgen's properties and even oversaw renovations. She also spent hundreds of thousands on luxury items for herself while she set up her clothing franchise at a luxury mall in Santo Domingo.

The battle escalated when Dorrejo called on Guido Gómez Mazara, a legal adviser to the Dominican president and leader of the Dominican Revolutionary Party, to intervene and help to lift the travel ban so that she could go to Florida and New York to buy merchandise for her clothing store.

When the travel ban was eventually lifted, Melgen flew into a rage, sending letters to the US Embassy in Santo Domingo and alleging interference by a government official. He threatened Gómez Mazara and told him that he had the power to revoke his visa to the United States by calling on his friend Bob Menendez.

"Melgen was a close friend of Menendez, and Menendez used his status as an influential politician to attack me, to mention my name, to affect my political career, and for that to end in a conflict to deprive me of my right to enter the United States," Gómez Mazara told Univision in 2013.

On October 10, 2002, at a hearing of the Western Hemisphere Subcommittee related to drug trafficking in the Dominican Republic and Guatemala, Menendez addressed questions about Gómez Mazara to the Drug Enforcement Administration's head of operations Roger Guevara and Undersecretary of State Otto Reich, both of whom had been invited to the hearing. Menendez wanted to know about the May 2002 death of Martín Abreu Pimentel, a suspected drug trafficker who had also been an adviser to the Dominican president and was known to Gómez Mazara.

"I would like to know what they know about Gomez Masara [sic]," Menendez said. "I would like to know if the administration is aware of any link that has been made between Mr. Pimentel and Mr.

Gomez Masara [sic], or between him and any of the other murdered officials."

Reich and Guevara seemed taken aback by the aggressive line of questioning. They said that the Dominican President Hipólito Mejía was cooperating with the United States by extraditing Dominicans suspected of being drug dealers to the United States. When neither man could answer his question about Gómez Mazara, even after making inquiries about him during a break in the subcommittee's proceedings, Menendez seemed to double down.

"Does anyone know who Mr. Gomez Masara [sic] is?" he asked.

When Guevara promised to look into the matter further, Menendez replied that he was "disappointed with what I have heard here."

"I hope that in the future, even in a closed session, I can hear what Mr. Guevara has to say about certain issues," he said

Weeks after the subcommittee meeting, Hans Hertell, the US ambassador to the Dominican Republic, visited Gómez Mazara at his office, ostensibly to discuss the extradition of three Dominican businessmen to the United States on drug trafficking charges. Gómez Mazara said he told Hertell that the charges against the men were related to money laundering and that the terms for their extradition had expired. The situation escalated with Hertell allegedly threatening to revoke Gómez Mazara's US visa.

"We had another altercation in front of the president of the Republic. He told me that I was disrespectful," Gómez Mazara told Univision. "I told him, 'look, if you want to take away my visa, take it away.' My wife is American, my children too . . . and I studied in the United States. Now, I am not going to reduce my personal dignity and the honor of my family because of your arrogant and haughty attitude."

In February 2004, the US government suspended Gómez Mazara's visa, citing his alleged links to illegal activities. A March 2004 WikiLeaks cable revealed that the removal of Gómez Mazara from his post, along with three other officials, was a priority for the US

Embassy in Santo Domingo, although there was no further explanation about why officials wanted him gone. For his part, Gómez Mazara hired three US lawyers who confirmed that there was no active criminal probe against him in the United States.

Later, a lawyer for Melgen said the eye doctor "did not request or seek to alter Gómez Mazara's visa status."[111]

In interviews with Dominican news outlets years later, Gómez Mazara maintained that it was Melgen's "skirt-chasing" that resulted in the diplomatic row and attacks against him.

Dorrejo also quickly found out that standing up to the well-connected doctor was a dangerous proposition. For one thing, the medical professional had a peculiar fascination for the occult.

"He would make calls to witch doctors, and he believed in all this esoteric stuff and cards and stuff, and he loved to call up people to have them say these strange things," she said.

Melgen also had the status of a diplomat. "I do know that when I was with him he was an ambassador," Dorrejo said.

In his own deposition in his company's case against Dorrejo, Melgen admitted that he was an "alternate ambassador" to the United Nations for the Dominican Republic, a post that allowed him diplomatic perks, including the use of a "presidential room" at the Santo Domingo international airport, a diplomatic passport, and pouches that were not subject to inspection by customs officials and allowed him to carry pretty much anything in and out of the United States and his native country. Alternate ambassadors fill in when the head of a country's permanent mission to the world body is indisposed.

Melgen's company eventually dropped the lawsuit against his ex-girlfriend. He became obsessed with a new business venture, one that was guaranteed to make him hundreds of millions of dollars. But he would need his old pal Menendez to pull the strings in both Washington and Santo Domingo.

Melgen might be the first to admit that he knew next to nothing about securing international ports, except that it was a lucrative business. Securing a port security contract for the whole country could see him rake in more than $500 million over twenty years in revenue.

Which is how the eye doctor came to take over the International Container Security System Inc. SA, a company that screened shipping containers going in and out of Dominican ports. The company had managed to secure a no-bid contract when it was set up in 2002 by the Beauchamp family, a Dominican clan close to Panamanian dictator Manuel Noriega. Sandra Noriega, the strongman's daughter, had married Jean René Beauchamp, the son of Juan René Beauchamp, former head of the Dominican Republic's armed forces, in 1987. Two years after Beauchamp senior was killed at his farm on the country's north coast in 2000, his widow, Belinda Beauchamp, and her children set up ICSSI, which was quickly condemned by the Dominican government for charging high fees for what officials said was ineffective technology. In 2004, the Dominican Customs authority filed a lawsuit in the country's courts to end the ICSSI contract.

Melgen got in on the multimillion-dollar deal two years later. In 2006, he purchased an option to secure 50 percent of the company, which he realized in 2011. By February 2012, he had bought the whole company and installed Menendez's old staffer Pedro Pablo Permuy as the CEO of the firm.

A month later, Permuy reached out to an aide in the office of William Brownfield, assistant secretary of state in the Bureau of International Narcotics and Law Enforcement Affairs, for help in brokering the standoff with the Dominican government and recommending the firm.

But the Dominican government was steadfastly refusing to honor the ICSSI contract. Miguel Cocco, then the Dominican customs director, had long said he had no faith in the firm.

In a letter to the president's legal adviser, Cocco said that the deal was "against the interests of the Dominican government, due to its

one-sided nature, exorbitant clauses, that it violates Dominican laws."
He also pointed out a "lack of transparency, commercial ethics in the
granting of the contract." The American Chamber of Commerce in
Santo Domingo backed up Cocco's claims.[112]

Menendez would have none of it. He was bent on helping his
benefactor end the contract dispute and took bold steps that raised
eyebrows in Washington, DC. Although he did not mention ICSSI
by name, he raised the issue of cargo screening in the Dominican
Republic at his subcommittee and brought up Melgen's security company at a 2012 meeting with Brownfield. Menendez issued a deadline and threatened to hold a formal hearing of the Senate Foreign
Relations Committee on the contract dispute. At the time, Menendez
was a member of the committee but not yet its leader.

"The senator noted displeasure very clearly with the current state of
affairs and threatened to hold a hearing on the matter if we don't meet
the deadline," said Todd Levett, an aide to Brownfield, in an email
to several State Department staffers following Brownfield's meeting
with the senator.

Menendez framed Melgen's contract as one of national security
importance, insisting that the Dominican ports were a vulnerable
entry point for illegal drugs bound for US ports. He was no doubt
hoping that the angle would play well with US agencies like the
Department of State and Customs and Border Protection, aligning
the contract with US priorities on drug interdiction in the region.

Brownfield said that he did raise Melgen's port security contact
with the president of the Dominican Republic in a fleeting exchange
in May 2012.

Letters and requests for meetings continued that year, even as
Menendez's insistent hands-on approach felt atypical for a senator,
especially since Melgen was not among his New Jersey constituents.

"Brownfield later learned that ICSSI had no connection to New
Jersey," said an appeal launched by Menendez in the US Court of
Appeals for the Third Circuit where the senator lost his bid to have

the ICSSI information tossed from an indictment, citing the "speech and debate clause" that protects federal lawmakers from divulging privileged government information.

"Brownfield advised it is very unusual to have a senator advocate on behalf of a non-constituent," the appeals court continued. "In Brownfield's experience, he is not aware of another example of a senator advocating for a non-constituent."

Menendez couched his insistence in terms of American national security, but the line between public duty and private interest grew more blurry with each pointed request.

In January 2013, he intervened with the Department of Homeland Security to end any donations of port security equipment to the Dominican Republic for fear that it might undermine Melgen's firm. In an email to Customs and Border Protection, a Menendez staffer did not mention Melgen's company by name when asking about whether the United States was planning to donate equipment to the country. Such a donation might actually help criminal elements in the country, allowing drugs and other contraband to move through the country's ports en route to the United States, the aide said.

"Apparently there are some efforts by individuals who do not want the increased security" in the Dominican Republic, the email from Menendez's office said. "These elements, possibly criminal, want C.B.P. [Customs and Border Protection] to give the government equipment, because they believe the government use of the equipment will be less effective than the outside contractor. My boss is concerned that the C.B.P. equipment will be used for this ulterior motive."

As his single-minded campaign to uphold the contract continued, the senator's office engaged directly with Dominican officials, urging them to recognize Melgen's security contract as essential. The message was clear: Aligning with this US-backed project would strengthen diplomatic ties, while resistance could mean less support. Menendez made a calculated play, knowing that a shift in US–Dominican relations would place added pressure on the country to comply. For their part, Dominican officials were caught in a political bind that extended beyond their own borders.

This period marked a turning point in Menendez's approach to foreign advocacy. The senator operated as if Dominican interests were extensions of his own, leaving a trail of communications that hinted at his willingness to act beyond his official duties. His close involvement became more than a matter of mere friendship or loyalty—it revealed the lengths he would go to as a fixer for his biggest supporter.

Menendez ramped up his communications with US agencies, pressing harder on the necessity of supporting the port contract. He contacted officials in the Department of State, suggesting that failing to back the security contract might signal weak drug enforcement at a key Caribbean point of entry. His argument went beyond persuasive lobbying; it implied that the United States was watching and waiting for the Dominican government to act favorably. Menendez played up the potential risks to US security, crafting a narrative that suggested failure to approve the contract would have far-reaching consequences. However, documents later revealed the central motivation had less to do with US security interests and more to do with Melgen's financial stake.

By the end of 2012, questions swirled about whether Menendez's support for the Dominican Republic's port security project was based on genuine US interests or merely personal loyalties. Melgen contributed $700,000 via his company, Vitreo-Retinal Consultants, to the Senate Majority PAC, a super PAC aimed at supporting Democratic senators. He directed these funds specifically to bolster Senator Menendez's 2012 reelection campaign.

In a reciprocating fashion, prosecutors later alleged that while Melgen was directing hundreds of thousands of dollars to Menendez politically, Menendez lobbied the Obama administration to modify Medicare reimbursement policies. These changes were intended to financially benefit Melgen significantly. In 2012, Melgen received $21 million from Medicare reimbursements. The line between official duty and private alliance was all but erased, replaced by a pattern of advocacy that left Dominican officials grappling with the weight of US pressure and the implications of Menendez's demands.

At the same time that he was aggressively backing the port security deal, Menendez was also going to bat for a group of New Jersey benefactors who were behind a controversial highway project in the Dominican Republic. Pedro Pablo Permuy was a key lobbyist behind Concesionaria Dominicana de Autopistas y Carreteras SA (CODACSA), a consortium of Spanish and US business interests behind building highways that would connect Santo Domingo to affluent resort communities, such as La Romana, where Melgen owned his villa. The new road system, dubbed the Coral Highway, would shorten travel between Santo Domingo and Punta Cana, another ritzy resort community, by thirty miles and connect the capital with tourist destinations in the eastern part of the country. Joseph Bonanno, a New Jersey businessman and supporter of Menendez's reelection campaigns, was the driving force behind the scheme, along with his wife, Ruby Pacheco. The couple had donated $19,800 to the senator since 2006.

The contract to build portions of a Dominican highway was worth $66 million, but was mired in corruption. The minister of public works demanded bribes from Odebrecht, the Brazilian construction giant building the roads. The Dominican government and CODACSA also disagreed over toll collection once the project was completed. After the parties went to international court, CODACSA lost the ability to collect tolls but won $42.5 million in damages. The decision came down in January 2012, and CODACSA needed help convincing the Dominican government to pay the cash.

At a July 31, 2012, hearing of the Foreign Relations Subcommittee on the Western Hemisphere, Menendez boldly called on the US government to pressure their Dominican counterparts to pay the judgment that CODACSA had won in arbitration.

"If these countries can get away with it, they will," Menendez said at the hearing. "They have, in our international arbitration, an award on CODACSA, which was building a road there; have US investors in it."

For federal investigators who already had the senator in their sights, his lobbying for ICSSI and CODACSA were major red flags. As the executive director at the government watchdog Citizens for Responsibility and Ethics in Washington noted at the time, "Menendez has a lot of explaining to do."

≈

CREW, along with another DC-area watchdog, the National Legal and Policy Center, had zeroed in on these anomalies while Menendez was in the midst of a firestorm that began as tiny embers back in the spring of 2012. The smear campaign to defeat Menendez on his first reelection bid for the US Senate began quietly enough in April 2012, while Permuy and Menendez were putting the finishing touches on their Jersey City business conference and while Menendez continued to lobby federal agencies to pressure the Dominicans into honoring the ICSSI contract and the CODACSA infrastructure project.

It's not clear who was behind the campaign to discredit the senator when "Pete Williams" reached out to CREW with an urgent message.

"My duty as a US citizen obligates me to report what I consider to be a grave violation of the most fundamental codes of conduct," said the email from the unknown whistleblower, who borrowed his identity from Harrison "Pete" Williams, a US senator from New Jersey who was convicted in 1981 of taking bribes and acting as a foreign agent in the Arab-sheikh-money-for-political-favors Abscam investigation that led to the conviction of several members of Congress on bribery and corruption charges in the late 1970s. The real Williams died in 2001.

"I have first-hand information regarding the reiterated participation of Senator Robert Menendez in inappropriate sexual activities with young prostitutes while on vacation in the Dominican Republic," the email continued.[113]

Officials at CREW tried for three months to reach "Williams" as well as one of the young women named in the email. When everything failed, they handed over the information to the FBI in July. The following month, FBI agents began to correspond with the tipster, demanding proof of the allegations against Menendez.

"As of the writing of this Amended Affidavit, Mr. Williams has refused to meet with the FBI, either by phone or in person," wrote FBI Special Agent Gregory J. Sheehy. "Mr. Williams has not disclosed enough information for the FBI to identify any minors."[114]

Although Sheehy said he confirmed that Menendez was indeed in the Dominican Republic at the same time as one of the unidentified women who said she had sex with Menendez, he couldn't verify that she had ever met the senator.

On November 1, 2012, days before the November 6 election, the conservative website *The Daily Caller* published an article based on interviews with three Dominican women who said that Menendez paid them for sex at a luxury resort. The article also mentioned that Menendez had used Melgen's private jet to travel to the Dominican Republic.

"We're not going to respond to a completely false accusation," said Tricia Enright, a spokeswoman for Menendez, in response to the report. Later, Menendez blamed Republican operatives for spreading false rumors about him to destroy his political campaign.

But the allegations, which were never proven, had little effect on the election. The Dominican women who initially said Menendez paid them for sex later recanted and said they were paid to make up the story about the senator. Menendez handily won against New Jersey State Senator Joseph Kyrillos in a chaotic election that took place days after Hurricane Sandy, one of the most destructive storms in US history, hit the East Coast and devastated parts of New Jersey and New York.

And while he celebrated his victory and must have breathed a sigh of relief, Menendez was about to face his own political storm—the biggest in his career. At the end of January 2013, *The New York Times*, with the help of Thomas Jason Anderson, published a story on its front page revealing Menendez's very close relationship with Melgen, and the senator's acrobatics in Washington over the port security deal in the Dominican Republic.

Around the same time as the bombshell article, FBI agents along with officials from the Office of the Inspector General of the Department of Health and Human Services, which investigates Medicare fraud, conducted the first of two raids at Melgen's West Palm Beach clinic. They cordoned off with yellow police tape the offices of Vitreo-Retinal Consultants and carted away thirty cardboard boxes of documents.

Publicly, both men shrugged off the allegations against them. But Menendez's office released a statement downplaying the extent of their relationship and the frequency of Menendez's use of Melgen's private jet, saying that Menendez had repaid the eye doctor $58,500 for two flights.

"This was sloppy," said a Menendez spokesman about the private jet flights. "I'm chalking it up to an oversight." But this was no oversight. Menendez would later have to admit to taking at least sixteen round-trip flights on two separate Melgen private jets. The pilot for both jets, Robert Nylund, testified to flying Menendez on an eight-seat Hawker and an eleven-seat Challenger with a couch that converted into a bed. "When they're ready to go, we go," Nylund recalled as he described the private jet flights on which Menendez traveled, "from point A to point B."[115]

That "oversight" would prove to be the tip of the iceberg that was about to hit the embattled senator.

CHAPTER SEVEN

Blame It on Cuba

Bob Menendez came up with a unique theory to explain the wild rumors that were circulating about him in the Dominican Republic: It was Fidel Castro's revenge and also linked to Cuban espionage. Although the seemingly outlandish theory had all the characteristics of a spy thriller, in the end, Menendez may have been right.

According to Menendez, it was the elderly Cuban leader who had fabricated the rumors of his participation in sex parties with prostitutes in the Dominican Republic. Castro handed over control of the government to his younger brother Raul Castro in 2006.

For the Cuban American lawmaker whose political career had been financed and supported by radical anti-Castro extremists in Union City and South Florida, and who had consistently opposed rapprochement with the Communist island in the House and in the Senate, it wasn't such a bad theory. Nor was it far-fetched. The allegations against the senator began at the same time that President Obama began secretly negotiating a thaw between the two countries that had been mortal enemies since shortly after Fidel Castro came to power in 1959. In 2016, Obama would achieve a huge milestone and would be the first US president to visit Havana since Calvin Coolidge in 1928.

Menendez bitterly opposed the normalization of diplomatic ties with the dictators in Cuba and imagined that he had long been a target of their operatives.

"The democracy of the people of Cuba—I have been outspoken in that regard, and I wouldn't be surprised that the regime would do anything it can to stop me from being in a position that ultimately would impede their hopes of getting a different relationship with the United States based upon their interest, not the interest of the American people," Menendez told *The Washington Post* in July 2014—five months before Obama restored full diplomatic relations with Cuba and opened an embassy in Havana for the first time in more than five decades.[116]

The newspaper reported that an unidentified former US official said that the CIA had obtained "credible evidence, including internet protocol addresses," that linked Cuban spies to the claims about Menendez and the underage prostitutes.

The CIA report indicated that spies working with Cuba's Directorate of Intelligence helped create the fake whistleblower "Pete Williams," the tipster who reached out to CREW, the FBI, and various news outlets, to plant the story that Menendez was involved in orgies with underage prostitutes while vacationing at Melgen's Casa de Campo villa.

"It is deeply disturbing that a foreign government whose intelligence service is an enemy of the United States might try to influence US foreign policy by discrediting an elected official who is an opponent of the Cuban regime," said Stephen Ryan, a lawyer for Menendez, in an April 2012 letter to the Department of Justice.

On first blush, it might have seemed an elaborate excuse on Menendez's part to deflect negative publicity with respect to his relationship with Melgen. But the sordid allegations strategically planted in the US media emerged at a time when Menendez and Melgen were enmeshed in a byzantine corporate and geopolitical struggle in the Caribbean. Hundreds of millions of dollars were at stake with respect to the port security contract and the development of the Dominican highway—multimillion-dollar projects that were both linked to Menendez.

In addition, the world's largest gold producer, Toronto-based Barrick Gold, found itself in an epic struggle over its mining concession in the Dominican Republic where their Pueblo Viejo mine contained the largest gold deposits in Latin America. And in a bizarre twist of fate, the newly appointed CEO of the mine was later unmasked as one of the longest serving Cuban spies in the history of the Communist island's General Directorate of Intelligence, known by its Spanish-language acronym DGI.

The Pueblo Viejo gold mine was in the crosshairs of the Dominican government when Victor Manuel Rocha became CEO in 2012. That struggle was led by a member of Melgen's family, who was also a close friend of Menendez. Pelegrín Horacio Castillo Semán, Melgen's cousin, was a member of the Chamber of Deputies and the chairman of the country's Commission on Mining who had big political aspirations of his own. He was a candidate for president in 2012. In 2014, he became the first ever minister of energy and mines. His father, Vincho Castillo, headed up the government's anti-narcotics division and was an important adviser to the Dominican president. When Melgen and Menendez were targeted with the allegations that they were partying with prostitutes in Casa de Campo, the Castillos were included in the photographs that appeared in the Dominican press. For Castillo Semán, the whole thing was a "dirty and illicit" campaign to scuttle all of their business deals.

"I've known Menendez as a friend of my cousin Salomon Melgen," said Castillo. "No one has come forward on the allegations and evil accusations. We spend every Easter together in Casa de Campo."[117]

A few years before the infamous photographs went public, the younger Castillo raised concerns over what he called "flaws" in the contract governing Barrick Gold's mining rights at Pueblo Viejo. Barrick Gold, which had entered into a 50 percent profit split with the Dominican government, had just spent billions to revitalize the mine and bring it up to international environmental standards. But the members of the mining commission felt there were no guarantees in place for the Dominican people. The mine would only split the profits after subtracting their expenses, and their corporate masters controlled the balance sheet. The Dominican government wanted more transparency and a cut on every ounce of gold that came out of the open-pit mine, regardless of how much the company paid to extract it.

The Pueblo Viejo mine was located in Cotui, one of the oldest cities in the New World, founded in 1505 by Spanish conquistadors who brutally enslaved the Taino community in their quest to extract gold and silver from the nearby mines. The Taino population declined precipitously in the century after the Spanish arrived on what was then called Hispaniola, the island that today includes both the Dominican Republic and neighboring Haiti. Millions of native people died from a lack of immunity to viruses brought by the Spanish, who also enslaved them in the plunder of riches from the region. In the sixteenth century, the area was considered the wealthiest in the New World and the first to be exploited by Spanish overlords.

Centuries later, the mine was inefficiently operated by a Dominican company whose extraction methods led to severe ecological issues that have contaminated nearby rivers and livestock and contributed to health problems among the local population. Toxic by-products of gold extraction, including cyanide, mercury, and other chemicals, have leached into the rivers and nearby farms, rendering much of the land infertile and transforming the nearby Pueblo Viejo valley into an industrial zone. Cotui's farmers found their soil unusable, their water unsafe to drink, and the natural resources they once depended on increasingly scarce by the time the government made the move to clear the entire valley. Environmental cleanup as well as extraction proved too costly for the Dominican government, and the mine ground to a halt in the 1970s. In the early aughts, the Dominican government entered into a special lease agreement with Canada's Placer

Dome in an effort to reopen the mine. In 2006, Barrick Gold bought Placer Dome and went into partnership with Goldcorp Inc., another Canadian mining company, to take over Pueblo Viejo's operations.

Six years later, Barrick Gold promoted one of Cuba's biggest undercover agents to head up its mining interests at Pueblo Viejo, proving perhaps that Menendez's Cuba espionage theory had real legs. Cuban spies were notorious for being some of the most intense and effective operatives in the world because they were largely driven by pure ideology.

Victor Manuel Rocha, a career US diplomat and leading expert on Latin America, was only unmasked as a longtime spy for Cuba in 2023, but he worked as an operative for the Communist island during the time that he was CEO of Barrick Gold's Dominican subsidiary and during the years that Menendez was involved with Melgen's projects in the country.

Born in Bogotá in 1950, he was raised in a housing project in Harlem after his widowed mother moved to the United States in 1960 when Rocha was ten years old. Rocha, his sister, and his brother crowded into an uncle's apartment. The Rocha family lived on welfare and food stamps while Rocha's mother worked as a seamstress in a sweatshop. But Rocha was a stellar student and a skilled soccer player. In 1965, he won a scholarship for minorities to attend the Taft School, an elite Connecticut boarding school.

Rocha's ties to Harlem also proved useful. He grew up in the neighborhood during a tumultuous time. In the summer of 1964, a race riot quickly spread from Harlem to other mostly black neighborhoods in the city after a white cop shot and killed a fifteen-year-old black teenager.

"Taft was the best thing that happened," he told the *Taft Bulletin* in 2004, adding that having lived through a race riot gave him entrée into the school's black student group, which made him its president. "My ghetto experience and my ability to deal in that world made me acceptable to all the black kids."

Rocha credited the school with opening the doors to an Ivy League education and a career in diplomacy.

Later, Rocha graduated cum laude from Yale University in 1973 and earned a master's degree in public policy from Harvard in 1976. Despite pleading guilty to spying for Cuba in 2024, Rocha is still listed on the "Prominent Alumni" page of the Walsh School of Foreign Service at Georgetown University, where he graduated in 1978. The list also includes Bill Clinton and Felipe VI of Spain, who was among the keynote speakers at the Jersey City meeting organized by Pedro Pablo Permuy and Menendez in the summer of 2012. The school has long been a recruiting ground for the Central Intelligence Agency, with more than two dozen ex-CIA operatives among the current teaching staff.

Was Rocha recruited as a CIA operative? It's not clear, but his federal criminal case was concluded with such speed that it's not known exactly what secrets he spilled to Cuba, with prosecutors insisting that those details remain classified even from the US District Court judge who sentenced him to fifteen years in prison. That sentence came six months after he was arrested at his home in Miami on charges that he engaged in "clandestine activities" to benefit Cuba since at least 1981, the year he joined the US State Department. Rocha entered into a plea agreement with authorities and blamed his years at various universities for his radicalization and for moving him closer to Cuba.

"During my formative years in college, I was heavily influenced by the radical politics of the day," he said. In 1973, the year he graduated from Yale, Rocha traveled to Chile where he met his Cuban handlers for the first time. At the time, Chile was run by Marxist President Salvador Allende, who had strong ties to Fidel Castro. Allende's government was overthrown in a bloody coup d'état, led by General Augusto Pinochet in September 1973.

"My deep commitment at that time to radical social change in the region led me to the eventual betrayal of my oath of loyalty to the

United States during my two decades in the State Department," Rocha told US District Court Judge Beth Bloom in Miami.[118]

Rocha became a naturalized US citizen in the same year that he graduated from Georgetown and before joining the State Department as a desk officer for Honduras in 1981. His Cuban handlers instructed him to assume a fictitious identity as a "right-wing person." For decades, Rocha was a registered Republican and later an early supporter of Donald Trump.

"Rocha secretly supported the Republic of Cuba and its mission of illegally gathering intelligence against the United States by serving as an agent of its secret services," according to the Department of Justice.[119]

Rocha's early career was spent largely in the Dominican Republic, where he met his wife and obtained Dominican citizenship. His first overseas posting was at the US Embassy in Santo Domingo where he was appointed as a political officer in 1982. Throughout the 1980s, he held posts in Honduras and Mexico before returning to the Dominican Republic as deputy chief of the US Embassy between 1991 and 1994. While in Honduras, he advised the Contra rebels in their battle against Cuba-backed Sandinistas in Nicaragua. In 1994, while working as the director of Inter-American Affairs at the National Security Council, he urged President Clinton to open trade with Cuba—a move blocked by Republicans as well as Democrat Bob Menendez in Congress. The lawmakers demanded that Clinton cut off all travel and remittances to the island and set up a military naval blockade to bring down the Castro regime. Clinton agreed to the increase in sanctions, but he refused the blockade. A year later, Menendez along with New Jersey Senator Robert Torricelli demanded that the Clinton administration reverse its policy of sending Cuban rafters back to the island.

At the time, Rocha was posted to Havana where he could meet with his Cuban handlers face-to-face while serving as the deputy principal officer of the US Interests section, then run out of the Swiss Embassy.

While Congress engaged in periodic battles over America's Cuba policy, Rocha rose through the ranks of the State Department and became a full-fledged ambassador and was posted to Bolivia in 2000.

It was during his time in the capital city of La Paz that he likely did his biggest favor for Fidel Castro when he intervened in the Andean country's elections that eventually ushered in leftist leader Evo Morales. At a diplomatic event at the US Embassy in 2002, he warned Bolivians that voting for Morales, a Marxist who headed up a union of coca growers, would cause the United States to end foreign aid to the country. It was a clever ruse, and Bolivians who resented the idea of the United States intervening in the Andean country's politics raced to the polls to vote for Morales. The long-shot candidate nearly won, but was beaten by his neoliberal opponent Gonzalo Sánchez de Lozada. Three years later, Morales was victorious, thanking Rocha for being his "best campaign chief."

Before taking up his post at Barrick Gold and following his retirement from the State Department, Rocha continued to wield important influence in Latin America, advising the US military on issues concerning Cuba and the countries under their influence in the region. Between 2006 and 2012, he was a leading adviser to the commander of the United States Southern Command, a Department of Defense agency that provides security cooperation to Latin America and the Caribbean.

Perhaps it was this mixture of diplomacy and military realpolitik that appealed to Barrick Gold's corporate executives in Toronto. Facing mounting pressure from environmentalists and the Dominican government over Pueblo Viejo, Barrick Gold's board of directors, which included such heavy hitters as the former Canadian Prime Minister Brian Mulroney, mining investor Peter Munk, and financier Nat Rothschild, likely figured that they needed a skilled diplomat in the Dominican Republic to start up the Pueblo Viejo project at a time when the company's shares were down by nearly 10 percent and earnings fell by $750 million.

Only an experienced diplomat with the type of access and experience Rocha had on issues within the sphere of Cuba's influence could take on government officials backed by the Menendez consortium of operatives and family members related to Melgen in the Dominican Republic. Barrick Gold didn't need a geologist or mining executive steeped in the knowledge of best practices for extraction of minerals. The company needed a skilled diplomat and operative who could deal with the machinations and sheer political power that a politician like Bob Menendez wielded in the Senate Foreign Relations Committee of the United States of America. This may explain why they hired Rocha in 2012, despite the fact that he had no expertise in mining.

The appointment of a former military attaché to head up Latin America's biggest gold mine was not lost on the leading environmentalist fighting the mine.

"Manuel Rocha is a military adviser who has had delicate military responsibilities in Latin America," said environmentalist Domingo Abreu Collado. "Nothing to do with gold, but a lot to do with political and military leadership."[120]

And espionage.

Although it's not clear whether Rocha himself was deployed against the Dominican government to push back against Castillo's attempts over Barrick's designs on Pueblo Viejo, he was certainly in the right place at the right time to cause havoc with Castillo, Melgen, Pedro Pablo Permuy, and Bob Menendez, their friend and powerful ally in the US Senate.

In April 2012, four months after Rocha became CEO of the gold company, the mysterious "Pete Williams" emerged in an email to CREW, spreading the story about Menendez having sex with underage prostitutes in the Dominican Republic.

Although a CIA source later confirmed to *The Washington Post* that Menendez was indeed the victim of a smear campaign organized by Cuba, the Williams emails had tarnished the senator's reputation and obstructed his objectives in the Caribbean, putting Melgen and

Permuy's interests in jeopardy. Every allegation cast a longer shadow, restricting Menendez's reach. By helping his friends with their myriad business deals, Menendez was making some powerful enemies.

≈

As Menendez contended with the fallout from Williams's email campaign, a parallel scandal began to emerge in Panama—one that involved some of the participants at his United States Spain Council meeting in Jersey City and Ricardo Martinelli, the corrupt president of the country.

Martinelli, who was partly educated in the United States and graduated with a business degree from the University of Arkansas in 1973, was already a billionaire by the time he was elected president of Panama in 2009. The head of a Panamanian supermarket chain, he also served as chair of the board of the Panama Canal between 1999 and 2003. Defeated at the polls when he first ran for president in 2004, Martinelli won national office in a landslide with 60 percent of the vote five years later. A year later, in 2010, he announced ambitious plans to invest $20 billion in local infrastructure to turn the country into a global powerhouse and enacted pro-business legislation to lure more foreign investment.

He also continued to enrich himself. In 2010, he became a silent partner and shadow hand controlling Petaquilla Minerals, a Canadian gold mining company that, under Martinelli's command, brought Pedro Pablo Permuy and a member of the Spanish royal house onto its board of directors. Cristóbal Colón de Carvajal was also a descendant of explorer Christopher Columbus and the current Duke of Veragua, a territory that encompasses Panama, Costa Rica, and Nicaragua. They joined the board in 2012, two years after Martinelli illegally took over the mine in Panama.

Under the guise of economic development in Panama, Petaquilla's business practices unfolded like a modern-day invasion in the dense rainforest where the mines were located, about one hundred miles west of Panama City. Petaquilla relied on loopholes in already weak environmental legislation to raze the rainforest near Petaquilla's gold and copper mines—a project whose scale was second only to the building of the Panama Canal between 1904 and 1914. And the geologists and engineers who descended on the region were dubbed the new conquistadors by members of the local native community. Petaquilla's drilling in the area contributed to environmental degradation and was reminiscent of the same disregard for native lands that Panama's indigenous communities faced when Christopher Columbus arrived in the country searching for riches in 1502. At that time, an indigenous leader who called himself Rey Quibian took on Columbus and eventually routed the conquistadors.

In 2012, an environmental group representing the Ngäbe-Buglé community took their inspiration from the native leader, naming their group after Rey Quibian and fighting the mining executives at every turn. Nueva Lucha, a small town located in Panama's lush rainforests, became a focal point of the battle against Petaquilla's mining operations. Rich in gold deposits and relatively untouched since the days of Columbus, the area held significant cultural and environmental value for its indigenous residents. The group saw Petaquilla's intrusion as emblematic of the same imperialistic ambitions that drove Columbus to claim lands in the name of the Spanish crown, disregarding the native inhabitants and the sanctity of their environment. The irony was that Petaquilla had on its board of directors a Spanish nobleman who was, in fact, a descendant of Columbus.

Fighting the mining giants proved a difficult undertaking. With Martinelli's backing, the company operated with relative impunity, using the president's influence to sidestep accountability and suppress opposition. Allegations of intimidation tactics surfaced as well as dubious land deals. Petaquilla's operations were not only environmentally destructive, they were socially disruptive. Moreover, by capitalizing on a web of corporate entities, the company avoided paying its fair share of taxes and contributed little to the local economy, mirroring the extractive nature of colonial exploitation.

Structurally, Petaquilla was a maze of shell companies registered in jurisdictions ranging from the British Virgin Islands to Panama, Portugal, and Canada. This intricate corporate web allowed stakeholders, including Martinelli, to conceal their control of the company and shield themselves from liability while exploiting natural resources and rigging share prices to enrich themselves at the expense of average shareholders. The company's operations involved systematic evasion of taxes, flouting of environmental regulations, and alleged bribery.

In Panama, the authorities were starting to take notice. At the end of 2012, Vernon Ramos, the federal deputy director of the Financial Analysis Division and auditor of the Superintendency of Securities, mysteriously disappeared after reporting irregularities in companies tied to Martinelli. Among those was High Spirit, the company that was used to manipulate shares of Petaquilla Minerals. By 2014, Martinelli's role in manipulating Panamanian industry for personal profit ballooned into a full-scale probe.

To consolidate his hold on power and protect his corrupt business dealings, Martinelli spent millions of government cash on advanced surveillance technology from Israel to spy on everyone from business partners to opposition politicians, journalists, and foreign diplomats, including staff at the US Embassy in Panama City.

Martinelli's corruption did not escape the notice of the US government. Ambassador Phyllis Powers, a career diplomat who had worked in Peru and Colombia before she was nominated by Obama to become the ambassador to Panama in June 2010, publicly criticized Martinelli. At a meeting organized by the US-Panama Business Council in Washington, Powers cited a "lack of judicial independence, corruption, and personnel in government institutions susceptible to influence."[121]

Her warnings were echoed by Menendez and others at the Senate Foreign Relations Committee. In addition to business dealings in the

Dominican Republic, Menendez, a prominent figure in the Senate Foreign Relations Committee in the years before he became chairman, had his sights set on ensuring that the State Department's diplomatic assignments aligned with the interests of his friends in Latin America.

Impressed with her tough talk and resolve, Menendez backed Powers to take over the US Embassy in Nicaragua, where another strongman, Daniel Ortega, was wielding absolute power and cracking down on political opposition. In doing so, Menendez scuttled the bid for Obama's handpicked ambassador for the Central American country. Obama had chosen Cuba hand Jonathan Farrar to take over the mission in Nicaragua, but Menendez had other plans for him.

In a leaked cable he wrote in 2009, Farrar, a career diplomat who had been in Cuba since 2008, said that Cuban dissidents had made little headway with people on the island. Menendez and fellow Senator Marco Rubio feared he would try to appease Marxist leader Daniel Ortega in the same way that they perceived he did with Fidel and Raul Castro.

But Farrar was anything but soft on Cuba. In leaked diplomatic cables, he railed against Australia, Canada, and several European countries for failing to put significant pressure on Cuba, accusing them of "kowtowing" to the regime and being members of the country's "best friends forever" camp.

"The truth is that most of these countries do not press the issue at all in Cuba," Farrar wrote in the November 24, 2009, cable to the State Department titled "Feisty Little Missions Dent Cuba's Record of Bullying Others to Silence on Human Rights." The email singled out the Vatican and the Order of Malta for their tough stands on Cuba and eviscerated the other countries for their weakness.

"The GOC [government of Cuba] . . . deploys considerable resources to bluff and bully many missions and their visitors into silence," Farrar wrote in the cable.

Despite his insights, Farrar was tasked with doing Obama's bidding on Cuba and implementing the first steps toward reestablishing relations with the United States. To this end, a giant electronic news ticker that streamed news and excerpts from the Universal Declaration of Human Rights to inspire the regime's opponents and annoy the Castros was taken down at the US diplomatic compound where it spread across twenty-five windows and rose three feet. Christmas decorations were also removed from the mission, lest they offend the atheist Communist leaders. If he was seen as being soft on Cuba, it wasn't entirely his fault. Farrar had been charged with implementing some of Obama's policies to broker diplomatic relations with the island of eleven million people, ninety miles south of Key West, Florida. At his hearing before the Senate Foreign Relations subcommittee on his appointment to Nicaragua, he defended his actions, saying that Cold War policies had failed miserably on the island.

Menendez and Rubio scuttled Farrar's Nicaragua posting but later approved his appointment to Panama where some of the high rollers he had assembled at his conference in Jersey City had huge financial interests in the gold mine that secretly benefited the country's corrupt president.

Was Menendez helping his old staffer Pedro Pablo Permuy, who was on the board of Petaquilla Minerals? Or was he truly concerned about Martinelli's corrupt hold on power when he lobbied to have Farrar sent to Panama and Powers sent to Nicaragua? On top of that, he must have known that Martinelli was wiretapping most of the foreign missions in the country.

On December 5, 2011, the State Department withdrew Farrar's appointment to Nicaragua and began the process of installing him in Panama City where he would remain until June 2015.

On January 2, 2013, Menendez was sworn in to a second term in the Senate, poised to become the chairman of the Foreign Relations Committee. Weeks later, on January 29, 2013, Pedro Pablo Permuy incorporated PTQ USA in Delaware, a limited liability company controlled by Petaquilla Minerals and, by extension, Martinelli. By then, Petaquilla Minerals owed millions to the Panamanian government, and the company's mining operations in Panama had ground to a complete halt.

It's not clear why Permuy formed the limited liability company when he did, but perhaps it was an effort to save Petaquilla as investigations swirled around the company in Panama. Permuy was never accused of any wrongdoing, but the giant house of cards that connected all the players in the Dominican Republic, Panama, and Cuba was about to collapse.

Two years later, Martinelli was charged with public corruption, illegally wiretapping more than 150 people, and embezzling more than $10 million in public funds in Panama. He fled to his villa in Miami as Panamanian authorities revealed that between 2009 and 2014, Petaquilla Minerals was part of one of the country's biggest stock manipulation scams.

And on April 1, 2015, Senator Bob Menendez was indicted on fourteen charges, along with Dr. Salomon Melgen who faced thirteen of his own. Combining the eight bribery charges, three counts of honest services fraud, and one count of violating the travel act, they faced 120 years in prison.

For Menendez it was nothing more than a cruel April Fools' Day trick. But he was defiant.

"I'm outraged that prosecutors at the Justice Department were tricked into starting this investigation three years ago with false allegations by those who have political motives to silence me," he told a crowd of cheering supporters in Newark after the charges were made public. "But I will not be silenced. I'm confident at the end of the day I will be vindicated and they will be exposed."

He reminded the crowd that he had been a corruption fighter his entire career and wore a bulletproof vest when he fought the Democratic Party boss William Musto in Union City.

"That's how I began my career in public service and this is not how my career is going to end," he said. "I am not going anywhere. I'm angry and ready to fight."

CHAPTER EIGHT

Resurrection

Resplendent in a gold silk tie, blue shirt, and sober charcoal suit, Bob Menendez walked with purpose into Newark's federal courthouse on the first day of his corruption trial. Flanked by his son and daughter, Menendez addressed a group of reporters and some supporters, reminding everyone that he had been there nearly forty years before.

"I started my public career fighting corruption, that's how I started," he said.

In 1981, he had marched into the same courthouse, a self-styled crusader for justice, prepared to testify against Bill Musto, the most powerful man in Hudson County who had propelled a young Bob Menendez into a brilliant political career. Perhaps there was some trepidation back then as he prepared to betray his mentor. After all, he had boasted so many times about being a marked man and wearing a bulletproof vest in the weeks leading up to his testimony at Musto's racketeering, extortion, and fraud trial that by the time he made his way into the courthouse on September 6, 2017, it had become a kind of urban legend.

Jim Plaisted, the assistant US attorney who prosecuted Musto, was adamant that there was no bulletproof vest, at least not when Menendez testified against the former Democratic Party boss. "I would have known about it," he said years later. "The FBI would have informed me if he had worn the vest in court."[122]

But it was a good story. The up-and-coming politician girded by Kevlar made for a great sound bite. Menendez reminded his constituents that he had once risked his life for the truth in the battle against public graft. Now the corruption fighter found the past repeating itself—except this time he was the protagonist battling for his political future.

Still, he was defiant. "I have never backed away from a fight that I didn't believe was right, even if it meant opposing my own president and my own party," he told the crowd on that cloudy Indian summer day outside the courthouse. "It's who I am, and I'm not going to stop now."

As he thanked his supporters, his voice caught and a hint of emotion crept in. But it was only a trace, and he instantly steadied himself, momentarily clearing his throat as he recalled the "countless New Jerseyans" who had called him or called his office offering their support.

"I have always acted in accordance with the law and I believe when all of the facts are known, I will be vindicated," Menendez told the crowd before ducking into the courthouse for the trial that would grind on for more than two months.

"These might be some of the most important weeks in Senator Menendez's life," said Abbe Lowell, the powerhouse attorney who headed his legal defense.

For Lowell, a white-collar and high-priced Washington attorney, the Menendez trial would prove his toughest challenge in a stellar career of defending some of the highest profile government players caught up in headline-grabbing scandals. His approach was almost surgical. He dismantled prosecutions by exploiting weak points in cases brought against his clients, turning legal battles into wars of attrition and grinding down his opponents. His command of the law—loopholes, procedural rules, and mastery of jury psychology—made him one of the most sought-after criminal defense attorneys in the country. He was also, by his own admission, a good actor in the courtroom.

"To be a trial lawyer," he said in a promotional podcast on his firm Winston & Strawn's website, "you have to have a desire to be a performer at some level. If I hadn't done this, it would have been on Broadway."

And he wasn't cheap. By the time he finished defending Menendez, the senator had paid him and his legal team more than $4.7 million in cash from his legal defense fund and campaign.[123]

Lowell was worth the expense. He had a reputation as a fixer—an attorney who could shift the trajectory of complex cases that might have seemed hopeless. During Bill Clinton's second term, he served as investigative counsel for the Democratic minority in the House Judiciary Committee during impeachment proceedings over the Monica Lewinsky affair. He helped Democratic Congressman Gary Condit during the high-profile investigation into the disappearance and murder of twenty-four-year-old intern Chandra Levy, with whom he was having an affair in 2001.

Lowell's handling of the case ensured that Condit never faced any criminal charges despite widespread speculation at the time. Although Washington's Metropolitan Police focused on his extramarital affair with Levy, they never named Condit as a suspect and later cleared him of any involvement. Still, a poll conducted by Fox News found that 44 percent of respondents believed that Condit was involved in the intern's disappearance. As a result of the intense media coverage over the missing intern and the affair, he lost his bid for reelection in 2002. The police found Levy's body a year later in Rock Creek Park. They charged a Salvadoran immigrant with the crime. Ingmar Guandique was convicted in 2010 and sentenced to sixty years in prison, but he later appealed the decision and a judge granted him a new trial in 2015. When prosecutors said they couldn't prove the case, charges were dismissed. Even so, Guandique was deported to El Salvador in 2017. Levy's murder remains unsolved.

In 2008, Lowell took on the defense of North Carolina Senator and presidential candidate John Edwards, a rising star in the Democratic Party. Edwards had been John Kerry's running mate in the 2004 race for the White House. During the Democratic primary for president in 2008, he was charged with six criminal counts, including conspiracy, making false statements, and using nearly $1 million in campaign cash to cover up his affair with Rielle Hunter, a filmmaker who had been hired to work on his presidential campaign. Edwards was having an affair with Hunter, who was pregnant with his daughter, while his wife was dying of cancer.

For Lowell, the question during the scandalous trial was whether Edwards was a federal criminal or just a bad husband. "John was a bad husband," said Lowell at Edwards's trial. "But there is not the remotest chance that John did or intended to violate the law. If what John did was a crime, we'd better build a lot more courtrooms, hire a lot more prosecutors and build a lot more jails."

Lowell also knew his way around New Jersey pols. He had been an attorney for Robert Torricelli, the New Jersey Democratic senator who had partnered with Menendez on Cuba when they were both in the House of Representatives. Lowell and Torricelli were longtime friends, and Lowell became one of the high-priced lawyers on his defense team when the senator was accused of accepting improper gifts—much like Menendez—from campaign donor David Chang, who had pleaded guilty to violating federal election laws, making $53,700 in illegal contributions to Torricelli's campaign and tampering with a federal witness. The federal probe was one of the most "exhaustive investigations" of a US politician, according to prosecutors. The investigation into a series of illegal donations to Torricelli's 1996 Senate campaign was dropped by US Attorney Mary Jo White in the Southern District of New York without seeking an indictment in January 2002 and with no explanation.[124] Months later, in October, Torricelli abruptly suspended his campaign, citing the distraction the probe into his campaign finances had caused for the Democratic Party.

It's not clear who recommended Abbe Lowell to Robert Menendez. Torricelli denied that he had had anything to do with it.

"Bob found him on his own," Torricelli told a New Jersey newspaper in 2015.[125]

Menendez needed the best lawyer money could buy. The senator, who had been charged with eighteen counts, including bribery and conspiracy, had a lot to lose as he joined the crooked pantheon of the other eleven US senators tried for corruption during their time in office. They included four-term US Senator Harrison Williams Jr.—the infamous "Pete" Williams—another native of New Jersey and a Democrat, who was indicted in 1980 on nine counts, including bribery and conspiracy to defraud the United States. Williams was caught up in the FBI's Abscam sting operation for taking bribes to help an undercover FBI agent posing as an Arab sheikh in exchange for a multimillion-dollar loan to a mining operation in which he had a secret financial interest. Like Menendez, Williams maintained his innocence and refused to leave the Senate during and even after his trial. He was found guilty in 1981, sentenced to three years in prison, and served twenty-one months. He only resigned during his expulsion trial in the Senate. He tried to receive a presidential pardon from President Clinton in 2000, but was unsuccessful. He died a year later.

For Bob Menendez, a conviction would force a resignation and spell the end of his career. For the US Senate, it would upset the balance of power and allow New Jersey Governor Chris Christie to appoint an interim replacement, likely a Republican. The Republicans already had a 52–48 majority in the upper house when Menendez went to trial.

During the trial, fellow Senators Cory Booker, a Democrat from New Jersey, and Lindsey Graham, a Republican from South Carolina, both came to his defense, testifying on his behalf. After their bipartisan show of support, Menendez had tears in his eyes, saying he was "honored" they had showed up at the Newark courthouse to support him.

"I know Bob Menendez doesn't just have my back but has their backs," said Booker, describing Menendez's concern for his constituents. Years later, after Menendez was convicted on sixteen counts of bribery and corruption at his second trial, Booker was among the first to demand Menendez's immediate resignation.

"He's someone you can go to as a Republican to see if you can find bipartisanship," Graham said, telling the court that they had teamed up to work on immigration reform and an Iranian nuclear deal in the past. "In very difficult circumstances he always keeps his word—a handshake is all you need from Bob." Graham was so fond of Menendez that he told reporters he had traveled on his own dime to the Garden State to stand up for him in court.

The allegations against Menendez had already taken a personal toll. Alicia Mucci, a New Jersey real estate agent, had ended their relationship before the charges were made public. Menendez had proposed to the stunning brunette in the US Capitol Rotunda on December 9, 2013, and announced their engagement with great fanfare at the White House congressional holiday ball, hosted by Vice President Joe Biden that same evening. The Obamas were not in attendance. They had rushed to South Africa to attend a memorial for Nelson Mandela.

"She didn't want the controversy," said a friend of Mucci's who did not want to be identified. "I think she was also a little annoyed with how he behaved. He would come from work, smoke a cigar, and constantly remind her that he was one of a hundred US senators. He kept repeating it, and it started to grate."

The trial opened with prosecutors cataloging the lavish gifts Menendez received from Salomon Melgen, including the hundreds of thousands of dollars in contributions the eye doctor had made to his campaigns. In exchange, he moved heaven and earth with various agencies of the US government to help Melgen secure his port security deal and avoid a reckoning for tens of millions in Medicare fraud.

"This is what bribery looks like," said lead prosecutor Peter Koski, deputy chief of the Justice Department's Public Integrity Section.

He went on to describe Menendez enjoying "a lifestyle that reads like a travel brochure for the rich and famous" thanks to Melgen, his co-accused. Menendez enjoyed sojourns at Casa de Campo, took flights on Melgen's private jet, and stayed in a luxurious hotel suite paid for by Melgen in Paris where the senator took one of his paramours.

"This case is about a corrupt politician who sold his Senate office for a life of luxury he couldn't afford, and a greedy doctor who put that politician on his payroll for whenever he needed the services of a United States senator," said Koski. "Make no mistake about it, Robert Menendez was Salomon Melgen's personal United States senator."

Beginning soon after he was elected to his second term in the US Senate in November 2012, federal agents put together their case against him, later accusing him of pocketing nearly $1 million worth of gifts and campaign contributions that included flights to Caribbean resorts on Melgen's private plane and a luxury suite in Paris. The gifts were in exchange for using the power of his Senate office to influence the outcome of tens of millions of dollars in Medicare billing disputes involving Melgen and to obtain visas for the doctor's harem of foreign models, among other favors. Menendez raised eyebrows in the Senate when he backed a $500 million port security project for the eye doctor as well as a highway development in the Caribbean country that would benefit a former staffer turned lobbyist as well as a New Jersey businessman who had been a major donor to his campaigns.

Melgen was also on trial, although he had already been found guilty in a separate criminal case of improperly billing the federal government for $100 million in insurance payments.

Menendez behaved throughout as if the trial was a nuisance, arriving every morning at the courthouse with his Senate staff to conduct the business of his office from Newark.

For his part, Lowell made everything sound as if Menendez and Melgen were just two very good friends exchanging big favors in his defense.

"It is that one word, 'friendship,' that the evidence will show was the true nature of their relationship," said Lowell in opening arguments at the trial.

"There's nothing illegal or corrupt if he acted out of that friendship," Lowell said, adding that they were so close that they referred to each other as *hermano*, Spanish for "brother."

The stars may have been aligned in the defense's favor. A year before Menendez's trial got underway, a Supreme Court ruling had made it harder to prosecute elected officials for corruption when the tribunal unanimously overturned the conviction of Bob McDonnell, former governor of Virginia. The court ruled that only the performance of definitive government actions—an explicit quid pro quo—could count as corruption, not arranging meetings for constituents even if gifts were involved. McDonnell and his wife, Maureen, had been convicted of taking bribes, including $170,000 in cash from a Virginia-based tech company and its CEO, in exchange for official favors. The Supreme Court said that prosecutors had relied on "boundless" definitions of public corruption.

"There is no doubt that this case is distasteful; it may be worse than that," Chief Justice John Roberts wrote. "But our concern is not with tawdry tales of Ferraris, Rolexes, and ball gowns. It is instead with the broader legal implications of the government's boundless interpretation of the federal bribery statute. A more limited interpretation of the term 'official act' leaves ample room for prosecuting corruption, while comporting with the text of the statute and the precedent of this Court."

Drawing on the high court's ruling, Lowell's straightforward defense strategy made a strong impression on the jury who couldn't reach a unanimous verdict after hearing nine weeks of testimony. On the fourth day of deliberations, the presiding US District Judge William Walls interviewed each juror individually, emerging from his chambers to tell the court that the seven women and five men who made up the jury were hopelessly deadlocked on every count.

"There is no alternative but to declare a mistrial," he said.

Later, one of the jurors told reporters that ten of the twelve members of the jury voted to find Menendez not guilty because prosecutors had failed to make the argument that the favors and gifts that Menendez exchanged with Melgen were actual bribes.

"I just didn't see a smoking gun," said Ed Norris, an equipment operator from Roxbury Township, who was on the jury. "They just didn't prove it to us."

The prosecutors put together a weak case against Menendez, but Lowell also made great strides to narrow the charges against his client and make sure that the senator would be tried in a jurisdiction favorable to him. Lowell was successful in ensuring the case would be tried in New Jersey where Menendez had an advantage. Prosecutors had originally wanted to try the case in the District of Columbia, but Lowell fought against it.

Prosecutors also mishandled a key piece of evidence, which was contained in an FBI report inserted as an exhibit in Lowell's Supreme Court challenge of the charges. In that case, Lowell invoked the Speech or Debate Clause, a constitutional protection given to lawmakers to allow them their independence from the executive branch of government to limit the scope of the prosecution against his client. Although Lowell's appeal to the US Supreme Court to kill the case didn't entirely succeed, it still benefited Menendez when prosecutors employed the wrong strategy.

The FBI had opened an investigation into Menendez, Permuy, and Melgen over the ICSSI port security deal. A draft of that file—dated March 3, 2013—prepared by Special Agent Gregory J. Sheehy revealed a bold attempt by Menendez and Permuy to pressure federal government officials into forcing the ICSSI deal on the Dominican Republic. Both Permuy and Menendez targeted William Brownfield, a career foreign service officer with the State Department—a government body Menendez had authority over through his chairmanship of the Senate Foreign Relations Committee. According to the report, Menendez made it clear that Brownfield's assistance in helping Melgen force ICSSI on the Dominican government would result in the senator approving additional funds to Brownfield's agency, the Bureau of International Narcotics and Law Enforcement Affairs (INL).

The FBI along with prosecutors in the Menendez case interviewed Brownfield in his C Street office at the US Department of State. A State Department employee since 1979, Brownfield had extensive experience throughout Latin America, having worked at postings in Chile, Venezuela, and Colombia. In 2011, he was promoted to assistant secretary of state at INL. He had also worked with Permuy in the past while they both served at the Department of Defense between 1999 and 2000 during the Clinton administration. According to Brownfield, it was Permuy who first contacted his office to ask for a meeting. Permuy said he needed Brownfield's help about an American company with ties to Menendez's home state of New Jersey that was involved in a contract dispute in the Dominican Republic.

During a lunch meeting, Permuy said that the Dominican Republic was not complying with a contract that would help INL meet its own responsibilities on drug interdiction and port security. Permuy was hoping that Brownfield could intervene on the company's behalf with the Dominican government.

Before his meeting with Permuy, Brownfield's staff had already done the research on Menendez's keen interest in the ICSSI contract, and after their meeting he told Permuy to contact another government bureaucrat. But both Menendez and Permuy continued to press the case with Brownfield, the FBI found.

"Around the same time period that Brownfield spoke with Permuy, Brownfield spoke directly with Menendez on the ICSSI issue on two occasions," the report said. "The first meeting between [them] involved discussions on port security in the Dominican Republic as well as everything else INL was doing in the Western Hemisphere. It was a big-picture conversation discussing INL projects and programs implemented throughout the Western Hemisphere. Menendez stated he was concerned about the Dominican Republic government not abiding by a contract between itself and an American company."[126]

Under pressure, Brownfield wondered about the senator's interests and the port security company's nonexistent ties to New Jersey. In his years in public service, he had never encountered a lawmaker pushing for an issue that did not directly involve his constituents, Brownfield told the FBI agents.

"Brownfield later learned that ICSSI had no connection to New Jersey," the report said. "Brownfield advised it is very unusual to have a senator advocate on behalf of a non-constituent."

In other words, there was no real reason for Menendez and Permuy to lobby the State Department so hard. No constituent services or legislative agendas were involved in their work on behalf of ICSSI. What made it worse was Brownfield went on to tell the FBI that he felt Menendez had positioned himself, through his power in the Senate, to engage in a quid pro quo, by dangling the promise of additional funds to the INL if Brownfield did his bidding on the port security contract.

"During the timeframe that Brownfield was dealing with Menendez on this issue, [he] viewed Menendez's interest in the Dominican Republic as potential to develop a congressional ally who might be able to assist INL in procuring funds and implementing desired programs," the report said.

The aggressive lobbying of Brownfield was the smoking gun the jurors needed, and it was available to prosecutors in the FBI file. But none of this came up during Menendez's trial. Instead prosecutors made the opposite argument, claiming that Menendez had threatened Brownfield when, in fact, he was really offering him a deal. At their joint trial, Melgen's attorney quickly pounced on this mistake.

"Was there ever any threat to you, sir?" Kirk Ogrosky asked Brownfield.

"[If] I use the word 'threat' in its technical term, no," Brownfield told the court. "By the same token, 'it's threatening to rain outside, my wife threatens to kill me if I'm late for dinner.' If we use it in a loose term, then perhaps so. But as the word has meaning in the English language, no."

Moreover, prosecutors did not use the information that the FBI provided in their case. Instead, they relied on notes of the meeting with Menendez and Permuy made by Todd Levett, a federal employee who worked as Brownfield's assistant. The notes described the senator threatening his boss.

"The senator noted displeasure very clearly with the current state of affairs and threatened to hold a hearing on the matter if we don't meet the deadline," wrote Levett, who died of brain cancer a year after the 2013 meeting.[127]

The prosecution's error to not highlight Menendez's pressure to push the ICSSI deal sealed the case. It was a fatal blow.

Even after a hung jury was declared, prosecutors had the ability to bring the evidence in the FBI report back up in a future trial to show the suggestion of a quid pro quo. They never bothered, and Menendez was able to claim victory.

Outside, on the steps of the federal courthouse, a jubilant Menendez addressed his supporters, comparing himself to Jesus Christ.

"Today is resurrection day," he proclaimed.

He broke down as he thanked his children for their support. But he couldn't help playing the victim, suggesting that he was unjustly prosecuted because of his minority status.

"The way this case started was wrong, the way it was investigated was wrong, the way it was prosecuted was wrong, and the way it was tried was wrong as well," he said. "Certain elements of the FBI and our state cannot understand or, worse, accept that a Latino kid from Union City and Hudson County can grow up to be a United States senator and be honest."

Prosecutors in the Trump Justice Department promised to retry the case, but ultimately decided not to do so. In January 2018, US District Court Judge William Walls acquitted Menendez and Melgen of seven of the eighteen corruption charges they had faced. Those charges related to official favors Menendez had made for Melgen in exchange for hundreds of thousands of dollars in contributions to Menendez's campaigns. In his opinion, Walls wrote that when it comes to bribery charges in exchange for political donations, prosecutors "must prove an explicit quid pro quo."

Months after their trial, Melgen was sentenced to seventeen years in prison for health care fraud. In April, before he went to trial with Menendez, he had been convicted on sixty-seven counts and ordered to repay tens of millions for overbilling Medicare.

"Salomon Melgen callously took advantage of patients who came to him fearing blindness," said a federal agent who had investigated the case. "Instead of treatment, they received medically unreasonable and unnecessary tests and procedures that victimized his patients and the American taxpayer."

Despite his victory in court, Menendez's reputation had taken a beating. Polls released as the trial was underway found that his approval rating had crashed. A Quinnipiac poll released in September showed that 50 percent of eligible voters in New Jersey did not believe he should be reelected.

The Senate Ethics Committee also weighed in on Menendez. In April 2018, the committee "severely admonished" Menendez. In a "Public Letter of Admonition" addressed to Menendez, the committee accused him of ignoring the Senate's highest standards of behavior.

"You demonstrated disregard for these standards by placing your Senate office in Dr. Melgen's service at the same time you repeatedly accepted gifts of significant value from him," said the four-page letter signed by three Democrats and three Republicans. "Your assistance to Dr. Melgen under these circumstances demonstrated poor judgment, and it risked undermining the public's confidence in the Senate. As such, your actions reflected discredit upon the Senate."

Despite the admonishment by the Senate Ethics Committee, Menendez forged ahead, announcing that he would run for reelection in the 2018 Senate race. Senator Cory Booker and New Jersey

Governor Philip Murphy stood behind him in the Union Hill High School gymnasium in front of a raucous crowd of supporters that included nearly the entire 2,800 students at the school who had been excused from four periods of classes to attend the rally.

"If you want to know who I am then you need to know where I came from," said Menendez to a cheering crowd of students from diverse immigrant backgrounds.

Brian Stack, the mayor of Union City, had been a loyal supporter of Bill Musto. He was also on hand to make a speech framed by a giant US flag. Booker spoke at such a high pitch during his own speech in support of Menendez that he came close to losing his voice. Members of the New Jersey Republican Party who were at the rally distributed cards made to look like Monopoly money, showing a caricature of Menendez as a prisoner and a photo of the senator and Melgen on vacation together.

It's a measure of just how angry New Jersey voters were with Menendez that Lisa McCormick, a New Jersey publisher and political unknown who did not raise enough in campaign contributions to meet a $5,000 disclosure rule, received nearly 38 percent of the vote in the June 2018 Democratic primary against Menendez.

Menendez defeated his Republican challenger Bob Hugin, a former pharmaceutical executive who was close to former Governor Chris Christie and who had served on the Union City school board with Menendez, in November, winning by a margin of only 11 percent.

Menendez, who spent much of the campaign attacking President Donald Trump, had to win back the trust of his constituents, and to do so he promised to target his enemies—the same people who had orchestrated a smear campaign against him and Melgen that eventually led to their prosecution.

"To those who were digging my political grave so that they could jump into my seat, I know who you are," he said in his impromptu conference outside federal court in Newark after his victory. "And I won't forget you."

It was a defiant senator who returned to Washington after the trial ended in November 2017. Not only was he gearing up for reelection, but he seemed bent on revenge. Among the most urgent matters on his to-do list was going after President Trump and his family.

The attacks, issued from the pulpit of the Senate Foreign Relations Committee, began with a swipe against Donald Trump Jr. in February 2018. In a letter to Kenneth Juster, then US ambassador to India, Menendez wrote a scathing letter about the first son's visit to the subcontinent to tour properties licensed by the Trump Organization.

"Given the potential to confuse Mr. Trump's private business visit with having an official governmental purpose, I write to ensure that the US Embassy presence in India will have no role in supporting Mr. Trump or the Trump Organization," wrote Menendez on February 21. He demanded that the Embassy confirm that their personnel would not be providing "any special assistance or support for this visit." Juster was instructed "to make clear" to the Indian government that Trump Jr. in "no way" speaks on behalf of the United States during a planned speech before the Global Business Summit, which would include speeches by Prime Minister Narendra Modi and several cabinet ministers.

Trump Jr., who had taken over the family company with his brother Eric while their father was president, canceled his address and opted for a "fireside" chat with a local journalist about his views on business in India.

The attacks against Trump and his family continued in Senate floor speeches in which Menendez lambasted the president's foreign policy, particularly the administration's "embrace" of Russian President Vladimir Putin. He also seemed to take Trump to task for his surprise victory over his political godmother, Hillary Clinton, in the 2016 election.

"I am stunned by President Trump's willful paralysis when it comes to holding Russia accountable about threats made crystal clear by our intelligence community," Menendez said. "Indeed, it's been more than a year since seventeen US intelligence agencies issued their report on how the Kremlin sought to—and I quote: 'Blend covert intelligence operations—such as cyber activity—with overt efforts by Russian government agencies, state-funded media, third-party intermediaries, and paid social media users, or trolls' in order to undermine our 2016 elections."

In another speech on the Senate floor on March 20, he blasted Trump for his "chaotic and incoherent approach to foreign policy" and the exodus of career diplomats from the State Department following his election in 2016.

"This is America," Menendez said. "Our government functions because of apolitical civil servants across agencies who dedicate their lives to advancing the interests of their fellow citizens—from distributing Social Security checks to negotiating nuclear arms treaties. It is outrageous. It is disgraceful. It is dangerous. We face challenges from every corner of the globe. We simply cannot confront them if we are not present. And we cannot overcome these challenges when the president himself does not acknowledge them."[128]

The campaign against Trump and the Trump Organization continued throughout that year, and this time Menendez uncharacteristically waded directly into a commercial dispute involving the Trump Ocean Club International Hotel and Tower in Panama City and a Cypriot businessman, attempting to turn it into a pressing matter of US foreign policy.

The compound—which features a hotel, five swimming pools, a casino, and luxury condominiums—opened in 2011 and is one of the tallest buildings in the region. Trump had licensed his name to the $400 million development in 2006, a deal that earned the Trump Organization nearly $14 million a year. The building was completed during Ricardo Martinelli's presidency when the country was awash in corruption.

In 2017, reporters began to dub the property "Narco-a-Lago" because most of the lavish condos were empty and allegedly bought by crooks looking to launder their ill-gotten cash. In an interview with NBC, Henrique Ventura Nogueira, one of the realtors who sold a third of the 666 preconstruction units in the building, said that most of his clients were Russian. Nogueira, a Brazilian, was under investigation in his own country for money laundering and later disappeared, according to reports.

By the time Menendez and the Senate Foreign Relations Committee entered the fray in the first months of 2018, the seventy-story hotel was already in the process of being taken over by Orestes Fintiklis, a private investor and head of the hotel's owners' association. Fintiklis, a colorful Oxford University grad who owned most of the units in the building, likened the Trumps to leeches who had attached to the property "draining our last drops of blood."

On March 1, Menendez's allies on the House Foreign Affairs Committee—Democratic Representatives Norma Torres and Eliot Engel—announced that they had fired off letters to Trump demanding accountability on the property and asking if he knew that it was being used to launder money.

"Given widely reported allegations of money laundering and drug trafficking in connection with the Trump Ocean Club Panama, we believe it is imperative to understand the Trump Organization's knowledge and role in sales at this property," the letter said. "If the president, in a previous role, failed to take reasonable steps to prevent the laundering of drug money, it would be of grave concern to us."

The duo later followed up with a letter to the Drug Enforcement Administration seeking a briefing on potential money laundering at the site. "This criminal activity may have tainted the Panama business interests of the Trump Organization, and by extension President Trump," the letter said.[129]

By March 5, 2018, a Panamanian court evicted the Trump management from the hotel and removed the Trump name from outside the building. The Trump family effectively surrendered physical control of the property.

Around the same time, Menendez sent a letter to the Trump Organization demanding that they hand over all financial documents related to foreign sources of revenue.

"The Trump Organization's announcement earlier this week provides no comfort to the American people that foreign governments are not spending money at Trump Organization properties to benefit or influence the president," wrote Menendez. "I urge you to immediately rectify this by providing a complete and transparent accounting of the Trump Organization's calculation of foreign profits." Menendez was particularly concerned about foreign dignitaries staying at the Trump International Hotel in Washington, DC, to curry favor with the president.

Two months later, after Trump company lawyers had asked the president of Panama to intervene in the company's dispute with Fintiklis over the ownership of the hotel, Menendez fired off another series of letters to President Trump, Commerce Secretary Wilbur Ross, the US Embassy in Panama, and the Trump Organization.

"Even if the Panamanian government rightfully refuses to intercede in the judicial proceedings, the letter's threatening tone may suggest to the Panamanian government that improper, and perhaps illegal, actions are effective means of influencing US policy toward the country," he wrote.

At the same time that he was using the Senate Foreign Relations Committee and his counterparts in the House Foreign Relations Committee to go after Trump and his family, the Department of Justice was going after Ricardo Martinelli for similar reasons—using the power of his office to get rich.

Martinelli fled Panama by a circuitous route in January 2015 as the country's Supreme Court opened probes into his phone-tapping and corruption scandals. Martinelli flew on a fifteen-seat Hawker jet to Guatemala and refueled in Florida, Canada, and Ireland before landing in Modena, Italy. Martinelli held both Panamanian and Italian citizenship and was good friends with former Prime Minister Silvio Berlusconi, who was himself facing criminal charges. Martinelli eventually landed in Miami in the summer of 2015 where he owned the condo that was featured in the 1983 Hollywood film *Scarface* and the TV series *Miami Vice*. A warrant for his arrest was issued by Panama's Supreme Court of Justice in December 2015, and the country sought his extradition from the United States.

In addition to the wiretapping charges, a Panamanian investigation into stock manipulation involving Petaquilla Minerals revealed that Martinelli used his position as president for insider trading—to purchase shares of the company at low prices and sell them for a profit through the brokerage firm Financial Pacific. Ignacio Fábrega, the former director of the federal Superintendency of the Securities Market in Panama, pled guilty in August 2015 to the scheme.

Martinelli called the charges a political smear job against him by his successor, President Juan Carlos Varela. He fought the extradition request for a year in the United States, but eventually lost. He was extradited to Panama on June 11, 2018. He was found guilty a year later and sentenced to ten years in prison. Martinelli attempted to annul the sentence and in 2024 fled to the Nicaraguan Embassy in Panama City seeking asylum.

Shortly after Martinelli's mad dash out of Panama in 2015, Petaquilla Minerals sued Panama in a World Bank court for $2.3 billion, alleging that the company had been stolen by Martinelli. "It was emphasized that in September 2009, Ricardo Quijano, as minister of commerce and industry representing Ricardo Martinelli, transmitted to Richard Fifer a verbal order to give up Petaquilla," court documents say. Fifer was CEO of Petaquilla Minerals.

Martinelli's theft of the gold mine occurred three years before Menendez's former staffer Pedro Pablo Permuy joined the company's board of directors in 2012 and created the limited liability company—PTQ USA Inc.—in Delaware in 2013.

PTQ remains in the Delaware database of companies, but appears to have been abandoned. It's not clear whether Permuy is still associated with the limited liability corporation or with Petaquilla Minerals since they have not filed any reports since June 30, 2013, according to the US Securities and Exchange Commission. The SEC suspended Petaquilla's trading on the US Stock Exchange on June 23, 2016.

Although the contents of Martinelli's wiretaps were never made public, Ismael Patti, an analyst hired by Martinelli's administration, testified that at least two Americans were recorded. Christian Ferry, a Republican political strategist who worked on Varela's campaign and once worked with Paul Manafort, Trump's former campaign manager, and Richard Downie, a retired colonel. Martinelli had also wiretapped American diplomats, foreign journalists, and lawmakers.[130] "Martinelli was obsessed with knowing what everyone was gossiping or saying about him," said Alvaro Alemán Healy, cabinet chief for Juan Varela. "He used to brag that he had a file . . . on everybody who was important here in Panama."

On June 14, three days after Martinelli was extradited to Panama, Menendez was back on the warpath against Trump. This time he went straight to the source, sending a missive to the US representatives of five foreign governments—Azerbaijan, Kuwait, Bahrain, Malaysia, and the Philippines—demanding to know about their transactions with the Trump Organization for events and visits to its hotel in Washington.

"President Trump has refused to completely divest from his business interests or place them in a blind trust, which creates the potential for conflicts of interest that may lead him to put his own financial interests above those of the US government and the American people," he wrote. "Our founding fathers had this concern in mind when they wrote Article 1, Section 9, Clause 8 of the United States Constitution, which prohibits federal officeholders from accepting emoluments from foreign states without first obtaining the affirmative consent of Congress."

The letter coming from the ranking member of the Senate Foreign Relations Committee (he would become chairman after the 2020 presidential election when the Democrats were back in power) would have been viewed as a direct threat. For with a stroke of a pen, Menendez controlled billions in US aid and arms sales to foreign countries.

In the end, the attacks against Trump seemed to evaporate into thin air. What had begun as an all-out war between Menendez and the Trump administration turned into a quiet retreat by Menendez that most observers failed to notice. Menendez went from multiple Senate floor broadsides in speeches that attacked the legitimacy of President Trump in addition to his two votes for impeachment, to barely a mention of the president after Martinelli was extradited.

Perhaps Menendez knew he had poisoned the well with the Trump administration after the Martinelli debacle, but there was little he could do to quell an aggressive administration that had no problem using the levers of power at their disposal to eliminate their political enemies. Even though Menendez had backed off from his confrontation with Trump, the administration was not done with Martinelli. An indictment was issued by the Department of Justice against both of Martinelli's sons. The administration's response to Menendez's attacks was to meet fire with fire.

"A criminal complaint was unsealed today in federal court in Brooklyn, New York, charging Luis Enrique Martinelli Linares and Ricardo Alberto Martinelli Linares for their roles in a massive bribery and money laundering scheme involving Odebrecht," said the complaint, referring to the Brazil-based construction conglomerate that had worked on the CODACSA project in the Dominican Republic.

"Luis Martinelli Linares and Ricardo Martinelli Linares were arrested today at el Aeropuerto Internacional la Aurora in Guatemala," read a press release filed by the United States Attorney's Office in the Eastern District of New York.

Martinelli's sons would eventually be deported from Guatemala where they were arrested after they fled Panama. They would plead guilty on December 14, 2021. During the plea hearing, Ricardo Martinelli Linares confessed to conspiring with his brother, Luis Alberto Martinelli Linares, and others to set up offshore bank accounts under the guise of shell companies. These accounts were used to funnel and obscure more than $28 million in bribes from Odebrecht, intended to benefit a high-ranking Panamanian public official who was a close relative. Ricardo further admitted to facilitating the transfer of these bribery funds both into and out of the United States as part of the scheme.

"Ricardo and Luis Martinelli Linares played integral roles in the corrupt scheme to funnel Odebrecht bribes to a high-ranking Panamanian government official," stated US Assistant Attorney General Kenneth Polite. "They used the US financial system to further their scheme, took steps to create shell company accounts at offshore banks to try to evade responsibility, and used some of the bribe proceeds for their personal benefit. The guilty pleas of Ricardo Martinelli Linares and Luis Martinelli Linares demonstrate that the Department of Justice remains committed to combating corruption at home and abroad."

The Martinelli brothers were sentenced to three years in federal prison, but were released in January 2023 after serving about two and a half years. The Martinellis—the brothers as well as the father—are banned from ever entering the United States.

—

Menendez seemingly dropped the war he was waging against Trump after Martinelli's extradition and moved on to more important things, including the leggy blonde divorcée he had dated years earlier. Nadine Arslanian, the sexy mother of two from Englewood Cliffs, New Jersey, was now back in his life after briefly dating him years before. She had texted him on New Year's Eve 2017 to congratulate him on his legal victory the month before and wish him happy birthday. Menendez would celebrate his sixty-fourth birthday on New Year's Day, and Arslanian wanted to take him to lunch.

"Would love to get together but as I said once before I don't want to interfere with your boyfriend," Menendez texted back. Perhaps he was being cautious, for years before Arslanian had broken his heart, two-timing him with her lawyer lover from Hackensack.

And then a month later, on the day that the Justice Department dismissed the remaining charges against Menendez, she wrote again, "Now reelection!!!"

The relationship seemed to start up after they met for dinner at a restaurant in New Jersey. "Enjoyed your company," Menendez texted after she thanked him for "a great night."

"We'll have to do it again," he wrote.

Weeks later, Arslanian sent Menendez a voice message that would seal the senator's fate.

"I have a favor to ask you, hopefully you can do it."

CHAPTER NINE

"Bubbles"

B ob Menendez had his eye on Nadine Arslanian for several years. According to friends, he first met the statuesque blonde divorcée at a fundraiser for his reelection campaign at the Saddle River home of Armenian American donors in 2010. The event was hosted by the Armenian National Committee PAC and featured both the Archbishop and Bishop of the Armenian Church in America. There was also a fleeting meeting at an IHOP where she used to take her two children for breakfast before driving them to the Lycée Français in Manhattan where they attended school.

But the meeting was not in 2018, as Arslanian claimed in an interview with *The New York Times*. It was years earlier, according to friends, who say they already enjoyed a friendship by 2012. Menendez and Arslanian knew each other well enough to dine together a few times a year. One of Arslanian's friends remembers the date of one of those meetings in 2012, because the three of them met for lunch in November to celebrate both Menendez's victory over Republican Joe Kyrillos in that year's Senate race as well as Barack Obama's win for a second term as president. Arslanian had claimed in the interview that when she first met Menendez, she had no idea that he was a senator.

"Oh please, she definitely knew he was a senator," said Kim De Paola, a former cast member of the reality show *Real Housewives of*

New Jersey and former owner of a high-end clothing boutique in New Jersey.[131]

Another former friend agreed. "Nadine was always impressed with power. When I heard she was dating Bob, I thought 'Oh my God!' But I wasn't all that surprised."

"She wants the world," a former boyfriend recalled. "She wants a seat at every campfire."[132]

And she was clingy with her boyfriends, often bringing them along for a girls' night out, said another friend. "She's the type who wants to be with her man 24/7, and the type who believes in fairy tales," said the friend. "She's really old fashioned when it comes to marriage. She is also totally naive—the kind of person who never gets a joke."

Another friend said that her naïveté made her incapable of manip-ulating anyone. "She's not a female Bond villain, but a struggling housewife trying to make it," said Pat Dori, a friend who said he lost touch with Arslanian after she started dating the senator.[133]

Others said she looked out for herself and could be vindictive when things didn't go her way. "She was known as 'psycho Barbie' in the Armenian community," said the former boyfriend, who did not want to be identified.

He said that, in 2010, Arslanian was so jealous after their relation-ship ended and he started dating another woman that she showed up at his home on Christmas Day with her two children, violating a "no contact order" lodged by the new girlfriend when Arslanian continued to show up at the house to leave pictures of her and the former boyfriend in the mailbox. She also keyed the new girlfriend's car. Restraining orders were filed against Arslanian for "harassment and communication in manner to cause alarm" on January 8, 2011.

"Nadine always believed she was above the law," the ex-boyfriend said.

Friends were not surprised when she started boasting about hang-ing out with a US senator. Although Arslanian was involved with Hackensack lawyer Douglas Anton, who once represented musician

R. Kelly during his sex trafficking and racketeering trial, she made a point of calling the senator every year on his birthday.

"Even when she was involved with Doug, she was always looking for the next best thing," said De Paola. "When she used to come to my events, she had her boobs hanging to her knees. We'd all look at her and say, 'What in the world?' She was always trying to be provocative. She had a way about her, always flaunting herself."

Arslanian was a regular at New Jersey book launches and parties featuring the casts of popular reality TV shows, such as the *Real Housewives of New Jersey* and *Mob Wives*. On Arslanian's social media accounts, which were scrubbed shortly after she was charged with corruption along with her husband, she is pictured at glamorous events with Karen Gravano (daughter of Salvatore "Sammy the Bull" Gravano) and Brittany Fogarty—daughter of convicted mobster John Fogarty—and her mom, Andrea Giovino, once nicknamed the "real-life Carmela Soprano." She also hung out with "Iron Chef" star Marc Forgione at the now-closed Englewood Cliffs branch of his American Cut steak houses and enjoyed nights out at upscale Manhattan restaurant Boulud Sud. Another friend was former Gambino family enforcer-turned-celebrity author John Alite, who testified against mobster John Gotti in 2008.

"We were friends," Alite said. "She used to help me pick out gifts for my girlfriends."[134]

Arslanian also volunteered with socialite and philanthropist Rosemarie "Ro" Sorce at Hackensack Meridian Health, the largest health care network in New Jersey, where Sorce, the well-connected wife of a New Jersey developer, was on the board of directors and its first woman chair. Arslanian, who was on an advisory board of the hospital, considered Sorce, who was also an important donor to Menendez, one of her closest friends, and the two would often head for boozy lunches after work at the hospital.

It was Sorce whom Arslanian called after she killed a man. On December 12, 2018, Arslanian was involved in a car crash in Bogota, a borough in Bergen County, that left a pedestrian dead and her Mercedes badly damaged. The windshield was shattered, and the front end of the car was dented because she veered into a parked vehicle after hitting Richard Koop, forty-nine, as he crossed the street to his home.

In the moments before and after the crash, while she was driving, Arslanian was texting her friend Ro Sorce. But instead of immediately dialing 911 after the accident, she placed a call to Sorce with whom she was scheduled to dine that evening.

"I am four miles away due to two detours," the first message said. The next, six minutes later at 7:34 p.m., said, "911, call me," and a third at 7:54 p.m. said, "I'm sitting in ambulance."

She called 911 at 7:37 p.m. Koop died almost instantly after Arslanian's black Mercedes slammed into him as he was crossing the street. A passerby had made the first 911 call that initially alerted the police. When she did call the emergency number, Arslanian said that a man had jumped onto her car while she was driving.

Bogota Patrolman Michael LaFerrera, writing in a police report, said he arrived at the scene and saw Koop "laying in the westbound lane of travel."

Koop "appeared to have severe head trauma, bleeding from the back of his head, bleeding from the face and possible fractured legs and arms."

His body was so mangled that his ex-wife, who was called to the morgue to identify him, could barely recognize him.

Arslanian told police she didn't see Koop. She was driving so fast that the collision flung his mangled body to the curb. It's a measure of how connected Arslanian was that police did not perform tests for drugs or alcohol, nor did they seize her cell phone. Shortly after a retired top cop acquaintance showed up within minutes of the crash, she was allowed to leave the scene. Michael Mordaga, the former director of Hackensack Police and an ex-chief of detectives in the Bergen County Prosecutor's Office, helped Arslanian take her belongings from the totaled vehicle after quizzing the patrolman about what he planned to do.

"I don't even know her," said Mordaga in a dash cam video recording, even though he was scheduled to dine with her and the Sorces that evening at I Gemelli in Hackensack. "That's my buddy's wife who's friends with her. He said, 'Could you do me a favor and take her up there, because her friend just got in a car accident.'"

Dash cam footage and 911 recordings do not show Arslanian asking after the victim, but they do show her refusing to have her cell phone searched.

"Ms. Arslanian was not at fault in this crash," a Bogota Police Department investigation report reads. "Mr. Koop was jaywalking and did not cross the street at an intersection or in a marked crosswalk."

Arslanian left the accident scene with Mordaga and headed to the Italian restaurant where she met the Sorces for dinner. Menendez was in Washington that evening.

—

Despite her social connections, as well as a closetful of designer shoes and handbags, Arslanian struggled after her divorce from her first husband, Raffi Arslanian, in 2005. "She was a good-hearted woman, but she was having a hard time financially," Alite said. For one thing, Arslanian had worked for her husband's property development business, and when they divorced, she was out of a job, friends said.

Nadine Arslanian may not have been born into fabulous wealth, but by US standards, she grew up in relative affluence and comfort in Beirut where she was born in 1967. She and her sister Katia each had their own governess. But after the country descended into civil war in 1975, the family fled—first to Greece and then to London and Palo Alto, California. They settled on a leafy street in Manhasset, New

York, a wealthy hamlet on the North Shore of Long Island where her parents, Ida and Garbis Tabourian, became loyal supporters of the Armenian community in New York. "I was educated by nuns and raised by righteous parents," wrote her father, Garbis Tabourian, in a handwritten letter to the federal judge who tried Menendez. "This is how I raised my children."

Arslanian graduated from New York University with bachelor's and master's degrees in international relations and French history. She married New Jersey real estate developer Raffi Arslanian, and the couple had two children. They bought a modest home in Englewood Cliffs across the Hudson River from Manhattan to tear down and build their dream home, according to Anton, who said he did legal work for her around the time of the separation from her husband. Nadine kept the house in the divorce, but had difficulty making ends meet. She moved her daughter, Sabine, and her son, André, from the Lycée Français, where tuition is now more than $48,000 a year, to a public high school near her Englewood Cliffs home when the money ran out.

"It was a great little family, really tight-knit," said Michael Mathews, who used to date Sabine. He and Sabine met when they both attended Cresskill High School. "Nadine was a sweetheart and a very caring mother who did everything she could for her kids, even though she barely had enough to get by."[135]

Mathews, who used to work as a paralegal in Anton's New Jersey law office, said he sometimes helped out by picking up Arslanian's kids from school.

"Sometimes she only had $20, and gave it to me for gas so that I could pick them up," he said. "She had a horrible financial situation and had to do odd jobs. She sometimes helped a friend who was a hairstylist."

Despite her precarious finances, she continued to be a fixture on the party scene, and continued her on-again, off-again relationship with Anton, who showered her with designer handbags and took her out for lavish dinners. On Christmas Eve in 2017, the couple lovingly sang Bon Jovi's "Always" together. But a few days later, Arslanian couldn't resist. She picked up the phone to wish her friend Bob Menendez a happy sixty-fourth birthday. The call changed both their lives.

≈

"It was 'Bob, Bob, Bob, Bob!' when she started dating him," a former friend said, adding that for at least a few months she seemed not to be able to decide between the two men in her life.

Menendez may have been right to be wary of Arslanian. He knew she was still involved with Anton because his driver saw her hanging out with the lawyer at a favorite cigar lounge in New Jersey, often on the same nights that she would later meet Menendez for dinner at Regina's Steakhouse and Grill in nearby Teaneck, said a friend of the couple.

Another friend said she often couldn't decide between the two men. At one time, she had "desperately" wanted Anton to propose. By the time he got around to asking her to marry him, she was already involved with Menendez.

"Nadine told Doug, 'You're too late,'" said the friend.

Things got so bad between the two men that the senator sent two Capitol Police officers to his love rival's office to "bully him out of the picture" in 2018, said John Alite. "The guy was hurt bad," Alite continued. "He [Bob] scared the shit out of Doug."

At one point, Menendez called off his relationship with Nadine.

"I cared for her a great deal, but I cannot get over her being with Doug while she was with me," the senator texted her younger sister, Katia Tabourian, who tried to persuade him to reconcile with Nadine. "Maybe time will heal wounds but not today. Wish it was different. Thanks."[136]

But by spring 2018, Arslanian had made her choice. This time, as she faced foreclosure on her property, the prospect of being the powerful senator's girlfriend seemed too good to pass up.

"He sold her a dream," said Alite. "I told her, 'Nadine, this guy's . . . not for you.' He really manipulated her. She thought she was going to marry Doug, but Menendez wooed her away. He manipulated her; he made her feel important. He was promising her the world."

Some of Menendez's friends were equally horrified—for his sake. "When he started dating her, he was extremely vulnerable," said a former girlfriend. "He had just escaped the indictment and was probably really lonely. He jumped into the relationship too quickly. I feel really bad for him. He really got caught up in a situation."[137]

They started dining together on a regular basis, and at the end of March 2018 went on a romantic weekend to the Dominican Republic, where Menendez had often taken his previous girlfriends. At one point Arslanian disappeared after setting up a rendezvous with Anton at her home just before Easter weekend. Anton said that Arslanian had been at his Hackensack office that night, and the two made plans to meet up later at her house for a drink. Anton said he arrived to find the lights on and TVs blaring. Arslanian left a "weird" typewritten note on the door, saying she needed "time to think," he said.

Anton said he wasn't too upset because he was also dating someone else at the time, "and the idea of a Nadine-free weekend was rather appealing." But when she didn't return on Monday, he began to worry, adding that he called her sister Katia, her adult children, and some of her friends, "who also had no idea where she was, that she left, and were very concerned." Her sister insisted he call the police.[138]

"It wasn't like her to do this, and days went by, so I went to the cops," he said. "I did a missing person report, and they had to come to the house to check to make sure that someone didn't kill her and put her in a closet."

Arslanian was found several days later.

"On the flight back from the DR [Dominican Republic], she could not get on the plane and had to call for a government check," Anton said. "That's when he [Menendez] first found out we were still 'seeing' each other on and off during the week when he was in DC. She later said he freaked out and was pissed."

In the meantime, police broke into Arslanian's home on April 3, 2018, after Anton filed the missing person report, and conducted an inventory of all the valuables found on the property during their search for her. According to an Englewood Cliffs Police Evidence Report obtained under freedom of information legislation, police listed $5,300 in cash in $100 and $20 bills, two safes that they said they could not open, and at least thirteen designer handbags, including Gucci, Prada, Dior, and Louis Vuitton. There were also three fur jackets and a Hermès scarf.

"She did like high-end things," said Mathews. "She cared about materialist things, and in many ways was a very gullible person, especially if someone had money and power."

When Arslanian was on the plane, she called police to say she was safe and asked them to send Anton a message to stay away from her. She returned to the United States on a Thursday, nearly a week after she had first "disappeared," said Anton.[139]

Under Menendez's orders, she stopped seeing Anton and embarked with Menendez on more trips—to Puerto Rico, Turks and Caicos, Colombia, and Greece. They were soon inseparable and texting regularly.

Arslanian addressed her new boyfriend in French, pronouncing him "*l'amour de ma vie*"—"the love of my life"—and "my very handsome senator." Menendez had his own nickname for the new woman in his life. He called her "Bubbles," in reference to her décolletage, said a friend.[140]

Arslanian bragged about dating Menendez to anyone who would listen, gushing to a reporter about one of the first times that she spoke to him. "He was very intelligent and had a great sense of humor, and he was very, very hot," she told *The New York Times*.[141]

Menendez described his new girlfriend in glowing terms—"beautiful and bright," he told the newspaper. "There was just this aura about her."

The fairy-tale romance soon turned to more practical matters as Arslanian struggled to pay her bills. Her home was in foreclosure, and months after returning from her secret trip with the senator to the Dominican Republic, she totaled her car in the accident that killed Richard Koop.

It's unclear if she communicated her financial woes to her new boyfriend, but in flirty phone calls and texts, Arslanian began to ask for favors. The former international relations major also asked Menendez to meet with her friends who had high-level connections with the Egyptian government.

"Hi, it's me, calling my very handsome senator," Arslanian said in a phone call. "I have a thing to ask you."

In one text, she asked about his "international position." Menendez told her that he was the highest ranking Democrat on the Senate Foreign Relations Committee. After that, it didn't take long for Arslanian to ask if he would meet with some Egyptian officials. The meeting would be good for the future relations of Egypt and the United States, she said. She added a few more details that seemed to stump the senator.

"Could you please discuss the country's relations with the International Monetary Fund and other large projects, such as the 'new Suez Canal,'" she said.

"Really???" Menendez texted back.

Moments later, Menendez went online and searched "Egypt and International Monetary Fund." He then clicked on a page titled "Frequently Asked Questions on Egypt and the IMF."

Most of the texts and phone calls took place in secret, on encrypted apps such as WhatsApp and Viber and private Gmail accounts, although sometimes Menendez added in members of his staff when he needed help answering a question. And many of the arrangements for meetings and favors with Egyptian officials were conducted on a cell phone that the couple referred to as their "007" phone, a reference to fictional spy James Bond.

In one such exchange with a member of his senate staff, Menendez wanted to know how many Egyptians and Americans worked at the US Embassy in Cairo. The aide seemed to betray a sense of unease about the query.

"Any idea how many Americans are posted to the embassy?" The question was directed to a Department of State employee from the Senate aide.

"Don't ask why I'm asking . . ."

CHAPTER TEN

Ghostwriter

A month before Menendez headed to India on his official state visit, he received an unusual visitor at his home in Englewood Cliffs. In the early evening of September 5, 2019, Menendez leaned back in his chair savoring the last drops of the bitter orange notes in his tumbler of brandy. Darkness was falling on what had been a perfect summer day. It was Thursday, and Menendez was in the final days of the Senate's summer recess. He had a few more languid days ahead of him with nothing to do but lounge in the relative peace of Arslanian's serene suburban backyard, puffing on a cigar and allowing himself to grow drowsy before the 116th Congress was set to resume on Monday.

On that evening, Jose Uribe, a Dominican American insurance executive, pulled up a metal patio chair and joined the white-haired politician in the tree-lined enclave of neat 1950s homes nestled among newly constructed, gaudy mansions. Uribe surprised Menendez with a bottle of Grand Marnier that they shared along with the cigars while Uribe reminded the senator of the purpose of his visit.

Uribe was worried. An investigation spearheaded by the insurance fraud unit of the New Jersey Office of the Attorney General threatened to ensnare his own family company. He already had a record of committing insurance fraud and had lost his license in the past. Now Uribe, a divorced father of four, had been served with subpoenas in the new probe. He was so distraught he had taken to popping Xanax to calm his nerves.

Like many before him, he pinned his last hope on the state's most powerful fixer—Bob Menendez.

Perhaps the senator was only half listening to Uribe's woes as he sat licking the fat stub of his cigar during that fateful summer of 2019. He had already heard some of them before: how the insurance broker had several brushes with the law, and how he had lost his insurance license in the process, and then started a handful of other companies, installing family members, including his son, and friends as licensed brokers and firm owners even as he continued to be in charge. The complicated setup allowed him to avoid paying taxes, but now he was heading for deep trouble after Elvis Parra, one of his friends who owned a trucking company, was in the crosshairs of state investigators. New Jersey state investigator Suzanna Lopez had already begun subpoenaing Uribe's son and daughter, who ran the insurance company with him, adding to his desperation.

A year earlier, in 2018, Uribe had laid out the sorry tale to his lawyer Andy Arslanian (no relation to Nadine) when he was overheard by Wael "Will" Hana, a stocky Egyptian American businessman, fond of bespoke suits, Rolex watches, gold jewelry, and the River Palm Terrace in Edgewater, a popular steak house. Hana shared offices with Arslanian, the attorney in Edgewater who also represented Egypt's department of defense in Washington, DC. It was Hana who suggested Uribe go to Menendez. The senator had "a way to make these things go away." For $250,000 Uribe's troubles could vanish, Hana told him.

"I am fucked, man," Uribe texted Hana in October 2018. "The whole thing is going bad. I have no face to talk to my family. . . . Please be sure that your friend knows about this, just as a last favor."[142]

Uribe was so desperate he would try anything to save his family, he told Hana, including bribing a senator. The best way to do that was to go through Hana's friend Nadine Arslanian, the busty blonde who was dating the senator and having trouble paying the mortgage on her home. Hana knew that she was desperate for a new Mercedes after she lost her car in a serious accident. If Uribe could help her out of her financial difficulties, she would forcefully make his case to the senator, Hana assured him.

Uribe didn't hesitate. Months before that backyard meeting, he had already met Nadine in a parking lot and handed over an envelope stuffed with $15,000—cash to help buy Nadine a new Mercedes-Benz convertible. He would continue with the car payments until June 2022.[143]

"I agreed with Nadine . . . and other people to provide a car for Nadine in order to get the power and influence of Mr. Menendez," Uribe said.

The car was parked at her Englewood Cliffs home the night Uribe arrived with the Grand Marnier.

Toward the end of his conversation with the senator, as he sat nervously nursing his glass of brandy, Uribe was startled when he heard the tinkling of a small bell that the senator used to summon the love of his life who was inside the house.

"*Mon amour!*" the senator called out. On cue, Arslanian appeared almost immediately, a piece of paper in hand.

Menendez motioned to Uribe to write down the name of his friends and the companies he believed were under investigation by the New Jersey Office of the Attorney General. The senator then took the paper, folded it, and tucked it into a pocket of his trousers.[144]

The next day, Menendez held a meeting with then New Jersey Attorney General Gurbir Grewal at his Newark district office. The suggestion was that Grewal's insurance fraud unit lay off Jose Uribe and his friends.

"I beg him to please do anything in his power to stop anything that could cause harm to my family," Uribe told a federal jury in the summer of 2024.

Grewal's aide, who attended the meeting, left disgusted.

"Whoa, that was gross," he said.

≅

Uribe worked in tandem with Hana and Fred Daibes, another New Jersey entrepreneur, to bribe the senator. All of them needed official favors from Menendez, and Hana's friend Nadine Arslanian seemed all too eager to help them.

Hana had met the senator's girlfriend through Andy Arslanian, the lawyer with whom he shared office space in Edgewater and who became his partner in IS EG Halal, a company they incorporated in November 2017 to certify meat in adherence with Islamic law. Andy Arslanian became a mentor to Hana after he met him in 2009. He represented him in court when Hana was charged with drunk driving in 2014 and introduced him to a coterie of fellow entrepreneurs. One of those businessmen was Daibes, a Palestinian American real estate developer fond of antique sports cars who was behind a collection of luxury high-rises along the Hudson River, overlooking Manhattan as well as a trendy French restaurant. Daibes had been so successful in Edgewater that a street—Daibes Court—had been named for him.

Daibes helped bankroll IS EG Halal and had a cozy relationship with both Hana and the Egyptian government. He provided his friend Hana with an apartment at one of his luxury rental buildings.

Hana, a Coptic Christian, had no experience certifying halal products, but he was a born risk-taker, a seasoned entrepreneur despite a string of failed business ventures he started after arriving in the United States on a green card lottery in 2006. Besides that, he was certain he could leverage his high-level connections in the Egyptian government to help him secure the rights to what could turn into a billion-dollar enterprise. By the time he met Menendez in 2018, he was driving a luxury car with diplomatic plates, courtesy of the Egyptian government, and showing off his collection of Rolex watches, recalled a friend.[145] It's not clear how Hana had made his high-level connections with the Egyptian government, but he rose fairly quickly from struggling immigrant who had enrolled in community college to learn English while working for a cleaning company. Once he gained his footing in America, he launched a trucking business, an Italian restaurant, a luxury car export company, and a limousine service.

But soon enough, Hana had a string of lawsuits against him for writing bad checks and had stiffed a former business partner for nearly $1 million when he ran the luxury car company that shipped Mercedes and Porsches to customers in China, Boston, and New York. The company that partnered with Hana wired him $3.6 million to make the car purchases on behalf of their customers in China. When Hana provided only $2.9 million worth of cars, they sued for the missing $700,000. The company won a judgment against Hana, but he never appeared in court or repaid the cash. At one point, he was so mired in debt that he couldn't afford to pay a $2,000 medical bill.[146]

Hana's fortunes seemed to change overnight after he began negotiating with the Egyptian government and secured the exclusive right to certify halal products for the country in the spring of 2019. The potential contract was massive, largely because Egypt imports 70 percent of its beef liver from the United States. When a delegation of Egyptian agricultural officials arrived in the United States for a trade mission in the spring of 2019 to visit slaughterhouses and halal certifiers, Hana inserted himself into the group, crashing their meetings and appointments with US officials, said James Tate, an official at the US Department of Agriculture. Tate recalled that Hana and his attorney were so unfamiliar with the halal process that they asked Tate to explain it to them. Despite his lack of experience, the Egyptian agricultural officials told their US counterparts in the Department of Agriculture that they would choose Hana's company as its sole importer of halal beef. Tate and others, including the US Meat Export Federation, were so concerned about Hana's monopoly that they demanded a meeting with the Egyptian government. Their concerns were realized when Hana's company increased the costs of the certification from $200 to $400 per shipping container to more than $5,000 per container.

"All the plants will either be: a) clamoring to get the services of the new certifier; or b) refusing to do business with a totally unknown character," a member of the federation wrote to the USDA. "The circumstances around this are very shady, and I think many companies are going to be reticent to do business with this group at all."[147]

Tate was so concerned about Hana's maneuvering that he called the FBI at the US Embassy in Cairo.

When the deal went through on the Egyptian side, Nadine Arslanian texted Menendez right away. "Seems like halal went through," she said. "It might be a fantastic 2019 all the way around."

Menendez got involved in the dispute with the US government in May 2019. He called Ted McKinney, chief executive of the National Association of State Departments of Agriculture, on his cell phone. The call was brief, but McKinney said he was startled by the senator's "serious" and "curt" tone of voice. When he tried to explain his concerns to Menendez about Hana's monopoly, the senator cut him off, he said.

"Stop interfering with my constituent," said Menendez.

The senator's concerns about his constituents didn't extend to another halal certification company based in New Jersey. After Hana scored his exclusive contract with the Egyptian government, Amana Halal went out of business.[148]

There were other favors that Hana needed for his pals in the Egyptian government in order to score his halal monopoly, and he had no qualms about asking Nadine Arslanian to help with her boyfriend—especially after he had helped Jose Uribe deliver her new Mercedes.

"Congratulations, *mon amour de la vie*, we are the proud owners of a 2019 Mercedes," Arslanian texted Menendez with a heart emoji and a photo of the new car, worth more than $60,000, that Uribe helped pay for between 2019 and 2022.

In addition to helping Hana secure his halal monopoly, Menendez was dispatched to aid the Egyptian government in overcoming their own problems with the US government, especially the block that the US had put on $300 million in military aid to the country.

The aid had been partly held up following a 2013 coup that installed a repressive military dictatorship that slaughtered dozens of the former Egyptian president's political supporters, censored the press, and jailed political opponents. The situation was so dire that international human rights groups, such as Amnesty International, called on the international community to impose sanctions and take other steps to protest the Egyptian government's authoritarian measures. At Arslanian's urging, Menendez edited and ghostwrote a letter for Egyptian military officials who were preparing to appear before his own Senate Foreign Relations Committee to plead their case. Arslanian told her boyfriend that she wanted him to help with the letter because Hana had gotten her "clearance for a project." Menendez sent the ghostwritten letter to Arslanian who sent it off to Hana who gave it to Egyptian officials, who would redraft it and present it to the senators on the committee.

"Will said please just speak about the IMF. That's important," she told Menendez, referring to Hana's anglicized first name.

In addition to helping Hana secure the halal contract, Menendez went on to do other favors involving Egypt. In one instance, Nadine Arslanian handed her phone to Hana's lawyer Andy Arslanian, who also worked for Egypt's Ministry of Defense in Washington, so that he could communicate directly with Menendez to arrange meetings. Subsequent texts show arrangements to set up meetings[149] between Menendez and Egyptian Major General Khaled Ahmed Shawky Osman, Egypt's defense, army, naval, and air force attaché to the United States and Canada.

Egyptian officials were also concerned about a troublesome lawsuit brought by an American skater against their government. April Corley, a professional roller skater who had appeared in commercials and trained the pop singer Katy Perry, had filed suit in federal court against Egypt for $14 million. This came four years after she was attacked while on holiday in the country. In September 2015, the Egyptian military launched a mistaken attack on a tour group using US-supplied Apache helicopters in the Western Desert that resulted in twelve dead. Corley was badly injured in the attack, and her Mexican boyfriend was killed. Although some of the victims were pulled from the wreckage, others had been burned to death. All that remained of tour guide Ahmed Uweis was an arm, leg, and a spine. Nine others also sustained serious injuries. Corley's family arranged for her immediate evacuation—a situation that led Egyptian authorities to question whether she was in fact one of the victims. Egypt later offered her $150,000 in compensation, which she rejected.

Menendez, Hana, and Nadine Arslanian met with an Egyptian intelligence official in Menendez's Senate office in May 2019 to discuss the Corley lawsuit. After the meeting, Menendez conducted a web search about the attack on the tourist group and Corley's lawsuit. Members of Congress wanted to hold off sending any military aid to Egypt until the matter was resolved. A week after the meeting, an unnamed Egyptian intelligence official sent Hana a text in Arabic, which said in part that if Menendez intervened, "he will sit very comfortably." Hana responded, "orders, consider it done." The Egyptian official then texted Hana screenshots of statements made by Corley's lawyers. Hana later forwarded them to Arslanian who sent them to Menendez, and later deleted her texts.

In the same month, a team of FBI agents happened to record a dinner attended by Menendez, Arslanian, Hana, and Egyptian officials at Morton's The Steakhouse, Menendez's favorite restaurant in Washington, DC, where he spent tens of thousands in campaign contributions. The senator could be found at the restaurant—which was a few blocks from the White House—on most nights tucking into a steak and finishing his meal off with a cigar and a snifter of brandy. In one year alone, his campaign billed more than $300,000 in meals at Morton's where his favorite dish on the menu is the New York Strip, which in 2025 went for $64.

The FBI agents were not at Morton's looking for Menendez and were surprised when he showed up with his party. The agents, posing as husband and wife, were eavesdropping on three Egyptian officials who were on the restaurant's outdoor patio. The undercover operatives had a concealed video camera and proceeded to take footage when Menendez, Hana, and Nadine Arslanian sat down with the three men. Another investigator was outside the restaurant with a camera posing as an Uber driver.

"What else can the love of my life do for you?" said Arslanian, who was overheard by one of the agents.

Although it's not clear to whom Arslanian was addressing her comments, the Egyptians were not shy about continuing to ask the senator for favors.

In exchange for all those favors, Hana helped Arslanian pay an outstanding mortgage debt, saving her home from foreclosure. He also asked Uribe to help front the $23,000 cost. When Uribe told Arslanian that Hana balked at the amount required to bring the mortgage current, Arslanian said in part, "When I feel comfortable and plan the trip to Egypt, he [Hana] will be more powerful than the president of Egypt."

Hana dispatched John Moldovan, a lawyer at IS EG Halal, to wire her the cash and sign a promissory note. But Arslanian was offended that her friend would entrust her business dealings to an attorney and refused to sign. Shortly afterward, Hana told Moldovan that he was giving Arslanian a $10,000 a month consulting job with his firm, and asked him to draft a contract between IS EG Halal and her newly formed Strategic International Business Consultants, a limited liability company that Menendez helped her set up. Moldovan later said that he never saw Arslanian come into work at IS EG Halal's offices.

"Every time I am a middle person for a deal I am asking to get paid and this is my consulting company," she told a relative in a text message.

In addition to the no-show job at Hana's firm, Hana helped broker the purchase of Arslanian's Mercedes convertible with Uribe, and showered Menendez with $150,000 in cash and gold bars after the senator met with Egyptian government officials to help secure the weapons purchase. After meeting with the Egyptians, Menendez told Arslanian to let Hana know that he had signed off on the sale of forty-six thousand 120mm target practice rounds as well as ten thousand rounds of tank ammunition worth nearly $100 million.

Included in the deal was the diamond ring that Menendez needed for the surprise proposal he planned while the couple was in India.[150]

But at one point Hana came close to blowing up the entire enterprise when he attempted to shortchange the couple on Arslanian's engagement ring. As part of the bribery scheme, Hana had been asked to use between $35,000 and $150,000 to buy the ring. Hana spent $12,000 on the ring, and used the rest of the cash to buy two watches, a bracelet, and a necklace for himself. He instructed the jeweler to write out a receipt for $35,000.

"The Hana associate also explained that Menendez knew that Hana shortchanged him with respect to the ring, and that Nadine Menendez (the 'gander') had taken the ring back to the jeweler and learned that it was worth less money," according to prosecutors. The "associate" was not named in court filings, and "gander" was a code name used for Nadine Arslanian.

"[Hana] was about to ruin things with Bob," a confidential source, who was in touch with Egyptian officials, told prosecutors. "Bob, who is starting to listen to us."

And he was also poised to finally remarry after nearly two decades as a bachelor following the divorce from his first wife.

"Bob told me I will know when I'm being proposed to because of a certain song he will sing when the time comes," said Arslanian in her interview with *The New York Times*. "I was very nervous because Bob is someone who sings all the time. He sings every morning, every night, and in between while he smokes his after-dinner cigar."

When Menendez began singing "Never Enough," from the film *The Greatest Showman*, in front of the Taj Mahal, Arslanian knew the time had come, and she began to cry.

"Will you marry me?" he said.

She said "yes" through her tears as Menendez struggled to put the engagement ring on her finger. "If you keep crying, I'm not going to be able to put this ring on your finger."

Two months later, Menendez found another way to declare his undying love for his fiancée when he finally passed a resolution to recognize the Armenian genocide, an important event for the Armenian community and for Arslanian's family, who lost thirteen "immediate members" of their family in the brutal Turkish attack that began in 1915 and left more than 1.5 million dead. The December 12, 2019, resolution came after three previous attempts.

"Menendez pushed to secure formal recognition in every session of Congress from 2006 to 2019, and in November 2019, Menendez took to the Senate floor every week to pursue adoption of the resolution," said a press release from the Senate Foreign Relations Committee.[151]

In a charcoal suit and a red-, white-, and blue-striped tie, Menendez stood on the Senate floor and outlined the horrors visited on the Armenian people by Ottoman forces who attacked them with "axes, shovels, and pitchforks" in 1915, smashed infants against rocks, and rounded up thousands of people in cattle cars. He described how US Ambassador Henry Morgenthau left his post in 1916 because the Ottoman Empire had become for him "a place of horror" when he was unable to do anything to stop the killing. And then Menendez stopped speaking, suddenly overcome with emotion. His final comments were barely audible, and he abruptly removed his microphone and left the lectern.

"To overlook human suffering is not who we are as a people," said Menendez, visibly emotional, in a speech on the Senate floor. "It is not what we stand for as a nation. We are better than that, and our foreign policy should always reflect this."

In a private message to his fiancée, Menendez wrote, "Truth, perseverance, and a commitment to a cause greater than yourself. In honor of your family and all who suffered. I hope your father was watching." He ended his text with "Never forget" written in Armenian script.

≈

Menendez, now a hero in the Armenian community, married Arslanian at an Armenian church in Queens on October 3, 2020. It was an "intimate and socially distanced" ceremony at the height of the COVID pandemic. The reception, with a small group of family and friends, was held outdoors. The bride wore a flowing white dress with an intricately beaded bodice and gauzy skirt, her blonde hair in a wispy chignon. She had two bouquets, the first of white roses and the second of white forget-me-nots, the national flower of Armenia, that became a memorial for the commemorations of the one-hundredth anniversary of the genocide in 2015. The flowers matched those in her new husband's boutonniere.

Steve Sandberg, a spokesman for Menendez, told an Armenian community newspaper that the couple bonded over "their shared interests of travel, love of family, pride for their respective heritage and ethnicity, and a mutual drive to improve access to quality health care and make lives better for the people of New Jersey." *The Armenian Mirror-Spectator* mentioned that the senator "has been prominent in efforts over many years to get the US government to officially recognize the Armenian Genocide."[152]

Meetings at high-end restaurants in New Jersey continued between the couple and Hana. In 2021, the Egyptians came to the group for help. Egyptian officials also called on their personal US senator—Hana referred to him as "our man" in correspondence with Egyptian officials—for advice in the summer of 2021 after reports emerged that Abbas Kamel, the chief of Egyptian intelligence, was going to face questions by the Senate Foreign Relations Committee about the country's role in the murder and dismemberment of Jamal Khashoggi. The Saudi journalist and *Washington Post* columnist was critical of Saudi Crown Prince Mohammed bin Salman. He was last seen on October 2, 2018, when he entered the Saudi consulate in Istanbul where he had gone to obtain documents for his upcoming wedding. Khashoggi was drugged and his body was reportedly dismembered and removed from the building. His remains have not been found. Before heading to Istanbul, the Saudi assassins, members of the notorious "Tiger Squad," flew to Cairo in a Gulfstream jet to pick up "illegal" drugs used to kill him. When he walked into the Saudi consulate, Khashoggi quickly realized what was going to happen and "tried to run away," according to secret notes obtained from Saudi prosecutors. He was forced to sit in a chair and was injected with the unknown drug the assassins had obtained in Egypt.

Two years later, a Saudi court jailed eight unidentified people for the murder, but human rights organizations and Khashoggi's fiancée were dissatisfied with the verdict, saying that the prisoners were not the only ones responsible for the grisly murder.

"The Saudi authorities are closing the case without the world knowing the truth of who is responsible for Jamal's murder," Hatice Cengiz wrote in a statement in 2020. "Who planned it, who ordered it, where is his body?"

By June 2021, human rights groups were also demanding answers. Democracy for the Arab World Now (DAWN), a nonprofit founded by Khashoggi shortly before he died, demanded a congressional investigation and wanted lawmakers to question Kamel while he was visiting the United States. Suddenly the Egyptians panicked. They needed help. They asked Arslanian to set up a meeting with Menendez in a hotel in Washington, DC, before his meeting with US senators the next

day. On the day of the meeting, Menendez provided Arslanian with
a copy of a news article reporting on questions that other US senators intended to ask the Egyptians about the murder of Khashoggi.
Arslanian, in turn, sent them the article. "I just thought it would be
better to know ahead of time what is being talked about and this way
you can prepare your rebuttals," she texted.

Menendez was among those who had been briefed by the CIA
about the murder in December 2018. At the time, he had demanded
that the United States take a hard line against the Saudis and blast
Saudi Crown Prince Mohammed bin Salman. After the Biden administration released an intelligence report on the murder in February
2021, Menendez blamed Trump for having covered it up.

"By ending Donald Trump's cover up of the murder of Jamal
Khashoggi, President Biden has demonstrated his commitment to
transparency and compliance with law," he said in a statement on
behalf of the Senate Foreign Relations Committee. "This was the only
appropriate first step, and I'm pleased that the Biden administration
has taken it. At the same time, I am hopeful it is only a first step
and that the administration plans to take concrete measures holding
Crown Prince Mohammed bin Salman personally responsible for his
role in this heinous crime."

Publicly, Menendez was on the side of justice—a crusader for
human rights. Privately, he was helping the Egyptians, who were
accessories to the crime. Two days after his private meeting with the
Egyptian intelligence official, Hana purchased twenty-two one-ounce
gold bars. Two of the bars were later found at the Englewood Cliffs
home Menendez shared with Arslanian.

Fred Daibes was also getting in on the action, asking his old friend Menendez to help get him out of a sticky criminal case and intervene on his behalf with a Qatari investment fund run by that country's royal family.

The prominent Edgewater developer and old friend of Menendez was counting on the senator to get him out of a fraud case involving Mariner's Bank where he was CEO and board chairman. Daibes was charged with sixteen counts of fraud, which were made public in 2018. He was accused of hatching a scheme to circumvent lending limits set by the bank in order to loan himself millions without the bank's knowledge.[153]

In 2020, Menendez called his friend Philip Sellinger to complain about Daibes's prosecution. At the time of the call, Sellinger was being considered for US attorney in New Jersey, and as a senior senator from the Garden State, Menendez was in a position to recommend candidates to the White House for federal appointments. Menendez tried to make the case to Sellinger that Daibes was being treated unfairly and asked him to look at his case "carefully" if he got the position. Sellinger informed Menendez he would be recused from Daibes's case because of a conflict of interest, which ultimately resulted in Menendez recommending another candidate for the job. Despite the senator's intervention, Sellinger went on to get the job, but was forbidden by the Department of Justice to handle the Daibes case. After Vikas Khanna, Sellinger's assistant, took over the case, he got a call from Menendez, ostensibly to praise Daibes's attorney.

In addition to his intervention with Sellinger, Menendez also went to bat for Daibes with the Qatari royal family. He had made numerous public statements supporting the government of Qatar. In one case, he sent Daibes a draft press release to present to his Qatari investors before it went public.

Menendez connected Daibes with Sheikh Sultan bin Jassim Al Thani, a member of the country's royal family, as well as Ali Al Thawed, the chief of staff of the emir's brother. The sheikh heads up the largest real estate development company in the tiny Gulf State, and is an important adviser on the emir's investments in the United States. When the sheikh's investment adviser did his due diligence and found out that Daibes had been accused of bank fraud in 2018, he urged the sheikh to seek out another partner. Menendez met with the sheikh and other officials, urging him to reconsider. "I hope that this will result in the favorable and mutually beneficial agreement that you both have been engaged in discussing," Menendez wrote to bin Jassim Al Thani in an encrypted WhatsApp message in January 2022.

To make sure that the Qataris were on his side, the senator introduced a resolution praising the country's humanitarian efforts to help house Afghan refugees after the United States pulled out of the country in August 2021.[154]

"You might want to send it to them," Menendez told Daibes. "I am just about to release."

Perhaps the Qataris were right to be worried about Daibes. The Palestinian American developer, who spent the first ten years of his life in a refugee camp, had gained "outsized power" and funneled cash to politicians in exchange for influence and contracts in his hometown of Edgewater, New Jersey, according to a state government report. Daibes arrived in New Jersey with his family from Lebanon in 1965 when he was eight years old. His father, Assad, set up an eponymous masonry company, which Daibes took over after his father died, transforming it into Daibes Enterprises in 1985 and expanding it into a sprawling group of companies.

"I didn't have much when my father passed," he told a New Jersey design magazine. "And in our culture, the oldest son is responsible. My mother didn't speak English, and I had siblings that were all younger than me. . . . I had to go out and work."[155]

The real estate mogul, who is fond of collecting sports cars, almost single-handedly developed a series of luxury high-rises creating Edgewater's "gold coast." Daibes's The Alexander, an ornate residential rental building featuring marble floors and faux Grecian statues in its carefully manicured gardens, is owned by the Egyptian government and was, at one point, home to Hana as well as other Egyptian government officials. In addition to a string of residential buildings, Daibes owned Le Jardin, a French restaurant boasting panoramic views of the Hudson River and the Manhattan skyline.

In May 2023, investigators with New Jersey's State Commission of Investigation (SCI) issued an extraordinary report about Fred Daibes—"a cautionary tale concerning the inherent dangers of enabling an influential, politically connected, and unelected private citizen to hold outsized power in government concerns."

The report disclosed that Daibes wrote personal checks for more than $100,000 to "the son and daughter of a high-ranking Genovese organized crime family member who was a key operative in an illegal gambling ring in northern New Jersey in the 2000s," then pleaded the Fifth Amendment when asked about them. Another Genovese associate, Richard Fischetti, lived rent-free in one of his apartment buildings for nine years and dined free at Daibes's restaurant. He was also married to a town council member, Duane Fischetti, whose son was the borough attorney, although Fischetti testified that the couple had lived separately for decades.

"The SCI found Daibes's power and influence within Edgewater were so strong he even held sway in local political decisions and other municipal concerns," said the May 2023 report. "The inquiry also revealed troubling findings related to Daibes's business operations, associates, and efforts to circumvent particular government regulations."[156]

But perhaps one of the most egregious parts of the report concerned Waterside Construction, a firm controlled by Daibes that won a $7.1 million city contract to clean up Veterans Field, a twenty-seven-acre waterfront park in Edgewater that had been closed since 2011 because of environmental contamination. Instead of cleaning it up, Daibes's firm contaminated the park even further, eventually costing the city nearly $30 million to rectify the situation. At first, another contractor let him take clean fill material from another construction site, but the report alleges that once that source dried up, Daibes's firm used contaminated fill instead, making the site more toxic than it was. Daibes said the fill his firm used was certified clean. As of early 2025, there was still litigation over the issue. When then-Mayor James Delaney, who had at first backed Daibes on the park project, moved to sue, the mayor's wife, Bridget, was fired from her job of fourteen years at Le Jardin.

"She told Commission counsel under oath that her family, including the couple's children, became outcasts in the community," according to the report. Daibes's attorney said she had quit and there was no revenge plot.

Despite his shady past, Daibes inked a $190 million deal with Heritage Advisors, a London-based investment concern founded by the sheikh in May 2022.

At about the same time that the deal went through with the Qatari firm, Daibes connected Bob and Nadine with a real estate agent in Tenafly, who began to schedule tours of luxury homes selling for more than $4 million in Alpine, a wealthy Bergen County enclave.[157] It's not clear if they had that kind of cash but perhaps they were expecting a big payday from Daibes and Hana, who had both continued to reward them with cash, gold bars, and even a recliner.

The senator felt so close to his Qatari benefactors that he thought nothing of asking them for free tickets[158] to Formula One's Miami Grand Prix—a three-day event—for his paramour's son and daughter-in-law. Menendez himself thanked the Qataris for the tickets.

"Thank you," the senator wrote in a text. "He is thrilled and so is his mother."

In the spring and summer of 2022, rumors swirled that Menendez was the subject of a federal bribery and corruption investigation. Between March and May of that year, Nadine Menendez headed to the nearby Edgewater Commons Shopping Center where she visited Vasken Khorozian, and cashed in four one-kilogram gold bars worth about $60,000 each, as well as four twenty-four-carat American Eagle coins worth $7,200. Khorozian, who had done business with Nadine in the past, didn't question her urgency for the cash, nor did he record the serial numbers of the bars that he was buying from her. Nadine said that the gold had been given to her by her family, and she needed to pay some bills. Khorozian sold the gold to a jeweler in New York's Diamond District where he had gotten his start in the jewelry business in 1979. The two gold merchants took a commission that added up to nearly $1,000 per bar of gold. Nadine didn't care that she was losing money, Khorozian later said. "You need money, you sell. You don't need, shut up and sit," he said.

A month after Menendez's communications with the Qataris, the FBI raided the couple's Englewood Cliffs property, carting out boxes of documents and items of suspicious monetary value. The search occurred on a Thursday morning while the Senate was in session. Later, Menendez complained that during that first search on June 16, 2022, federal agents "ransacked" his home, rifling through drawers, filing cabinets, and closets and left the couple's belongings scattered throughout the property.

"I was shocked to find my belongings and furniture in complete disarray," he said.

The night of that first search, prosecutors acquired a second search warrant to return to the house. "To obtain several of these search warrants, the government actively distorted the evidence and withheld key exculpatory information, misleading well-meaning magistrate judges into granting warrants that should never have been issued," Menendez's lawyers wrote.

But the protests fell on deaf ears. Between 2022 and the fall of 2023, federal agents returned three more times to search the house in Englewood Cliffs and Menendez's home in Washington, DC.

There were five federal raids of Menendez homes in New Jersey and Washington, DC, in total, between June 2022 and September 2023. His lawyers dismissed them as so much "exploratory rummaging," but federal agents hauled away an exercise machine—the One Vision Fitness Elliptical—a Blueair Air Purifier Classic 605, thirteen gold bars, a Mercedes convertible, and nearly $500,000 in cash.

Most of the cash was found in envelopes and plastic bags in a locked closet in the house, although agents also found cash stuffed into the pockets of coats and shoes. They found $5,350 stuffed in a right red shoe and $20,000 in cash in a left red shoe in the basement. They also found $7,000 in a left brown boot and $6,000 in cash in an envelope in a black leather jacket. Another jacket featuring a Congressional Hispanic Caucus logo had an envelope containing $4,300. The gold bars bore the imprint of Credit Suisse, Valcambi Suisse, and Asahi, among other stamps of gold refineries around the world. Some of the bars and envelopes contained the DNA and fingerprints of Daibes as well as his driver.

In a strange twist, agents traced four of the gold bars found at the Menendez home directly to Daibes.[159] In 2013, Daibes reported to police that he had been a victim of a vicious robbery at his home in the twenty-five-story St. Moritz (later renamed The Riello), one of the "gold coast" Edgewater residential developments that his company had built. On November 26, 2013, at just after 4:00 a.m., three masked men and a woman entered the developer's duplex penthouse, pulled him out of bed, and spent hours ransacking his apartment. During the robbery, Daibes's shoulder and ribs were broken.[160]

After the robbery, Daibes reported to police that twenty-two gold bars, worth $3 million, as well as diamonds, gemstones, and $500,000 in cash, were taken. The loot was eventually found in another apartment, and police determined that the whole thing had been "a classic inside job" planned by one of Daibes's most trusted employees.

To get his property back, Daibes signed releases, swearing that the gold bars belonged to him. "Each gold bar has its own serial number," Daibes said to investigators in a 2014 transcript made by prosecutors and police who recovered—and returned to Daibes—the stolen valuables. "They're all stamped . . . you'll never see two stamped the same way."

Years later, the FBI found some of those bars during their raids of the Menendez residence.

CHAPTER ELEVEN

Under the Bus

A few days after investigators raided his home, Menendez called Abbe Lowell, the super lawyer who had successfully defended him at his New Jersey corruption trial in 2017.

Lowell agreed to represent the senator during the investigation and asked for a confidential meeting with federal prosecutors to quash the case against his powerful client. He made an initial presentation in June 2023, a year after the first raid, and another presentation three months later.

Before each of his meetings with federal prosecutors, he discussed the potential charges with Menendez and made his legal arguments based on what the senator told him. Lowell lectured the prosecutors, who included US Attorney Damian Williams, for ninety minutes, meticulously going through slide after slide that purported to show legitimate legal transactions. Normally, during such a meeting, prosecutors would engage with the defense attorney, asking questions, seeking clarifications. This particular meeting was notable for the uncomfortable silence that pervaded the conference room, according to Geoffrey Mearns, a paralegal who recorded the proceedings. Prosecutors sat stone-faced, and the great white-collar criminal defense attorney appeared more than a little bit flustered.

"Can you tell us more about what you are thinking, where your heads are at, so we can do a better job of explaining where we're at?" said Lowell, according to Mearns's memo of the meeting. The memo went on to say that Lowell realized that prosecutors "were not going to be asking many questions or show their hand."

The tone shifted, and Lowell seemed unhappy, "trying to convince" the prosecutors to give him more information.

But the problem Lowell had was not so much a team of prosecutors who were refusing to play ball with him, but an angry group of legal professionals who felt he was lying to them.

It soon became clear to Lowell that there was no room for negotiation. These federal prosecutors meant business and were determined to send his client to prison. On top of that, Menendez hadn't been entirely honest with Lowell. He told his attorney that the mortgage and car payments made to his wife by Hana and Uribe were loans, and that he only became aware of them after the investigation against him and his wife began. In the indictment, the prosecutors said that the senator "well knew" that those payments were bribes.

Eleven days after the PowerPoint presentation, the indictment was unsealed. Menendez, his wife, Wael Hana, Jose Uribe, and Fred Daibes were charged with bribery and corruption as well as conspiring to act as foreign agents of the Egyptian government. Later, prosecutors also charged the group with conspiring to work as foreign agents of Qatar. They each faced more than twenty years in prison, and all of them initially pleaded not guilty.

The case was mired in legal complexities from the start. Not only did Menendez begin preparing his defense, he launched a legal defense fund, encouraging his donors to help pay his legal costs. By the time he got through with his trial, which would go on for nine weeks, Menendez's campaign and legal defense fund shelled out almost $9 million on lawyers, nearly double the $5.16 million that they jointly spent on his 2017 corruption trial.[161]

Early on, in November 2023, Lowell's firm, Winston & Strawn, asked Judge Stein to allow them to withdraw from the case. No explanation was given, but months later when Stein allowed prosecutors to use Lowell's PowerPoint presentation as evidence, it became clear that the firm couldn't represent Menendez because he had lied to Lowell, causing Lowell to lie to prosecutors.

In March 2024, Menendez and his wife were each charged with three counts of obstruction of justice in a superseding indictment, for characterizing the bribes they received from Hana and Uribe as "loan payments." On the eve of the federal raids, Menendez wrote a $23,000 check to Nadine "for car payments," but when Nadine exchanged that cash for a $21,000 check to Uribe, she noted that it was a "personal loan" in the memo field.

"Menendez and Nadine Menendez wrote checks and letters falsely characterizing the return of bribe money to Wael Hana . . . and Jose Uribe as repayments for loans," the new indictment said. It also said the couple "caused their counsel to make statements regarding the bribe money from Hana and Uribe," which they "knew were false, in an effort to interfere with an investigation." Although the indictment did not name the lawyers involved, in Menendez's case he was represented by Lowell during June, August, and September 2023—the period specified by the indictment. Lowell was not charged or accused of any wrongdoing.

Nadine Menendez had a separate team of lawyers, and they also withdrew from the case shortly after Lowell's departure. Nadine's four attorneys filed a motion to withdraw when prosecutors told the judge that they would call David Schertler, one of her lawyers, as a witness. Just as Lowell had to recuse himself from Menendez's case because he could be called as a witness, Nadine's lawyers were also forced to recuse themselves over this conflict of interest. They had passed on lies that their client had given them to the prosecutors in her case, causing an obstruction of justice. In a hearing, Stein informed Nadine that her lawyers could be disqualified by the court from representing her if they were deemed to have a conflict of interest.

Menendez next hired the Paul Hastings law firm. His new team of criminal lawyers included Washington-based attorney Robert Luskin. Ironically, Luskin had once accepted his $500,000 legal payment with forty-five gold bars while appealing the 1993 conviction of Stephen Saccoccia, a Rhode Island precious metals dealer who was convicted of laundering money for Colombian drug cartels.[162] Saccoccia was slapped with a 660-year prison sentence, while in 1998 Luskin agreed to forfeit $245,000 in his fees to settle a case brought by federal prosecutors against him.

Luskin had also represented Lance Armstrong in the disgraced cyclist's doping case, as well as a host of Washington insiders, including political consultant Karl Rove and Mark Middleton, a former aide to President Bill Clinton with ties to billionaire pedophile Jeffrey Epstein. Middleton committed suicide at his home in Arkansas in 2023.

The other lawyers on Menendez's team were Adam Fee and Avi Weitzman, who had represented former New Jersey Governor Chris Christie during an independent investigation of the infamous Bridgegate affair (also known as the Fort Lee lane closure scandal). The scandal, which took place between 2013 and 2014, saw some of Christie's aides create traffic jams in Fort Lee, a New Jersey borough across the George Washington Bridge from Manhattan, by shutting down traffic lanes as revenge against the city's Democratic mayor, Mark Sokolich, who did not support Christie as a candidate for governor in the state's 2013 gubernatorial race.

As Menendez assembled his new legal team, he also declared that he would not run for reelection as a Democrat in the 2024 race. In a one-minute video posted on social media, he said he would resign.

"I am hopeful that my exoneration will take place this summer and allow me to pursue my candidacy as an independent Democrat in the general election," he said.

The senator was likely bowing to pressure from his own party, which had largely distanced itself from the corruption trial. Polls showed that he was almost certain to lose in a primary race against congressional Representative Andy Kim and Tammy Murphy, the wife of New Jersey Governor Phil Murphy.

Still, many Democrats feared that if he did run as an independent he would take votes away from the Democratic candidate in a close race and help usher in a Republican victory, upsetting the tenuous balance in the upper chamber.

More than likely, his insistence on staying in the race had more to do with raising funds for the legal defense for him and his wife than anything else. Menendez had already spent more than $2.6 million on attorneys from his campaign and legal defense fund combined since the indictment was unsealed. And the case had not yet even gone to trial.

The first order of business for Menendez's new legal team was to separate Menendez's case from that of his wife. There was no advantage to trying them together, and every advantage for Menendez to secure a separate trial, largely so he could blame everything on his wife. The couple had not even been legally married when most of the bribes took place, the defense attorneys said.

At first, prosecutors fought against the split, noting that they would essentially be trying the same case twice, recalling "dozens of witnesses," and picking a new jury. But when Nadine's lawyers informed the court that she was suffering from a "serious medical condition that will require a surgical procedure in the next four to six weeks as well as possibly significant follow-up and recovery treatment," the judge ruled in favor of the split. Menendez later announced that his wife was battling breast cancer. Nadine Menendez's case would be delayed for months while she received treatment.

For some of Nadine's friends, the split was unconscionable, especially after her diagnosis was revealed. "How can he just throw his wife under the bus like that?" said Pat Dori. "She's naive and vulnerable and now she has cancer. It's just completely wrong."[163]

The defense didn't care, and likely neither did Menendez. His only goal was proving his innocence so that he could hold on to his political power, and he wasn't about to let anything, including his new wife, stand in his way.

Opening arguments began on a rainy day in May 2024. A few camera crews had set up outside the Daniel Patrick Moynihan Courthouse on Pearl Street in Lower Manhattan, but it was hardly the media presence one might expect for the historic trial of one of the most powerful elected officials in the country.

Menendez had competition. Less than five hundred feet away, dozens of reporters and camera crews crowded the sidewalk across the street from the Manhattan Criminal Court for another historic trial—the *People of the State of New York v. Donald J. Trump*. The former president had been charged with thirty-four felony counts of falsifying business records to conceal hush money payments to porn actress Stormy Daniels. Manhattan District Attorney Alvin Bragg had also charged Trump with falsifying the records in order to commit other crimes, including tax fraud, violating campaign finance rules, and unlawfully influencing the 2016 presidential election. The indictment was the first against a former president.

Outside the courthouse, Trump regularly denounced the proceedings against him while a steady stream of both supporters and protestors tried to drown each other out in demonstrations. Supporters waved US flags and held up signs emblazoned with images of the former president and the message "Never Surrender" while protestors chanted "No one is above the law" and waved signs that read, "Slept with a porn star, screwed voters."

Among Trump's defenders outside the courthouse was Andrew Giuliani, the son of former New York Mayor Rudy Giuliani. When a reporter asked him about the other high-profile trial going on nearby, he seemed momentarily confused. "Oh yes, of course," he said. "Forgot about that."[164]

Perhaps Menendez welcomed the lack of intense press attention. Unlike Trump, who regularly disrupted the proceedings during his trial, rolling his eyes and making comments under his breath, Menendez sat in quiet attention in the courtroom. He often made his way into the courthouse without an entourage and without a gaggle of reporters waiting outside to shout questions. The only clue that he was on his way through the main doors came from the court officers manning the security scanners at the entrance. "Menendez just arrived" was the only alert that the marshals needed to guide the senator through the metal detectors.

As his own trial began, Menendez continued to vehemently declare his innocence and refuse to resign his Senate seat, although he did step down from the chairmanship of the Senate Foreign Relations Committee on September 22, the same day that charges against him were announced. The move was viewed as temporary, "until the matter has been solved," said Senate Majority Leader Chuck Schumer. Menendez was allowed to remain on the committee.

To address the large amounts of cash that were found in his home, Menendez's legal defense fund paid more than $4,000 to hire a Manhattan forensic psychiatrist as an expert witness who he hoped would testify that he suffered from "intergenerational trauma" with respect to stashing cash at his home and related to his father's suicide, which took place after Menendez stopped paying his gambling debts.

But Menendez could not get the expert's testimony, and so the defense attorneys argued that the senator's personal health information should have been redacted from the prosecution's filing, because it included "deeply private and sensitive details about Senator

Menendez's personal history and mental health diagnosis." Menendez didn't want his personal medical history to be used against him by prosecutors, who would likely use it in the worst light possible. He wanted his expert to frame his mental health issues in a way that could benefit his defense.

At a press conference shortly after the charges were announced, Menendez would go on to confess that as a result of the "confiscation" of his parents' assets in Cuba, he developed the habit of storing cash at home.

"For thirty years I have withdrawn thousands of dollars in cash from my personal savings account, which I have kept for emergencies because of the history of my family facing confiscation in Cuba," he said at a news conference shortly after the indictments against him and his wife were unsealed. "This may seem old fashioned, but these were monies drawn from my personal savings account based on the income that I have lawfully derived over those thirty years."

But Menendez was again playing with the facts and leading people to believe that the family had been political refugees fleeing the 1959 revolution led by Fidel Castro, whose government seized their assets before allowing them to leave. In fact, Menendez's mother, father, and two older siblings had already been in the United States for years before the revolution.

The bank withdrawal excuse would later blow up in his face when prosecutors demonstrated that some of the cash was wrapped in bands that showed it had been taken out in $10,000 increments at a bank where the Menendezes "had no known depository account."

Still, during the trial, defense attorneys drilled down on the Cuba confiscation excuse, making it a key part of his criminal defense to explain why federal agents found nearly $500,000 in cash when they raided his Englewood Cliffs home in June 2022. The defense attorneys put Menendez's sister, Caridad, on the stand to elaborate on the family custom of storing cash at home. Their mother, Evangelina, stored cash in the doorframe of a closet, Caridad said in her testimony. Their father, Mario, kept cash in a shoebox that he stored on a shelf in a closet, she added.

Gonzalez said that in the 1980s, when she worked in her brother's law office, he asked her to retrieve cash that he kept in a shoebox.

"It was a Cuban thing," said Caridad Gonzalez, describing a habit of storing cash at home that her brother had developed from childhood.[165]

"Daddy always said, 'Don't trust the banks,'" continued Gonzalez. "If you trust the banks, you never know what can happen, so you must always have money at home. And this was something, so to speak, that they say to you and say it to you so many times that it's—it sort of forms a law inside of you."

Menendez also had a ready excuse for the gold bars. They were customary gifts in Middle Eastern cultures, his defense attorneys argued. Attorney Larry Lustberg, who represented Hana, said that Hana had given his friend Nadine the bars in recognition of their fifteen years of friendship.

"Will's gifts got nicer as his business succeeded," Lustberg said.

Later, Nadine's younger sister, Katia Tabourian, testified that the thirteen gold bars and jewels the FBI found at the couple's house were consistent with traditional Lebanese family gifts. Tabourian said that her parents had left the sisters an inheritance in gold, which she also said belonged only to Nadine. The bedroom closet at the Englewood Cliffs home that Nadine shared with her husband was kept locked, she said, because a nanny had stolen from her sister years before.

≈

The most sensational part of the trial took place when the prosecution's star witness took the stand. In February 2024, several weeks before the trial was set to begin, Jose Uribe flipped for the prosecution, further complicating the case. Although he still faced seven charges for bribery, fraud, and tax evasion, the plea deal would likely help him secure a more lenient sentence from Judge Stein.

A day before Uribe took the stand in June, prosecutors questioned Gurbir Grewal, New Jersey's former attorney general, whom Menendez contacted after the backyard meeting with Uribe to press his case, which included having a state probe against his associate Elvis Parra thrown out. Parra, who owned a trucking company, was scheduled to stand trial for insurance fraud in New Jersey. His case was linked to Phoenix Risk Management, an Uribe-controlled brokerage, which had secured insurance for Parra's company.

Menendez summoned Grewal to his Newark office, Grewal said, adding that he thought the meeting was about policy issues such as reducing the number of opioid deaths in New Jersey and stemming gun violence. When Menendez began speaking about the investigation, Grewal testified that he immediately cut him off. He said he told the senator to have the accused's defense attorney speak directly to the judge or the prosecutors in the case. The meeting ended minutes later, Grewal said.

"I didn't know the case. I didn't want to know the case," Grewal testified. "It's not something I was comfortable speaking to him about."

Grewal said that he didn't know the name of the defendant that Menendez needed help with. He never asked him the name and did not speak to anyone in his office about what he called the senator's "unprecedented request," he told the court, adding that Menendez was polite during the short meeting and made no "explicit ask."

"What I understood the upshot of this conversation to be was that he didn't like how this matter was being handled by our office and wanted it handled differently," Grewal said.

Still, Grewal told the court that he was careful with what he said to Menendez, concerned about being on the senator's "bad side." Menendez was close to New Jersey Governor Phil Murphy, whose office provided half of the attorney general's $1 billion budget.

The next day, Judge Stein's twenty-third floor courtroom was packed when Uribe took the stand, providing bombshell details about bribes paid to the senator. In more than two and a half hours of testimony, the failed insurance executive and divorced father of four described his struggles as an immigrant from the Dominican Republic and how he built a successful family business specializing in insurance for transportation firms. He described how he met Wael Hana in 2007, when he provided insurance for the short-lived trucking company he ran at the time.

The bribery scheme began in 2018 when Hana overheard Uribe speaking to his attorney about Parra's case and the subpoenas he had received as the widening state investigation threatened his own company.

He also described in detail the first private meeting he had with the senator in the backyard of his Englewood Cliffs home over glasses of Grand Marnier and imported cigars.

In addition to admitting that he had provided the senator's wife with a 2019 Mercedes-Benz C 300 convertible, he also admitted to organizing a fundraiser for Menendez's reelection campaign in the summer of 2018. He raised $50,000 and contributed $5,000 of his own money.

"I wanted to be in the good graces of the senator because it was my best avenue at this point," he told the court, referring to enlisting the senator to stop the New Jersey investigation into his insurance company.

"I agree[d] . . . to provide a car to Nadine to get the power and influence of Senator Menendez, for positive resolution for a colleague, and to stop and kill investigations," Uribe said in testimony at Menendez's trial.

Menendez's defense counsel tried to portray Uribe as "a sophisticated liar" who had repeatedly ripped off his customers. They also tried unsuccessfully to introduce evidence that he was a deadbeat dad who had skipped out on child support payments, frequented strip clubs, and struggled with credit card debt. Defense attorneys also emphasized Uribe's past crimes, including insurance fraud, for which he had pled guilty.

"So, you would agree that you have been committing frauds and other crimes for at least the last thirteen years, correct?" Fee asked him.

Uribe answered, "Yes."

≈

But the jury believed everything Uribe had said about Menendez and his wife. After the nine-week trial, which included thirty witnesses and three thousand exhibits, including the gold bars that the jurors held in their hands, the deliberations took three days. The jury convicted Menendez of all sixteen counts. Hana was convicted of giving Nadine Menendez a no-show job and paying her mortgage in exchange for the senator's help with his halal monopoly. Daibes was also convicted of providing envelopes stuffed with cash and at least two one-kilo gold bars in exchange for helping him secure funding for an Edgewater development project from the Qatari royal family and intervening to stop a federal bank fraud case against him.

For Damian Williams, the first black US attorney in the history of Manhattan's Southern District, the Menendez case was a triumph. His team had already secured convictions in some of the court's biggest cases under his tenure, including the successful prosecution of cryptocurrency wunderkind Sam Bankman-Fried, who was sentenced to twenty-five years in prison on multiple fraud charges in 2024. But the Menendez case was a huge victory, especially because prosecutors in New Jersey had failed to achieve a conviction at his 2017 trial.

"This case has always been about shocking levels of corruption—hundreds of thousands of dollars in bribes in the form of cash, gold bars, a Mercedes-Benz," said Williams in an impromptu press conference outside the courthouse immediately following the conviction. "This wasn't politics as usual. This was politics for profit. Now that a jury has convicted Bob Menendez, his years of selling his office to the highest bidder have finally come to an end."

"Gold Bar Bob"

D ays before his sentencing, Menendez's attorneys filed nearly four hundred pages of documents that included letters from more than 130 people, extolling his sacrifice and exemplary public service in a political career that spanned more than fifty years. There were letters from his high school buddies, including convicted drug dealer Manny Diaz, Donald Scarinci, and Abraham Antun, as well as letters from the relatives of the young children he had helped by using his Senate office to secure visas for lifesaving medical care in the United States.

A handwritten letter to the judge from his father-in-law, Darius Tabourian, praised him for his "integrity and commitment," thanking him for pushing the Senate to recognize the Armenian genocide in which he'd lost several family members.

"There was nothing more that I wanted to see at the age of ninety-four before I die than the recognition of the Armenian genocide and the remembrance of my grandparents' lives and those of 1.5 million Armenians who were slaughtered," Tabourian wrote.

In a curious letter to Judge Stein, Menendez's daughter spoke of how, during the "darkest days of his own life, he has navigated his wife's breast cancer diagnosis with a type of grace and forgiveness I honestly do not understand, but admire."

Perhaps the "forgiveness" was meant to evoke the defensive tactic Menendez took at his own trial, which amounted to blaming most of his wrongdoing on his ailing wife. Through his lawyers, Menendez blamed his wife, saying that Hana and others involved in the bribes were friends of hers, not his. Nadine never publicly responded to the allegations. Friends said that as soon as she was indicted in the fall of 2023, she stopped communicating with them and changed her cell phone number.

But Alicia Menendez was the only letter writer who even mentioned Nadine Menendez's illness. Letters from Nadine's family, including her sister, brother-in-law, and young nephew, only spoke of Menendez's greatness and current state of humiliation. "It kills me that the outcome has destroyed his life," said Katia Tabourian, Nadine's sister, who goes on to describe the consternation of her young son who now googles his beloved Uncle Bob and finds only stories of "how bad of a human being he is."

Also missing from the numerous letters are missives from his political supporters, including Bill and Hillary Clinton and Joe Biden, who had served with him in the Senate. There was no letter from Pedro Pablo Permuy, his devoted former staffer who had made great strides in the Caribbean with the former senator's help. No doubt, they wanted to stay as far away as possible from a convicted felon—the first sitting member of Congress to be convicted of conspiracy to act as a foreign agent in US history.

Menendez's legal team had hoped that the letters of support would show that the good Menendez did during his more than half century as a lawmaker would outweigh his corruption. In voluminous court papers, the legal team had fought against the prosecution's request to sentence Menendez to at least fifteen years in prison, a punishment prosecutors said would fit the egregious crimes he was convicted of and act as a deterrent to other elected officials about engaging in public corruption. Menendez's defense team argued that he should be sentenced to only two years in prison, and even floated the idea of having their client engage in community service rather than being locked up in a federal jail. He was seventy-one, after all, and devoted to his four grandchildren, they argued.

But by the time they took their places in Judge Stein's courtroom on a blustery day in January 2025, defense attorneys quickly changed their tune. They saw that the judge wasn't likely to let their client off lightly after sentencing his codefendants Fred Daibes and Wael Hana to seven years and eight years in prison, respectively. The judge also ordered Daibes to fork over $1.75 million in fines. Hana's fine stood at $1.3 million.

Now Adam Fee, Menendez's attorney, asked the judge to sentence Menendez to no more than eight years in prison. "Bob is not a typical defendant," Fee told Judge Stein. "He is unique because of his good work."

To drive home the point, the defense quoted from letters thanking the senator for saving the lives of their loved ones.

In 2011, Menendez was instrumental in obtaining a humanitarian visa for the seven-year-old Salvadoran sister of Yarelis Bonilla, a five-year-old New Jersey girl who needed a bone marrow transplant for her leukemia treatment. Gisselle Bonilla Ramirez, who had been denied entry by the State Department on her first try, managed to obtain a humanitarian visa with Menendez's help after her family appealed to the senator. The sisters had never met each other until Gisselle arrived in the United States to help her sister.

"I remember him saying he would do everything in his power to . . . save Yarelis's life," said Gertrudis Ramirez, the girls' grandfather. "It is the reason that my entire family will continue to support Bob Menendez."[166]

Six years after helping Yarelis Bonilla, Menendez stepped in to obtain a visa for the mother of a New Jersey woman who needed a kidney transplant. In 2017, after the State Department had repeatedly refused a visa for Nina Saria's mother to travel from her home in Georgia to save her daughter by donating a kidney, Menendez helped the family qualify for "humanitarian parole," which allows foreigners to travel to the United States for a short period to address "a compelling emergency."

"No other government representative in New Jersey would even just hear my story or how their involvement would make a difference," said Nina Saria.[167]

In addition, Menendez has been a longtime advocate for immigration reform, and spearheaded legislation to provide relief for 9/11 families who were previously excluded from a federal fund for victims of terrorism. He advocated for often ignored minority groups, authoring legislation that no other member of Congress with his stature would ever consider touching as a matter of American foreign policy.

Like Katia Tabourian, Fee seemed to suggest that because his client had already been "ridiculed and shamed publicly" during the trial that he should not have to serve a lengthy sentence. "Despite his record of service, he is now known more widely as 'gold bar Bob,'" Fee told the crowded courtroom echoing a letter from Alicia in which she said her father had "been reduced to a punchline about gold bars."

The prosecution, led by Paul Monteleoni, continued to argue for a fifteen-year sentence. Although he had been barred from bringing up the previous corruption charges that had ended in a hung jury in 2017 into the most recent case, Monteleoni did note that Menendez had been publicly admonished by his fellow senators and the Senate Ethics Committee in 2018. "He also brought shame to the Senate years before he even began this scheme," said Monteleoni. As Monteleoni made clear, the offenses committed by Menendez this time around were even more "extraordinary" and "a truly grave breach" of the trust of his fellow senators, his constituents, and the people of the United States whom he had promised to serve. They were also historic. Menendez was the first senator in US history to abuse the sovereign power of the United States. He conspired to use the power invested in him as chairman of one of the most powerful committees in Congress to work for foreign governments. He acted as a foreign agent for Egypt, helping their intelligence chief respond to pointed questions from his fellow senators about their role in the murder and dismemberment of a journalist. He used his power to ghostwrite letters for Egyptian authorities eager to obtain hundreds of millions in US weapons despite the fact that the Middle Eastern country had been globally condemned for human rights violations and had used those weapons against foreign tourists, including an American citizen. In addition, Menendez helped his developer friend Fred Daibes to secure investments worth tens of millions from a company connected to the royal family of Qatar to develop property in New Jersey. In exchange, he was rewarded with gold bullion and hundreds of thousands in cash.

"He believed that the power he wielded belonged to him," Monteleoni continued. "It belongs to the people."

Menendez stood at the defense table behind a large box of Kleenex, which one of his lawyers had placed there, anticipating the sobs that would accompany the former senator's pleas for mercy from Judge Stein.

"Your honor, you have before you a chastened man," Menendez said, stopping a few times to compose himself as he outlined the work he had done on behalf of his constituents. "I have dedicated my entire life to the service of others. I am far from a perfect man, but I believe in my half-century of public service, I have done more good than bad."

Perhaps Judge Stein was moved by the elderly former pol's plight when he sentenced him to eleven years in prison, because he disposed with charging him a hefty fine, largely because he knew that Menendez didn't have the cash to pay it. Following his conviction, Menendez faced financial ruin. In addition, he would be forced to forfeit to the court nearly $1 million in cash and gold bars that he received as part of the corruption scheme.

"Somewhere along the way, you became, I'm sorry to say, a corrupt politician," Stein told Menendez. "You stood at the apex of our political system. Somewhere along the way, I don't know where it was, you lost your way, and working for the public good became working for your good."

But remorse may not be Menendez's strong suit. Shortly after the sentencing hearing, Menendez was back to his old combative self, addressing a group of journalists outside the federal courthouse in Lower Manhattan, insisting that he is innocent, that he will surely appeal his conviction, and calling his prosecution "a witch hunt." It's not clear what he meant since the prosecution was conducted by a team under the command of crusading US Attorney Damian Williams, a Biden appointee and, like Menendez, a member of the Democratic Party.

Still, he attacked Williams and the Southern District of New York, "the Wild West of political prosecutors."

"President Trump is right," he continued. "This process is political and has been corrupted to the core. I hope President Trump cleans up the cesspool and restores integrity to the system."

Was he invoking Trump to seek a pardon?

His attorneys and moneyed supporters had tried repeatedly to obtain a pardon from Biden before he left office in January 2025. Although Biden controversially pardoned members of his own family and thousands of others before leaving office, he seemed to have nothing to gain in helping Menendez.

Which is why Menendez was playing all sides. Months after his conviction, sources said that the former senator was seeking a pardon from Donald Trump, who had pardoned Menendez's old friend Salomon Melgen in 2021, following pleas from a handful of Bay of Pigs veterans, former patients, and Menendez himself. Menendez admitted that he had played a small part in seeking the pardon for Melgen but had had "no expectation that [Trump] would act," he said in a statement.

"I don't pretend to know what motivates President Trump to act, but I am pretty sure it's not me," Menendez said after Melgen was granted the pardon.

In another X post, Menendez praised Trump for his position on Iran, no doubt in an effort to appeal to the pro-Israel lobby and the American Israel Public Affairs Committee (AIPAC), a powerful benefactor in the past. "I applaud President Trump for working to insure Iran does not obtain a nuclear weapon," he posted in April 2025. "It would negatively change the entire paradigm of the Middle East and would be an existential threat to Israel."

Trump is not likely to act for Menendez. During Trump's first term in office, Menendez repeatedly said he was "unfit" to rule. He voted twice to impeach him, and even went against Donald Trump Jr. when he sought to do business in India during his father's first term in office.

"Not once did I hear the president's team make a compelling defense," said Menendez in a statement entered into the Senate record after the first impeachment vote in December 2019. "I heard a damning case from the House managers. A case that laid out, in sobering detail, how the president of the United States subverted our national security interests and solicited interference from a foreign power for his own personal political benefit."

And then a week before Trump's first term ended, Menendez slammed his Republican colleagues in the Senate for their "political cowardice" in refusing to impeach Trump and bar him from ever holding elected office in response to the January 6, 2021, attack on the US Capitol by his supporters.

"In private, they complain about feeling trapped by President Trump's poisonous grip on the Republican Party and yet refused to free themselves by voting to bar him from running for future office," Menendez said in a statement after the vote. "This is pure political cowardice and I fear their refusal to hold Donald Trump accountable will have lasting negative and even dangerous consequences for the future of our country."

Whether Trump agreed to pardon Menendez or commute his sentence would have no effect on his ability to secure his federal pension. Following his conviction in July 2024, Menendez resigned from the

Senate although he continued to receive his federal pension, which, considering his years in both the House and Senate, could be worth up to $300,000. He continues to receive $1,066 per month in a pension from New Jersey, but the state's attorney general has been in talks to pull the cash and seek a court order to bar Menendez from ever holding public office in the state following his conviction.

A tough new law, the No Corruption Act—which was signed shortly before Biden left office—cuts off pension payments upon the initial finding of guilt, with the pension restored only if an appeals court overturns the conviction.

"A presidential pardon is not enough to restore a lawmaker's pension," the law says.

The bipartisan legislation, which was introduced by Nevada Senator Jacky Rosen and her Florida counterpart Rick Scott, seemed tailor-made for Menendez. It was introduced in the House in 2023 just as Menendez, his wife, and three other defendants were indicted for corruption and bribery, but was signed into law in December 2024, five months after Menendez was convicted.

"If you are a member of Congress and convicted of a crime involving public corruption you should lose all pension benefits provided to you by taxpayers and hardworking families, period," said Scott after the act was signed by Biden and became law.

Still, for perhaps the first time in his political life, the cards seemed stacked against Menendez, although longtime observers of his career found it difficult to believe that he was actually on his way to prison.

"He has weaseled his way out of everything. I'm shocked that the weasel doesn't have another way out, and I just can't believe he's finally going to prison," said Paul Mulshine. The longtime columnist worked at the storied *Star-Ledger* until its owners pulled the plug in February 2025, effectively leaving Hudson County, a bastion of political corruption that spawned William Musto and his protégé Menendez, without a newspaper.

"I keep waiting for him [Menendez] to pull something else," Mulshine continued.

But Bob Menendez would need a miracle to pull himself out of the hole he has dug.

Without cash coming into his campaign and legal defense fund, how will he afford to appeal his conviction, which he has promised to do, if he is financially ruined? And how will he pay for his wife's ongoing legal expenses?

≈

Nadine Menendez arrived at the courthouse alone, a frumpy shadow of the statuesque blonde bombshell. On most days, she wore a black ski jacket, dark glasses, her hair pulled back in a scruffy ponytail and a pink mask decorated with Breast Cancer Awareness ribbons hiding her mouth and nose. It was a visual reminder for the jury of the health struggles that had delayed her trial. In the early days of the trial, she clutched a legal notepad and handbag to her chest like a protective shield as she entered Judge Stein's twenty-third-floor courtroom and took her seat next to her legal team.

"They were partners in crime, partners in corruption, and partners in greed," Assistant US Attorney Laura Pomerantz told the court in the prosecution's nearly hour-long opening arguments. "She did the dirty work."

But in court, at least, her partner was visibly absent. Nadine Menendez was very much alone. Bob Menendez was listed as a defense witness in her case, and was conveniently barred from accompanying her to trial.

"Robert Menendez: If we call him, would testify about every aspect of the indictment as it relates to his wife, as well as his relationship with her and her character and reputation for truthfulness," defense attorneys said. Fred Daibes and Wael Hana were also listed as witnesses for the defense.

Though the disgraced senator wasn't in the courtroom, he was there in spirit and via social media where he continued to appeal to Donald Trump and slam the Southern District of New York.

"My wife, who had breast cancer reconstructive surgery just days ago, is being forced by the government to go to trial tomorrow. Only the arrogance of the SDNY can be so cruel and inhumane. They should let her fully recover! @realDonaldTrump," he posted on his X account in the early days of the trial, still describing himself as "senator."

Once again, Jose Uribe was the prosecution's star witness, and under cross-examination Nadine's attorney Barry Coburn used the text messages between them to insinuate that Uribe was in love with Nadine when he showered her with cash and paid for her Mercedes.

"You said to her, 'I want to be your slave'?" Cobum asked Uribe.

"Sitting here today, I don't have a recollection of saying that to Nadine," Uribe said.

Coburn attempted to show Nadine as a naive divorcée, an innocent woman pursued endlessly by a group of criminals who constantly showered her with lavish dinners and gifts to win her affection.

But Uribe's testimony was interrupted when Nadine called in sick, delaying the trial by yet another week.

During the break in court proceedings, Menendez went back to social media to express his disdain and gain sympathy for his wife. "This is the second time in one week that my wife Nadine's trial had to be postponed because of her physical pain and illness," Menendez posted on X. "As I said previously, the Prosecution should have never rushed her to trial after her breast cancer operations. This is not Justice!"

Nadine's trial seemed to prove Menendez was using it as another opportunity to game the system to avoid having to serve prison time for as long as possible. Not only did he convince Judge Stein to delay his prison date so that he could support his cancer-stricken wife, he also managed to get a delay to attend his stepdaughter's wedding in June 2025. In the end, Nadine was convicted on all fifteen bribery counts. Her defense lasted only one day with her sister, Katia Tabourian, as the most significant character witness. The aim seemed to be to gain as much sympathy as possible with the jury—a strategy that ultimately failed.

—

"What is past is prologue" from William Shakespeare's *The Tempest* has been a favorite quote of Menendez's since his time in high school. He used it in his lofty yearbook messages about working for a just future, and he began his 2009 book with the quote from the play. In *Growing American Roots*, he wrote about how as a US senator he was fond of walking from his Senate office down Pennsylvania Avenue to the National Archives building, which houses the country's most sacred documents—the Declaration of Independence, the Constitution, and the Bill of Rights. He often stopped to contemplate his favorite sculpture: the massive image of a young woman holding an open book, carved from a piece of Indiana limestone that sits outside the building. It's called "The Future" and features the dramatic line from Shakespeare inscribed on its pedestal.

"We are products of our history," wrote Menendez in the introduction.

The notion that the past shapes our future actions is an apt metaphor for Menendez's entire life. The "scrappy" son of Cuban immigrants may have become the first in his family to go to college and worked hard to reach the pinnacle of power in the US Senate, but he was also a creature of a different set of circumstances. He came of age in a culture of machine politics and bossism in Union City, and he learned everything from his powerful mentor, William Musto. Like Musto, Menendez was beloved for finding jobs for his supporters, for helping new immigrants navigate government services, for helping them obtain health care and other rights. And like Musto, he was convicted of corruption.

Yet, to this day, there are homages to Musto in Union City. In 2011, the local library was renamed the William V. Musto Cultural Center. It houses three museums, an art gallery, and a concert space.

"I don't know of a better person that this could be named for," said Union City Mayor Brian Stack, who admired Musto so much that he attended every day of his corruption trial in Newark federal court, and wrote him letters in prison when he was a teenager in the early 1980s. "No one has done more for this city than William Vincent Musto."

It's a testament to Musto's sheer charisma that the article about the opening of the eponymous community center makes no mention of his corruption trial, conviction, or imprisonment. "I don't think that I've seen a man more dedicated and who cares more about people, the city, the community, and even the state," said former US Congressman Frank Guarini, who was first elected in 1978. "He was a wonderful man, I love Bill Musto."

Menendez is not so lucky. An elementary school named for him in West New York in 2013 abruptly changed its name after his conviction in 2024.[168]

Just where did he go wrong?

Like his mentor, he became mayor of Union City, a powerful position he continued to hold when he was elected to the state assembly and the New Jersey State Senate, following closely in Musto's footsteps before launching his career in national politics.

But along the way, he betrayed the boss, using his political father's demise as the springboard to launch an even bigger career for himself. Bob Menendez might have started his illustrious career as an earnest corruption crusader sporting a bulletproof vest, but he ended a caricature of the political boss, tucking into massive steaks at Morton's in Washington, DC, and chomping on a fat cigar.

His betrayals of Musto, his constituents, his family, and the aides who believed his social justice rhetoric were epic. They were Shakespearian, and they don't have a happy ending.

In Act 2, scene I of *The Tempest*, the treacherous and conniving Antonio goads Sebastian into committing murder.

"Whereof what's past is prologue, what to come / In yours and mine discharge," says Antonio, rationalizing the wrongdoing in his quest for power, taking advantage of a shipwreck to assert his control, no matter whom he hurts along the way.

Like Antonio, Menendez showed no remorse for his or his wife's schemes. The couple happily helped the government of Egypt hush up their part in the murder and dismemberment of a journalist at the Saudi Embassy in Istanbul, and a military attack that left twelve tourists dead and an American woman permanently scarred. They exchanged Menendez's power for gold bars and cash. And when he was called to account, Menendez did what he had done decades before: He simply blamed everything on someone else. And perhaps he is partly right to blame his wife. After all, this is a woman who showed no remorse after she killed a man on a dark New Jersey street, and then promptly went on to enjoy a dinner with friends.

For Menendez, the past events of his life helped set the stage for his own demise. He was a legislator formed in the furnace of the Union City political machine and learned how to manipulate government agencies into vehicles for the acquisition of personal power.

In the beginning, before all of the trappings that came with the power of being an incumbent member of Congress and a senator, a combination of ambition and dishonesty about who he fundamentally was is what put Menendez on the witness stand to testify against his mentor William Musto. The bulletproof vest he claimed to wear was likely never needed to protect his mortal body. It was more like armor for his soul. The betrayal of Musto laid the foundation for the betrayal of an entire nation that he was elected to serve. It was a sacred code that politicians like Musto understood and never broke. Men like Musto were war heroes and legends who doled out political patronage, broke the law but never turned on those closest to them, and they never violated their own rules of conduct. Musto was never a "rat," and his code of loyalty to his community and his country perhaps kept his soul intact, which is why to this day his memory is still celebrated by the people of Union City.

After Musto went down at his trial, Menendez continued to play the system by becoming a corrupt agent of it. The once idealistic high school student leader gradually became increasingly emboldened when he was able to get away with corruption in Union City. Leasing a property he owned at inflated rent to a local nonprofit whose mission was to help the poorest members of his community was one example. Menendez got away with it in Union City, and later took those lessons to Congress where he became a leading Hispanic member of the Democratic Party in the 1990s. He became a kind of understudy of another disgraced former senator from New Jersey, Bob Torricelli.

Menendez increasingly saw his own path to power carved out of his hatred for Castro's Cuba, winning the backing of Bill and Hillary Clinton as well as Republican and hard-line anti-Castro activist Jorge Mas Canosa. For Menendez, it was like being handed a lottery ticket. He only needed to perpetuate the lie that he was a persecuted Cuban whose family fled the Castro regime to win the big prize. Embracing a rabid anti-Castro ideology helped him rise politically in Union City and did wonders for him on the national stage.

He had also learned early in his career that America's political system wasn't designed to bust corrupt politicians and that he could enrich himself while leveraging the political power he was accumulating to project his status onto the global stage. In so doing, he provided cover for evil regimes and terrorists around the world in his role as member and then the powerful chairman of the Senate Foreign Relations Committee, ultimately becoming a foreign agent for brutal violators of human rights and financiers of terror.

During his nearly half century in politics, Menendez became so adept at the dark arts of high-level political corruption that he was able to climb to the pinnacle of the DC power structure. He became a leader, whether purposefully or not, of the party of Thomas Jefferson wielding nearly absolute power over foreign policy in the Western Hemisphere, while maintaining a firm grip on the Department of Justice, and the Securities and Exchange Commission in his role as a high-ranking member of powerful committees such as Judiciary, and Banking, Housing and Urban Affairs, as well as Foreign Relations. Menendez used his legislative prowess to turn the Democratic Party in the United States Senate into a Union City patronage mill. For nearly a generation, Menendez controlled the levers of promotion and advancement, discouraging those of honest intent and a true passion for representing the voters who were electing them, and instead creating a machine that benefited those who were willing to turn a blind eye to the corruption at the top of the party.

For Menendez's rise in the Democratic Party coincides with its betrayal of the principles of "Hope and Change"—a rallying cry repeated during Barack Obama's rise to power in 2008. "Hope is making a comeback!" said former First Lady Michelle Obama at the 2024 Democratic National Convention. But as the election showed, "Hope and Change" has become little more than an empty mantra for a party whose leadership resembles a hapless group of entitled empty suits scrambling for solid footing in a Make American Great Again world. Under the influence of Menendez and his former Senate colleagues, Hillary Clinton and Joe Biden, the Democratic Party went from the party representing the union worker and immigrant fighting for fair wages and freedom to a party that sold out its constituents for the corrupt pursuits of its leadership.

On the world stage, during the peak of Menendez's power and influence on the Foreign Relations committee, Vladimir Putin was emboldened to invade Ukraine in 2014 and again in 2022. Russia continued to push into Africa, the Middle East, and central Asia ushering in the turmoil that has become the new world order. On Menendez's watch, China and Iran created economic footholds in America's backyard—in Central and South America. The situation led to the rise of Mexico's drug cartels who began using Chinese base chemicals to fuel the fentanyl crisis that has killed more than 250,000 Americans.

The story of Bob Menendez's rise to power is a cautionary tale of how someone with a brilliant future, who sets out to do good in the world, can embrace corruption and think nothing of receiving the perks that come with power and a lavish lifestyle—trips on private jets, stays at luxurious resorts, gold bars, and wads of cash—in exchange for official favors. When his 2017 corruption and bribery trial ended in a hung jury, Menendez likely thought he was untouchable. Rather than serving as a wake-up call, this close brush with the law emboldened him and reinforced a sense of invincibility. And when his well-connected girlfriend arrived on the scene, singing his praises and treating him like a king who could summon her with the tinkle of a bell, he likely thought he was truly on top of the world and above the law.

At Menendez's sentencing, Judge Stein merely scratched the surface when he pondered the questions of what drove Menendez to become a corrupt politician. In addition to greed, was it also hubris that drove him? Stein seemed to be thinking out loud, because he was hardly expecting an answer.

"I don't know what led you to commit these crimes," Stein said. "You'll have to figure it out yourself over time."

ACKNOWLEDGMENTS

We both owe a debt of gratitude to Ken Boehm, to whom this book is dedicated. Ken, a former Pennsylvania state prosecutor, congressional aide, and radio talk show host, was the ultimate researcher, fearlessly going after corruption wherever he saw it. Ken uncovered evidence that ultimately led to the Boeing tanker scandal at the Pentagon in 2003, which resulted in criminal penalties for two of the company's executives. He started investigating Democrat Robert Menendez's relationship with his Palm Beach benefactor Salomon Melgen as early as 2010.

Ken worked closely with Thomas to compile an exhaustive research file on Menendez when he became a researcher at the National Legal and Policy Center, a government watchdog cofounded by Ken in Virginia. By 2012, when rumors of Menendez partying with political donors on Caribbean junkets began making the rounds, Ken and Thomas began working with *The New York Times* and, later, the *New York Post*.

We would both like to acknowledge the *New York Post* and its incredible staff, past and present, particularly Melissa Klein, Hugh Dougherty, Shelly Ridenour, Andy Tillett, Steve Lynch, Margi Conklin, Paul McPolin, and Keith Poole, who supported fearless investigative work on Menendez.

We also want to thank our sources, most of whom did not want to be identified for fear of reprisals. Thanks for pointing the way and trusting us with your stories.

Thank you to Frank Weimann, our agent, who believed that the story of Menendez's incredible rise and precipitous fall was the stuff of Shakespearean tragedy and could make a compelling book. Thank you to the team at Diversion Books, particularly Evan Phail, who saw the merits of this story and supported us on our long journey.

For Thomas: The journey would not have been possible without the support of friends like Mike Walsh, Joyce Press, and my children—Audrey, Cyrus, and Penelope—an endless source of love and encouragement, offering the strength I needed to continue the watchdog grind. And of course, Jessica Morris, the silent hand who kept me grounded, honest, and focused—her unwavering support was vital.

For Isabel: Thank you to my family, particularly my daughter, Hannah, who cheered me every step of the way, and Ray Dowd, whose inspiration is on every page of this book.

Ken Boehm did not live to see Menendez convicted in the summer of 2024. He died in April 2018, months after Menendez's first corruption prosecution ended in a hung jury. He was disappointed the government decided not to retry the case.

NOTES

Authors' note: In many cases, sources would only consent to speak to us on the condition of anonymity. They are indicated by the generic term "source" throughout these endnotes.

1. Charles Bethea, "Robert Menendez's Golden Pipes," *New Yorker*, October 30, 2023.
2. Alicia Menendez. Letter to Judge Sidney H. Stein, undated.
3. Donald Scarinci. Letter to Judge Sidney H. Stein, January 14, 2025.
4. Danny O'Brien. Letter to Judge Sidney H. Stein, August 19, 2024.
5. Hank Sheinkopf. Interview, July 18, 2024.
6. Paul Monteleoni. Comments made in closing arguments. *USA v. Robert Menendez et al.*, US District Court for the Southern District of New York, July 8, 2024.
7. Source. July 29, 2024, by author.
8. Eusebio Rodriguez. Interview with the authors, Union City, New Jersey, August 21, 2024.
9. Presentment of the Special Hudson County Grand Jury—Panel A, In the Matter of an Investigation into Corrupt Activities and Influence in the Union City Police Department and City Government, February 6, 1986.
10. Joanne Palmer, "Coming to America: Senator Menendez Tells His Family's Immigration Story," *Jewish Standard*, September 19, 2014.
11. Bob Menendez, *Growing American Roots: Why Our Nation Will Thrive as Our Largest Minority Flourishes* (New York: Penguin Group, 2009).
12. Paul Mulshine. Interview with the authors, July 16, 2024.
13. Source. Interview with the authors, August 21, 2024.
14. Bob Hugin. Interview with the authors, Summit, New Jersey, December 6, 2024.
15. Caridad Gonzalez. Letter to Judge Sidney H. Stein, August 19, 2024.
16. Alicia Menendez. Letter to Judge Stein, undated.
17. Donald Scarinci. Letter to Judge Sidney H. Stein, January 12, 2025.
18. Menendez, *Growing American Roots*.
19. Union Hill High School Yearbook, 1972.
20. Menendez, *Growing American Roots*.
21. *Star-Ledger*, July 30, 2006.
22. Menendez, *Growing American Roots*.
23. Source. Interview with the authors, July 19, 2024.
24. Alan Jay Weiss. Interview with the authors, August 26, 2024.
25. Source. Interview with the authors, August 19, 2024.
26. Willam E. Geist, "Man in the News: The Man Union City Believes In," *New York Times*, May 13, 1982.
27. Scarinci. Letter to Judge Stein, January 12, 2025.

28. Jeffrey Gettleman, "A Congressman Is Ready to Step Up in New Jersey," *New York Times*, September 19, 2005.

29. Fred Snowflack, "Context: In 1974, Menendez Seemed Mature Beyond His Years," *Insider NJ*, November 16, 2017.

30. Jeffrey Gettleman, "The Menendez Story, with All the Chapters," *New York Times*, December 25, 2005.

31. Robert Hanley, "Jersey State Senator Is Indicted in 'Conspiracy,'" *New York Times*, November 18, 1977.

32. Joseph F. Sullivan, "Witness Said He Heard of Plotting to Tie Senator Musto to Gamblers," *New York Times*, March 31, 1978.

33. Robert D. McFadden, "Cuban Refugee Leader Slain in Union City," *New York Times*, November 26, 1979.

34. Dan Geringer, "City's Managing Director Turns Loss of Dad, Daughter into Mission to Make Others' Lives Better," *Philadelphia Inquirer*, February 3, 2012.

35. Jeff Stein, "An Army in Exile," *New York Magazine*, September 10, 1979.

36. Peter Kihss, "Three Castro Foes Arrested in Firing of Bazooka at UN," *New York Times*, December 23, 1964.

37. CIA: "Pinochet Personally Ordered Letelier Bombing," National Security Archive, September 23, 2016.

38. Stein, "An Army in Exile."

39. Agustin Torres, "Menendez Fears His Link to Omega 7," *Jersey Journal*, October 8, 1987.

40. Jonathan Miller, "In New Jersey Contest, a Senator with Tough Friends," *Observer*, November 6, 2006.

41. Stein, "An Army in Exile."

42. Camille Kenny and Paul Moses, "Negrin: Cops Ignore Threats Against My Life," *The Dispatch*, March 28, 1979.

43. Camille Kenny, "Police Skeptical of Omega 7 Claim to Negrin's Murder," *The Dispatch*, November 27, 1979.

44. Alfonso Narvaez, "Witness Testifies in Jersey Bribery," *New York Times*, November 22, 1981.

45. Jim Dwyer, "In Bygone Days, Menendez Fought Graft with Courage," *New York Times*, April 2, 1015.

46. Jim Dwyer, "New Jersey Senator's Rival Faults Him in '80s Corruption Case, but History Disagrees," *New York Times*, June 25, 2006.

47. Alfonso A. Narvaez, "Summations Begin in Extortion Trial of Union City Mayor and 7 Associates," *New York Times*, March 17, 1982.

48. Eusebio "Chi Chi" Rodriguez. Interview with the authors, Union City, New Jersey, August 19, 2024.

49. Dwyer, "New Jersey Senator's Rival Faults Him."

50. Source. Interview with the authors, Union City, New Jersey, August 19, 2024.

51. Joe Hayden. Interview with the authors, July 29, 2024.

52. Hayden. Interview.

53. Dwyer, "New Jersey Senator's Rival Faults Him."

54. Jim Plaisted. Interview with the authors, July 30, 2024.

55. Jeffrey Gettleman, "Robert Menendez, a Politician Even at 20," *New York Times*, December 10, 2005.

56. New Jersey District Court, "Art of the Jury Trial Newark," March 21, 2024.

57. United Press International, "A Jury, One of Whose Members Changed Her Mind . . . ," March 27, 1982.

58. *United States v. William V. Musto*. US District Court for the District of New Jersey—540 F. Supp. 318 (D.N.J. 1982), May 12, 1982.

59. *United States v. William V. Musto*. US District Court for the District of New Jersey.

60. Menendez, *Growing American Roots*.

61. Alfonso Narvaez, "Another Musto May Run," *New York Times*, June 27, 1982.

62. Alfonso Narvaez, "Musto Reflects on His Career," *New York Times*, June 6, 1982.

63. Source. Interview with the authors, Union City, New Jersey, August 19, 2024.

64. Dwyer, "New Jersey Senator's Rival Faults Him."

65. Alicia Menendez. Letter to Judge Stein, undated.

66. Rob Menendez. Letter to Judge Sidney Stein, December 26, 2024.

67. Pete Donohue, "Feds Want Refund from Union City; $600,000 Spent on Office Work Instead of Poor," *Jersey Journal*, May 27, 1992.

68. Torres, "Menendez Fears His Link to Omega 7."

69. Miller, "In New Jersey Contest, a Senator with Tough Friends."

70. Torres, "Menendez Fears Impact of His Link to Omega 7."

71. Paul Mulshine, "More on Bob Menendez: Some Never-Before-Seen Evasions on the 2006 Rowhouse Scandal | Mulshine," *Star-Ledger*, March 8, 2015.

72. Jerry Gray, "In Hudson, 2 Democrats in Spotlight," *New York Times*, May 28, 1992.

73. Menendez, *Growing American Roots*.

74. Stephen Kimber, "Field Notes 1: Livio de Celmo Remembers" and "The Murder of Fabio di Celmo," stephenkimber.com, undated.

75. Ann Louise Bardach and Larry Rohter, "A Bombers Tale: Taking Aim at Castro; Key Cuba Foe Claims Exiles' Backing," *New York Times*, July 12, 1998.

76. BBC, "Cuba Anger at US Posada Carriles Verdict," April 10, 2011.

77. Jose Pertierra, "Day 25 in the Trial of Posada Carriles—Follow the Money," *Venezuela Analysis*, March 16, 2011.

78. Evelyn Nieves, "A New House District Could Make History," *New York Times*, October 29, 1992.

79. T. J. English, *The Corporation: An Epic Story of the Cuban American Underworld* (New York: Harper Collins, 2018).

80. Kenneth M. O'Connor, Special Agent, Federal Bureau of Investigation, Government Exhibit J-AVO-6, March 29, 1998.

81. Eusebio Rodriguez. Interview with the authors, Union City, New Jersey, August 29, 2024.

82. Source. Interview with the authors, August 19, 2024.

83. Alberto Canal, "Manny Diaz, Once Considered for the Top, Hits Bottom," *Jersey Journal*, November 13, 1989.

84. Canal, "Manny Diaz."

85. Bill Cotterell, "New Documentary Recasts the 2000 Presidential Vote in Florida as the Elian Election," *Tallahassee Democrat*, October 20, 2020.

86. Washington Bureau, "Starr Delivers Critical Report," *Chicago Tribune*, August 11, 2021.

87. Bob Herbert, "In America: House of Arrogance," *New York Times*, December 20, 1988.

88. Source. Interview with the authors, August 21, 2024.

89. Jeffrey Gettleman, "A Swift Climb Up the Ladder, from Lowly Assistant to Highly Paid Lobbyist," *New York Times*, July 17, 2005.

90. Deborah Howlett, "Menendez Buddy's Past Under a Microscope," *Star-Ledger*, July 27, 2006

91. Jill Colvin and Colleen Long, "Kushner Pardon Revives 'Loathsome' Tale of Tax Evasion, Sex," Associated Press, December 23, 2020.

92. Staff Report. "Menendez Mendacity," *New York Post*, January 21, 2007.

93. David Kocieniewski, "Inquiry Focuses on Former Aide to Menendez," *New York Times*, August 28, 2007.

94. Kocieniewski, "Inquiry Focuses on Former Aide to Menendez."

95. Paul Mulshine. Interview with the authors, February 8, 2025.

96. Laura Manners and David W. Chen, "New Jersey Attorney General Quits," *New York Times*, August 16, 2006.

97. Cynthia Burton, "Florida Broadcaster Gives Major Backing," *Philadelphia Inquirer*, April 2, 2006.

98. Jim Dwyer, "Kean Campaign Cancels Film on Menendez," *New York Times*, November 3, 2006.

99. *New Jersey Lawyer*, February 3, 2003.

100. Veronique E. Hyland, "Queen Bee," *Harvard Crimson*, December 16, 2004.

101. Ken Silverstein, "Menendez Case Heats Up," *Harper's Magazine*, November 9, 2007.

102. Hillary Clinton. Personal email to Lona Valmoro and Huma Abedin, "Where did we leave departure time on Sunday?" June 15, 2012.

103. *Puerto Rico Herald*, "Clinton Calls for Puerto Ricans to Decide Territory's Ultimate Status," April 11, 2003.

104. *Puerto Rico Herald*, "Clinton Calls for Puerto Ricans to Decide . . ."

105. Miguel Rodriguez. Personal email to Cheryl Mills and Roberta S. Jacobson, "Farrar-Update," July 25, 2011.

106. Alexandra Navarro Clifton, "Matriarch in Coma after Simple Surgery Goes Wrong," *Palm Beach Post*, April 7, 2001.

107. Press Release, Department of Justice. "South Florida Doctor Indicted for Medicare Fraud," April 14, 2015.

108. Elizabeth Rosner and Kaja Whitehouse, "Menendez's Former Chief of Staff Refutes Prosecutor's Allegations," *New York Post*, October 18, 2017.

109. Katie Thomas, "Polo Ponies Were Given Incorrect Medication," *New York Times*, April 23, 2009.

110. *Progreso Weekly*, " Melgen's and Menendez's Companion Was a Ukrainian Actress," February 8, 2013.

111. *Dominican Today*, "'Skirts' Fueled Menendez-Melgen Scandal: Dominican Republic TV Host," April 23, 2015.

112. Ray Hernandez, and Frances Robles, "Senator Has Long Ties to Donor Under Scrutiny," *New York Times*, January 31, 2013.

113. Matt Friedman, "Menendez Denies Prostitution Claims, Says Claims Are 'Politically Motivated,'" New Jersey Advance Media for NJ.com, January 30, 2013.

114. Nick Corasaniti, "Fact Check: Did Senator Menendez Hire Underage Prostitutes?" *New York Times*, October 17, 2018.

115. Laura Jarrett and Sarah Jorgensen, "Private Jet Pilot Details Bob Menendez Flights," CNN, September 13, 2017.

116. Carol D. Leonnig and Manuel Roig-Franzia, "Sen. Robert Menendez Seeks Probe of Alleged Cuban Plot to Smear Him," *Washington Post*, July 7, 2014.

117. *Dominican Today*, "Menendez Scandal Linked to Dominican Republic Drug Trafficking," February 4, 2013.

118. Jay Weaver, "Convicted Ex-U.S. Diplomat Says, 'Radical Politics' at Yale Turned Him into Cuban Spy," *Miami Herald*, April 15, 2024.

119. Press Release, Department of Justice. "Former U.S. Ambassador and National Security Council Official Admits to Secretly Acting as Agent of the Cuban Government and Receives 15-Year Sentence," April 12, 2024.

120. Domingo Collado Abreu, "Barrick detrás de Barrio," *Observatorio Latinoamericano de Conflictos Ambientales*, October 5, 2012.

121. *Newsroom Panama*, "US Ambassador Warns of Justice and Corruption Problems in Panama," March 17, 2012.

122. Jim Plaisted. Interview with the authors, July 29, 2024.

123. Lia Eustachewich, "Menendez Racked up More Than $4.7 Million in Legal Fees," *New York Post*, February 26, 2018.

124. David Kocieniewski and Tim Golden, "Charges Ruled Out as US Concludes Torricelli Inquiry," *New York Times*, January 4, 2002.

125. The Auditor, "Menendez Lawyer Represented Torricelli, Other High-Profile Pols," New Jersey Advance Media, March 25, 2015.

126. The encounter with William Brownfield and the FBI is outlined in an exhibit in *United States Supreme Court, Robert Menendez v. The United States of America*, "On Petition for a Writ of Certiorari to the United States Court of Appeals for the Third Circuit," Appendix K.

127. Ryan Hutchins, "Menendez Trial Focuses on Dominican Port Dispute, Contract with Friend's Firm," *Politico*, September 26, 2017.

128. Robert Menendez, speech, Senate Foreign Relations Committee, March 20, 2018.

129. Eliot Engel and Norma J. Torres. Letter to Alan Garten, General Counsel of Trump Organization, February 27, 2018.

130. David Gagne, "Wiretaps Paint Unflattering Picture of Former Panama President," *Insight Crime*, March 8, 2016.

131. Kim De Paola. Interview with the authors, April 18, 2024.

132. Source. Interview with the authors, June 23, 2024.

133. Pat Dori. Interview with the authors, May 17, 2024.

134. John Alite. Interview with the authors, September 27, 2023.

135. Michael Mathews. Interview with the authors, September 27, 2023.

136. Dana DeFilippo, "Defense Attorneys Offer Ordinary Explanations for Sen. Menendez's Hoarded Riches," *New Jersey Monitor*, July 1, 2024.

137. Interview with the authors, June 18, 2024.

138. Doug Anton. Interview with the authors, April 29, 2024.

139. Anton. Interview.

140. Nina Burleigh, "Nadine and Bob Menendez's Flashy, Allegedly Corrupt Romance," *New York Magazine*, October 31, 2023.

141. Vincent Mallozzi, "How They Proposed," *New York Times*, January 21, 2021.

142. The description of Jose Uribe's meeting with Robert Menendez is recounted in *USA v. Robert Menendez et al.*

143. Josh Russell, "Key Witness in Menendez Bribery Trial Says He Made Senator's Wife's Car Payments for 3 Years," Courthouse News Service, June 10, 2024.

144. Dana DiFilippo, "Businessman Describes Asking Sen. Menendez for Help in Killing Criminal Probe," *New Jersey Monitor*, June 10, 2024.

145. Source. Interview with the authors, May 15, 2024.

146. Nicole Hong, Tracey Tully, William K. Rashbaum, "Menendez Co-Defendant's Curious Path from Bad Deals to a Meat Monopoly," *New York Times*, October 1, 2023.

147. Dana DiFilippo, "A 'Very Shady' Meat Monopoly in Egypt Dominates Day in Menendez Corruption Trial," *New Jersey Monitor*, May 17, 2024.

148. Ry Rivard, "USDA Official Explains Early Worries About Meat Monopoly in Menendez Case," *Politico*, May 17, 2024.

149. Caitlin Yilek, "Prosecutors Unveil Cache of Menendez Texts in Bribery Trial: 'It Is Extremely Important That We Keep Nadine Happy,'" CBS News, May 30, 2024.

150. Memorandum of Law of the United States of America in Opposition to the Defendants' Motions to Suppress, *United States of America v. Robert Menendez et al.*, February 12, 2024, p. 17.

151. Senate Foreign Relations Committee, "Senators Menendez, Blackburn Introduce Armenian Genocide Education Act," April 27, 2023.

152. *Armenian Mirror-Spectator*, "US Senator Bob Menendez and Nadine Arslanian Married," January 3, 2021.

153. Sophie Nieto-Munoz, "Judge Rejects Plea Agreement for Sen. Bob Menendez's Co-Defendant," *New Jersey Monitor*, October 5, 2023.

154. Senate Foreign Relations Committee, "Chairman Menendez Statement on Qatar's Efforts to House Afghans Seeking Refuge in the United States," August 20, 2021.

155. Michael Scivoli, "Local Developer Fred Daibes: A Reflection of Community," VUE New Jersey, undated.

156. State Commission of Investigation, State of New Jersey. "Public Matters, Private Interests: An Inquiry into Local Government Ethics and Integrity Issues in the Borough of Edgewater," May 2023.

157. Dana DiFilippo, "Prosecutors in Senator Menendez's Corruption Trial Shift Focus to Qatar," *New Jersey Monitor*, June 21, 2024.

158. Tracey Tully and Benjamin Weiser, "Formula 1 Tickets and a Fixation on Gold: Menendez Trial Takeaways," *New York Times*, June 24, 2024.

159. Jonathan Dienst, Courtney Copenhagen, and Tom Winter, "Gold Bars Featured in Bob Menendez Bribery Case Linked to 2013 Robbery, Records Show," NBC, December 4, 2023.

160. Kristie Cattafi, "Gold Bars Stolen 10 Years Ago in 'Inside Job' Resurface in Sen. Menendez Investigation," NorthJersey.com, December 6, 2023.

161. Chris Marquette, "Campus Notebook: Sen. Menendez Spent over $5 Million in Legal Fees Associated with Corruption Scandal," Roll Call, January 17, 2020.

162. Isabel Vincent, "Senator Bob Menendez Splits from Super Lawyer," *New York Post*, December 1, 2023.

163. Dori. Interview.

164. Gregory Krieg, "Trump Circus Overshadows Menendez Trial," CNN, May 21, 2024.

165. *USA v. Robert Menendez et al.*, July 1, 2024.

166. Gertrudis Ramirez. Letter to Judge Sidney H. Stein, September 24, 2024.

167. Nina Saria, Letter to Judge Sidney H. Stein, August 31, 2024.

168. David Wildstein, "Robert Menendez Elementary School Will Get a Name Change, Mayor Says," *New Jersey Globe*, July 25, 2024.

BIBLIOGRAPHY

ARTICLES

Abreu, Domingo Collado. "Barrick detrás de Barrio," *Observatorio Latinoamericano de Conflictos Ambientales*, October 5, 2012.

Adames, Fausto Rosario. "Familia Beauchamps y Cotecna defienden beneficios de rayos en los puertos," *Acento*, December 3, 2013.

Adams, David C. and Gerardo Reyes, Juan Coopery, Daily Camacaro. "Exclusive: Panama's Ex-President Wiretapped Americans, According to Court Documents," Univision News, June 24, 2017.

"A Jury, One of Whose Members Changed Her Mind . . ." United Press International, March 27, 1982.

Bardach, Ann Louise and Larry Rohter. "A Bombers Tale: Taking Aim at Castro; Key Cuba Foe Claims Exiles' Backing," *New York Times*, July 12, 1998.

Becker, Jo. "Cash Flowed to Clinton Foundation Amid Russian Uranium Deal," *New York Times*, April 23, 2015.

Bennett, George. "North Palm Beach Eye Doctor Salomon Melgen Lost $68 Million in Investments," *Palm Beach Post*, Feb. 10, 2013.

Bethea, Charles. "Robert Menendez's Golden Pipes," *New Yorker*, October 30, 2023.

"Bill Clinton visits big wind farm in western Panama," Associated Press, November 10, 2015.

Burleigh, Nina. "Nadine and Bob Menendez's Flashy, Allegedly Corrupt Romance," *New York Magazine*, October 31, 2023.

Burstein, Jon. "Nurse Accused of Negligence in Death; Surgery Wasn't Monitored, Authorities Say," *South Florida Sun Sentinel*, May 10, 2002.

Burton, Cynthia. "Florida Broadcaster Gives Major Backing," *Philadelphia Inquirer*, April 2, 2006.

Byrd, Mary Lou. "Clients of Top Donor to Bob Menendez Awarded Millions in Taxpayer Funds," *Daily Caller*, November 21, 2012

Canal, Alberto. "Manny Diaz, Once Considered for the Top, Hits Bottom," *The Jersey Journal*, November 13, 1989.

Caputo, Marc and Jay Weaver, Amy Sherman, "So. Fla. Eye Surgeon Under Scrutiny with Sen. Menendez Frequently Prescribed Expensive Drug," *The Miami Herald*, Feb. 08, 2013.

Cattafi, Kristie. "Gold Bars Stolen 10 Years Ago in 'Inside Job' Resurface in Sen. Menendez Investigation," NorthJersey.com, December 6, 2023.

Clifton, Alexandra Navarro. "Matriarch in Coma After Simple Surgery Goes Wrong," *Palm Beach Post*, April 7, 2001.

"Clinton Calls for Puerto Ricans to Decide Territory's Ultimate Status," *Puerto Rico Herald*, April 11, 2003.

"Clinton Opens Solar Park Providing Power to 30,000 Families," *Newsroom Panama*, February 1, 2019.

Colvin, Jill and Colleen Long. "Kushner Pardon Revives 'Loathsome' Tale of Tax Evasion, Sex," Associated Press, December 23, 2020.

"Copolad: Dominican Republic is the command center for drug trafficking," *VOXXI*, January 22, 2013.

Corasaniti, Nick. "Fact Check: Did Senator Menendez Hire Underage Prostitutes?" *New York Times*, October 17, 2018.

Cotterell, Bill. "New Documentary Recasts the 2000 Presidential Vote in Florida as the Elian Election," *Tallahassee Democrat*, October 20, 2020.

"Cuba Anger at US Posada Carriles Verdict," BBC, April 10, 2011.

DiFilippo, Dana. "A 'Very Shady' Meat Monopoly in Egypt Dominates Day in Menendez Corruption Trial," *New Jersey Monitor*, May 17, 2024.

DiFilippo, Dana. "Businessman Describes Asking Sen. Menendez for Help in Killing Criminal Probe," *New Jersey Monitor*, June 10, 2024.

DeFilippo, Dana. "Defense Attorneys Offer Ordinary Explanations for Sen. Menendez's Hoarded Riches," *New Jersey Monitor*, July 1, 2024.

DiFilippo, Dana. "Prosecutors in Senator Menendez's Corruption Trial Shift Focus to Qatar," *New Jersey Monitor*, June 21, 2024.

Dienst, Jonathan and Courtney Copenhagen, Tom Winter. "Gold Bars Featured in Bob Menendez Bribery Case Linked to 2013 Robbery, Records Show," NBC, December 4, 2023.

Donohue, Joe and Josh Margolin. "Former McGreevey Fund-Raiser Indicted (US Sen Menendez, Puerto Rico Gov, in Alleged Dim Conspiracy)," *Star-Ledger*, March 27, 2008.

Donohue, Pete. "Feds Want Refund from Union City; $600,000 Spent on Office Work Instead of Poor," *Jersey Journal*, May 27, 1992.

Duret, Daphne. "Melgen Medicare Fraud Trial Resumes After Judge Denies Mistrial Motion," *Palm Beach Post*, March 13, 2017.

Dwyer, Jim. "In Bygone Days, Menendez Fought Graft with Courage," *New York Times*, April 2, 2015.

Dwyer, Jim. "Kean Campaign Cancels Film on Menendez," *New York Times*, November 3, 2006.

Dwyer, Jim. "New Jersey Senator's Rival Faults Him in '80s Corruption Case, but History Disagrees," *New York Times*, June 25, 2006.

El Diario. "X-Ray Contract Has Been in Court for 8 years," March 14, 2012.

Eustachewich, Lia. "Menendez Racked Up More Than $4.7 Million in Legal Fees," *New York Post*, February 26, 2018.

"Former U.S. President Clinton Visits Panama," *Newsroom Panama*, June 5, 2011.

Friedman, Matt. "Menendez Denies Prostitution Claims, Says Claims are 'Politically Motivated,'" *New Jersey Advance Media* for NJ.com, January 30, 2013.

Gagne, David. "Wiretaps Paint Unflattering Picture of Former Panama President," *Insight Crime*, March 8, 2016.

Geist, Willam E. "Man in the News: The Man Union City Believes In," *New York Times*, May 13, 1982.

Geringer, Dan. "City's Managing Director Turns Loss of Dad, Daughter Into Mission to Make 'Other Lives Better,'" *Philadelphia Inquirer*, February 3, 2012.

Gettleman, Jeffrey. "A Congressman Is Ready to Step Up in New Jersey," *New York Times,* September 19, 2005.

Gettleman, Jeffrey. "A Swift Climb Up the Ladder, from Lowly Assistant to Highly Paid Lobbyist," *New York Times,* July 17, 2005.

Gettleman, Jeffrey. "The Menendez Story, with All the Chapters," *New York Times,* December 25, 2005.

Goodman, Alana. "Defunct Foundation of Controversial Democratic Donor Engaged in Highly Unusual Practice, Experts Say," *Washington Free Beacon,* March 22, 2013.

Goodman, Alana. "Menendez Sponsored $3.5M Earmark for Major Donor in 2010, Records Show," *Washington Free Beacon,* March 5, 2013.

"Gran Apertura Nosotros Centro De Servicios al Inmigrante!," *Nosotros,* May 20, 2010.

Gray, Jerry. "In Hudson, 2 Democrats in Spotlight," *New York Times,* May 28, 1992.

Hanley, Robert. "Jersey State Senator Is Indicted in 'Conspiracy,'" *New York Times,* November 18, 1977.

Herbert, Bob. "In America: House of Arrogance," *New York Times,* December 20, 1988.

Hernandez, Ray and Frances Robles. "Senator Has Long Ties to Donor Under Scrutiny," *New York Times,* January 31, 2013.

Hong, Nicole and Tracey Tully, William K. Rashbaum. "Menendez Co-Defendant's Curious Path from Bad Deals to a Meat Monopoly," *New York Times,* October 1, 2023.

Howlett, Deborah. "Menendez Buddy's Past Under a Microscope," *Star-Ledger,* July 27, 2006

Hutchins, Ryan. "Feds: Menendez Named on 9 Pages in 'Ledger' Found in Melgen's Office," *Capital New York/Politico,* April 24, 2015.

Hutchins, Ryan. "Menendez Trial Focuses on Dominican Port Dispute, Contract with Friend's Firm," *Politico,* September 26, 2017.

Hyland, Veronique E. "Queen Bee," *Harvard Crimson,* December 16, 2004.

"Is the FBI's latest probe of the Clinton Foundation a 'witch hunt' – or something more?," The Conversation, January 19, 2018.

Jorgensen, Sarah. "Witness Describes 'Hostile' Conversations with Menendez, Reid, Sebelius," CNN, October 2, 2017.

Kenny, Camille and Paul Moses. "Negrin: Cops Ignore Threats Against My Life," *The Dispatch,* March 28, 1979.

Kenny, Camille. "Police Skeptical of Omega 7 Claim to Negrin's Murder," *The Dispatch,* November 27, 1979.

Kihss, Peter. "Three Castro Foes Arrested in Firing of Bazooka at UN," *New York Times,* December 23, 1964.

Kimber, Stephen. "Field Notes 1: Livio de Celmo Remembers" and "The Murder of Fabio di Celmo," stephenkimber.com, undated.

Kocieniewski, David and Tim Golden. "Charges Ruled Out as US Concludes Torricelli Inquiry," *New York Times,* January 4, 2002.

Kocieniewski, David. "Inquiry Focuses on Former Aide to Menendez," *New York Times,* August 28, 2007.

Krieg, Gregory. "Trump Circus Overshadows Menendez Trial," CNN, May 21, 2024.

Kumar, Anita and Marisa Taylor and Kevin G. Hall. "Inside Panama Papers: Multiple Clinton connections," *McClatchy Washington Bureau,* May 20, 2016.

Jarrett, Laura and Sarah Jorgensen, "Private Jet Pilot Details Bob Menendez Flights." CNN, September 13, 2017.

Lantigua, John. "Florida Doctor Was Paid $21 Million by Medicare; No. 1 in U.S.," *Palm Beach Post*, April 10, 2014.

Leahy, Michael Patrick. "Despite High Powered Lawyers and Intervention by Reid and Menendez, Controversial Doctor Still Owed $8.9 Million for Overbilling Medicare," *Breitbart*, March 14, 2015.

Leahy, Michael Patrick. "DOJ Drops Bombshell in Menendez Corruption Trial: Dozen More Unreimbursed Flights Paid for by Co-Defendant Melgen," *Breitbart*, August 30, 2017.

Leahy, Michael Patrick. "The Corrupt Origins of the Melgen-Menendez Dominican Port Security Deal," *Breitbart*, February 10, 2013.

Leahy, Michael Patrick. "The Manuel Noriega Connection to the Family Behind the Melgen-Menendez Dominican Port Security Deal," *Breitbart*, February 26, 2013.

Leonnig, Carol D. and Jerry Markon, "Sen. Menendez Contacted Top Officials in Friend's Medicare Dispute," *Washington Post*, February 6, 2013.

Leonnig, Carol D. and Manuel Roig-Franzia. "Sen. Robert Menendez Seeks Probe of Alleged Cuban Plot to Smear Him," *Washington Post*, July 7, 2014.

Llorente Elizabeth. "Children from Northern Ireland in U.S. Cease-Fire Spreads Optimism Menendez Sees Hope in IRA Talks," *The Record*, July 22, 1997.

Mallozzi, Vincent. "How They Proposed," *New York Times*, January 21, 2021.

Manners, Laura and David W. Chen. "New Jersey Attorney General Quits," *New York Times*, August 16, 2006.

Marquette, Chris. "Campus Notebook: Sen. Menendez Spent over $5 Million in Legal Fees Associated with Corruption Scandal," *Roll Call*, January 17, 2020.

McFadden, Robert D. "Cuban Refugee Leader Slain in Union City," *New York Times*, November 26, 1979.

McGrory, Kathleen and Melissa Sanchez. "Following the Trail of Sen. Robert Menendez Scandal Leads to Dead End in Dominican Republic," *The Miami Herald*, Feb. 02, 2013.

"Medicare Fraud Doctor's Sentence Gets Commuted," *Palm Beach Post*, January 21, 2021.

"Melgen's and Menendez's Companion Was a Ukrainian Actress," *Progreso Weekly*, February 8, 2013.

Menendez, Bob. "Saving Our Neighborhoods from Foreclosures; Testimony and Discussion," United States Senate Field Hearing, February 10, 2012.

Mercurio, John. "Prosecutor Purge, Take Two," NBC News, October 18, 2007.

Miller, Jonathan. "In New Jersey Contest, a Senator with Tough Friends," *Observer*, November 6, 2006.

Morrissey, Ed. "Menendez Judge: Say, Corruption Suspects Sure Are Getting Off Easy These Days," *Daily Caller*, August 18, 2016.

Mulshine, Paul. "More on Bob Menendez: Some Never-Before-Seen Evasions on the 2006 Rowhouse Scandal | Mulshine," *Star-Ledger*, March 8, 2015.

Musgrave, Jane. "High-Stakes Trial for Harry Sargeant, Who Faces Allegations of Iraqi War Profiteering, Starts Monday," *Palm Beach Post*, July 10, 2011.

Narvaez, Alfonso. "Summations Begin in Extortion Trial of Union City Mayor and 7 Associates," *New York Times*, March 17, 1982.

Narvaez, Alfonso. "Witness Testifies in Jersey Bribery," *New York Times*, November 22, 1981.

Nieto-Munoz, Sophie. "Judge Rejects Plea Agreement for Sen. Bob Mendez's Co-Defendant," *New Jersey Monitor*, October 5, 2023.

Nieves, Evelyn. "A New House District Could Make History," *New York Times*, October 29, 1992.

"Noriega's Family in the Dominican Republic," *South Florida Sun Sentinel*, March 18, 1988.

"Noriega's Family Will Be by His Side in Court," UPI, August 31, 1991.

O'Connor, Kenneth M. Government Exhibit J-AVO-6, Federal Bureau of Investigation, March 29, 1998.

"Panama Intermediaries Each Sentenced to 36 Months in Prison for International Bribery and Money Laundering Scheme," US Department of Justice Archives, May 20, 2022

Parti, Tarini and Kenneth P. Vogel. "Menendez Donor Courted Obama, Reid," *Politico*, March 19, 2013.

Pertierra, Jose. "Day 25 in the Trial of Posada Carriles—Follow the Money," *Venezuela Analysis*, March 16, 2011.

"Petaquilla Minerals: Beyond Mining, Pursuing Social Responsibility," *VOXXI*, December 6, 2012.

"Prosecutor Told Man Disappeared While Investigating Martinelli Accounts," *Newsroom Panama*, August 28, 2014.

"Puerto Rican Governor, Ally of Menendez, Indicted," NJ.com, March 27, 2008.

Ragu, Manu. "A Senator's Puerto Rican Friendship Draws Scrutiny," *The Hill*, October 23, 2007.

Rimbach, Jean and Peter J. Sampson, "Tenants Don't See Imam as 'Healer,'" *Jewish World Review*, August 30, 2010.

Rivard, Ry. "USDA Official Explains Early Worries About Meat Monopoly in Menendez Case," *Politico*, May 17, 2024.

Robles, Frances. "Port Deal Pushed by Menendez Could Benefit Former Aide, Not Just a Major Donor," *New York Times*, February 4, 2013.

Robles, Frances. "Doctor With Big Medicare Billings Is No Stranger to Scrutiny," *New York Times*, April 9, 2014.

Robles, Frances. "Ecuador Family Wins Favors After Donations to Democrats," *New York Times*, Dec. 16, 2014

Rosner, Elizabeth and Kaja Whitehouse. "Menendez's Former Chief of Staff Refutes Prosecutor's Allegations," *New York Post*, October 18, 2017.

Russell, Josh. "Key Witness in Menendez Bribery Trial Says He Made Senator's Wife's Car Payments for 3 years," Courthouse News Service, June 10, 2024.

Scivoli, Michael. "Local Developer Fred Daibes: A Reflection of Community," *VUE New Jersey*, undated.

"Sen. Robert Menendez Holds a Hering On Doing Business in Latin America," Political Transcript Wire, August 1, 2012.

Sherman, Ted. "Wealthy Menendez Donor Gave Big to Own Charity That Benefitted Brazilian Girlfriend," NJ.com, April 17, 2015.

Silverstein, Ken. "Menendez Case Heats Up," *Harper's Magazine*, November 9, 2007.

"'Skirts' Fueled Menendez-Melgen Scandal: Dominican Republic TV Host," *Dominican Today*, April 23, 2015.

Snowflack, Fred. "Context: In 1974, Menendez Seemed Mature Beyond His Years," *Insider NJ*, November 16, 2017.

Stein, Jeff. "An Army in Exile," *New York Magazine*, September 10, 1979.

Sullivan, Joseph F. "Witness Said He Heard of Plotting to Tie Senator Musto to Gamblers," *New York Times*, March 31, 1978.

The Auditor. "Menendez Lawyer Represented Torricelli, Other High-Profile Pols," *New Jersey Advance Media*, March 25, 2015.

"The Tainted History of the Father of Panama Mining," *Newsroom Panama*, February 28, 2016.

Thomas, Katie. "Polo Ponies Were Given Incorrect Medication," *New York Times*, April 23, 2009.

Torres, Augustin. "Menendez Fears His Link to Omega 7," *Jersey Journal*, October 8, 1987.

Tully, Tracey and Benjamin Weiser. "Formula 1 Tickets and a Fixation on Gold: Menendez Trial Takeaways," *New York Times*, June 24, 2024.

"US Senator Bob Menendez and Nadine Arslanian Married," *Armenian Mirror-Spectator*, January 3, 2021.

Weaver, Jay. "Convicted Ex-U.S. Diplomat Says, 'Radical Politics' at Yale Turned Him Into Cuban Spy," *Miami Herald*, April 15, 2024.

Wildstein, David. "Robert Menendez Elementary School Will Get a Name Change, Mayor Says," *New Jersey Globe*, July 25, 2024.

Winston, Hannah. "Medicare Fraud Doctor's Sentence Gets Commuted," *Palm Beach Post*, January 21, 2021.

XVII United States-Spain Council Forum. Forum Agenda. June 22-24, 2012.

Yilek, Caitlin. "Prosecutors Unveil Cache of Menendez Texts in Bribery Trial: 'It Is Extremely Important that We Keep Nadine Happy,'" CBS News, May 30, 2024.

COURT RECORDS

"Art of the Jury Trial Newark," New Jersey District Court, March 21, 2024.

Robert Menendez v. The Supreme Court of the United States of America On Petition for a Writ of Certiorari to the United States Court of Appeals for the Third Circuit.

State of Florida Board of Pharmacy Case No: 2008-17152.

United States District Court for the Southern District of Florida, Case No: 1:17-cv-22197-EGT In the Matter of the Extradition of Ricardo Alberto Martinelli Berrocal.

United States District Court for the Southern District of Florida, C&K Grocery LLC, a Florida Limited Liability company, Plaintiff, vs. Jean Beauchamp, an individual, Defendant.

United States v. Robert Menendez, et al, District Court District of New Jersey, April 1, 2015 — January 31, 2018.

United States v. Robert Menendez et al., US District Court for the Southern District of New York, September 21, 2023 to May 28, 2025.

United States vs Salomon E. Melgen Case number: 15-80049-KAM Entire Docket April 14, 2015.

United States v. William V. Musto. US District Court for the District of New Jersey—540 F. Supp. 318 (D.N.J. 1982), May 12, 1982.

GOVERNMENT REPORTS

CIA: "Pinochet Personally Ordered Letelier Bombing," National Security Archive, September 23, 2016.

Englewood Cliffs Police, Evidence Report, I-2018-005047, obtained under Open Public Records Law (24-203).

Lobbying Disclosure ACT of 1995 Lobbying Reports for Greenburg Traurig (2002-2014) and Pedro Pablo Permuy 1999-2025.

Presentment of the Special Hudson County Grand Jury—Panel A, In the Matter of an Investigation into Corrupt Activities and Influence in the Union City Police Department and City Government, February 6, 1986.

State of New Jersey Commission of Investigation, "Public Matters, Private Interests: An Inquiry into Local Government, Ethics and Integrity Issues in the Borough of Edgewater," May 2023.

US Food and Drug Administration Inspections, Compliance, Enforcement, and Criminal Investigations Franck's Lab Inc dba Franck's Compounding Lab 7/9/2012.

UNITED STATES SENATE FOREIGN RELATIONS COMMITTEE CHAIRMAN'S PRESS

CSPAN Digital Library 1,809 videos for Bob Menendez as both a Senator and Member of the House of Representatives.

Data.cms.gov Medicare Physician and Other Practitioner Look-Up Tool.

https://data.cms.gov/tools/medicare-physician-other-practitioner-look-up-tool

Democratic Rep. Norma Torres Official House of Representatives Website Lawmakers question Trump ties to Panama project linked to laundering, trafficking, March 01, 2018.

FAA Aircraft Registry Files for N200CC.

Florida Office of Insurance Regulation Medical Malpractice Reports for Dr. Salomon Melgen

File numbers: M200221269, M200325082, M200536407, M201161109, M20126321 May 10, 2002.

Menendez Leads Series of Floor Speeches Condemning Trump Administration's Foreign Policy Agenda, March 20, 2018.

Menendez Probes US Ambassador to Ensure Trump Jr.'s Trip to India Was Not Assisted by State Department, February 21, 2018.

Menendez Raises Questions After Chinese State-Owned Company Receives Multimillion Contract for Trump Golf Club, June 22, 2018.

Sal Melgen Foundation Inc. IRS 990 for years 2008, 2009, and 2010.

United States Department of Transportation FAA Aircraft Bill of Sale for N150SA April 18, 2003.

FEDERAL ELECTIONS COMMISSION FILINGS:

Menendez for Senate, Committee Number C00264564, All Filings, April 9, 1992- April 15, 2025.

Menendez Victory Fund, Committee Number C00479501, All Filings, March 26, 2010–October 15, 2024.

New Millenium Pac, Committee Number C00349233, All Filings, September 30, 1999–February 12, 2025

CONGRESSIONAL FINANCIAL DISCLOSURE FILINGS:

United States Senate, May 9, 2012–December 17, 2024.

LEGAL DEFENSE FUND FILINGS:

Menendez Legal Defense Fund, All Filings, January 31, 2024–April 9, 2025.

Robert Menendez Legal Expense Trust, All Filings, January 31, 2014–January 16, 2020.

CONGRESSIONAL HEARINGS:

Sen. Robert Menendez, Chairman, "Sen. Robert Menendez Holds a Hearing on Caribbean Narcotics Trafficking," Committee Hearing: Senate Committee on Foreign Relations, Subcommittee on Western Hemisphere, Peace Corps, and Global Narcotics Affairs, December 15, 2011.

Sen. Robert Menendez, Chairman, "Sen. Robert Menendez Holds a Hearing on Caribbean Narcotics Trafficking," Committee Hearing: Senate Committee on Foreign Relations, Subcommittee on Western Hemisphere, Peace Corps, and Global Narcotics Affairs, July 31, 2012.

S. Hrg. 112-57 - A Shared Responsibility: Counternarcotics and Citizen Security in the Americas Congressional Hearings. General. Foreign Relations, Subcommittee on Western Hemisphere, Peace Corps, and Global Narcotics Affairs. Thursday, March 31, 2011.

S. Hrg. 112-55 - U.S. Policy Toward Latin America Congressional Hearings. General. Foreign Relations, Subcommittee on Western Hemisphere, Peace Corps, and Global Narcotics Affairs. Thursday, February 17, 2011.

S. Hrg. 112-83 - Navigating a Turbulent Global Economy: Implications for the United States Congressional Hearings. General. Foreign Relations. Thursday, March 3, 2011.

S. Hrg. 112-90 - The State of Democracy in the Americas Congressional Hearings. General. Foreign Relations, Subcommittee on Western Hemisphere, Peace Corps, and Global Narcotics Affairs. Thursday, June 30, 2011.

S. Hrg. 112-370 - The U.S.-Caribbean Shared Security Partnership: Responding to the Growth of Trafficking and... Congressional Hearings. General. Foreign Relations, Subcommittee on Western Hemisphere, Peace Corps, and Global Narcotics Affairs. Thursday, December 15, 2011.

S. Hrg. 112-607 - Doing Business in Latin America: Positive Trends but Serious Challenges Congressional Hearings. General. Foreign Relations, Subcommittee on Western Hemisphere, Peace Corps, and Global Narcotics Affairs. Tuesday, July 31, 2012.

S. Hrg. 112-744 - Anatomy of a Fraud Bust: From Investigation to Conviction Congressional Hearings. General. Finance. Tuesday, April 24, 2012.

S. Hrg. 114-27 - Oversight of the State Department and Agency for International Development Funding Priorities for . . . Congressional Hearings. Oversight. Foreign Affairs, Subcommittee on the Western Hemisphere. Tuesday, March 24, 2015.

S. Hrg. 114-69 - Deepening Political and Economic Crisis in Venezuela: Implications for U.S. Inter- Ests and the . . . Congressional Hearings. General. Foreign Relations, Subcommittee on Western Hemisphere Transnational Crime, Civilian Security, Democracy, Human Rights, and Global Women's Issues. Tuesday, March 17, 2015.

S. Hrg. 114-70 - Understanding the Impact of U.S. Policy Changes on Human Rights and Democracy in Cuba Congressional Hearings. General. Foreign. Tuesday, February 3, 2015.

S. Hrg. 114-705 - Review of Resources, Priorities, and Programs in the FY 2016 State Department Budget Request Congressional Hearings. General. Foreign Relations, Subcommittee on Western Hemisphere Transnational Crime, Civilian Security, Democracy, Human Rights, and Global Women's Issues. Tuesday, May 5, 2015.

S. Hrg. 114-795 - Overview of U.S. Policy Towards Haiti Prior to the Elections Congressional Hearings. General. Foreign Relations, Subcommittee on Western Hemisphere Transnational Crime, Civilian Security, Democracy, Human Rights, and Global Women's Issues. Wednesday, July 15, 2015.

BOOKS

English, T. J. *The Corporation: An Epic Story of the Cuban American Underworld* (New York: Harper Collins, 2018).

Ingle, Bob and Sandy McClure. *The Soprano State: New Jersey's Culture of Corruption* (New York: St. Martin's Griffin, 2008).

Menendez, Robert. *Growing American Roots: Why Our Nation Will Thrive as Our Largest Minority Flourishes* (New York: Penguin Group, 2009).

Union Hill High School Yearbook, 1971, 1972.